Neruda's
Ekphrastic Experience

Neruda's Ekphrastic Experience

Mural Art and *Canto general*

Hugo Méndez-Ramírez

Lewisburg
Bucknell University Press
London: Associated University Presses

Associated University Presses
440 Forsgate Drive
Cranbury, NJ 08512

Associated University Presses
16 Barter Street
London WC1A 2AH, England

Associated University Presses
P.O. Box 338, Port Credit
Mississauga, Ontario
Canada L5G 4L8

The paper used in this publication meets the requirements of the American National Standard for Permanence of Paper for Printed Library Materials Z39.48-1984.

Library of Congress Cataloging-in-Publication Data

Méndez-Ramírez, Hugo, 1953–
    Neruda's ekphrastic experience : mural art and Canto general / Hugo Méndez-Ramírez.
        p.   cm.
    Includes bibliographical references and index.
    ISBN 0-8387-5398-1 (alk. paper)
    1. Neruda, Pablo, 1904–1973.   Canto general.   2. Neruda, Pablo, 1904–1973—Knowledge—Mexico.   3. Mexico—In literature.
    4. Ekphrasis.   5. Mural painting and decoration—Mexico.   I. Title.
PQ8097.N4C1736   1999
861—dc21   98-47708
                                                                           CIP

To Vialla and Alexandra

Contents

Acknowledgments

THIS BOOK IS THE RESULT OF NUMEROUS CONTRIBUTIONS FROM many different people and institutions, spanning several years. First, my deepest gratitude and appreciation go to my wife Vialla to whom this book is dedicated for her clear, brilliant mind, her extensive and dedicated editorial work, but most importantly, for her loving and unconditional support throughout all these years. This book is also hers in many ways. To Alexandra, our daughter, I also dedicate this book for all the joy she brings into our lives.

This work would never have been possible without the encouragement of Albert and Jean Huber, and particularly Carl Huber, whose timely and smart intervention in the early stages of this project was crucial. I am grateful to my dear friend and mentor Donald L. Shaw, who gave me the inspiration and thirst to write and to follow the academic life. I am also indebted to Linda Maier for her careful and meticulous reading of early versions of the manuscript, and for her thoughtful suggestions. Special thanks to my parents, Juan and Celia, for their efforts and patience as my first teachers, and to my brother Marcos, whose professional expertise in taking many of the mural photographs contained in this book is deeply appreciated.

This book also owes its existence to several institutions that provided financial support and time to conduct research in Mexico and to prepare the manuscript for publication: to The City College of New York and the Research Foundation of the City University of New York for granting me the PSC-CUNY Research Award, which allowed me to complete my research in Mexico City and Guadalajara in the summer of 1991; and to Georgia State University and the Center for Latin American Studies for their support in preparing the manuscript for publication.

My acknowledgments to the Fundación Neruda for permission to reproduce several verses and poems from *Canto general* and to the University of California Press for permission to use their English translation of the book. I wish to thank the Museum of Modern Art for allowing me to reproduce *Ethnography* of David Alfaro Siqueiros; and the Hood Museum of Art for their permission to reproduce *Ancient Human Sacrifice* from the murals of José Clemente Orozco at Dartmouth College. Finally, I am grateful to the Instituto Nacional de Bellas Artes in Mexico City for allowing me access to their photographic archives; and to the Mexican government and the government of the state of Jalisco for their permission to photograph murals in various public buildings.

Neruda's
Ekphrastic Experience

Introduction: Neruda in Mexico (1940–1943)

Pablo neruda's return to america in 1937 prefigures a fundamental change in his poetry, a shift from a tone of existential
despair to hope through social and political commitment. Beginning with *Canto general* (1950), and even as early as the fifth section of the *Tercera residencia* (*Third Residence*) (1942), Neruda's
poetry adopts a very different manner of expression from that of
his earlier writings. This change has been previously attributed
to Neruda's Spanish Civil War experience and the outbreak of
World War II, but it has more recently been argued that the major
transition in Neruda's poetry occurs only after his return to
America and his residence in Mexico.[1] A careful and detailed
study of Neruda's writings during his years as Chilean consul in
Mexico (1940–43) confirms that it is during this period that his
poetic expression crystallizes and achieves maturity, and his perspective widens from personal and local concerns to encompass
continental issues. The Mexican mural movement, at its apex at
the time of Neruda's stay, was key in this development.

From 1940 to 1943, Pablo Neruda represented the Chilean government as consul to Mexico. Neruda was well acquainted with
Mexico's history and participated in the intellectual and political
life of the country during his years there. As Frank Reiss has
stated, "Neruda's stay in Mexico and his contact with a well-
established social, historical and literary tradition must have
played an important part in shaping the *Canto general*."[2] Hernán
Uribe writes that it was precisely in Mexico where Neruda's political positions are solidified and where a good part of his artistic
work was conceived: that the poet frequently finds poetic inspiration in the land of the Aztecs, especially in his treatment of Latin
American themes.[3] It is often overlooked that Neruda originally
published many poems of *Canto general*, composed between 1940
and 1950, in Mexican journals and newspapers, particularly between 1940 and 1943. Clearly, Neruda's Mexican years were vital
to his artistic development and shaped his future production.

Until now, no formal systematic analysis has been undertaken
to examine Neruda's Mexican experience, though several studies

13

treat it in a cursory way.[4] Wilberto Cantón's essay, "Pablo Neruda en México" (1950), remains the most comprehensive study of Neruda's years in Mexico. Filled with personal anecdotes, it offers essential information regarding Neruda's political, artistic, and private activities in Mexico. The other studies utterly fail to explain the significance and scope of this period of Neruda's poetry.

It should be noted at this point that the intent of this book is not to present a catalog of anecdotes or correspondence between Neruda and his friends and acquaintances; that has been done by the critics just mentioned. My objective is to examine precisely the other aspects that have been ignored or overlooked: the aesthetic and formal which then can be linked to the thematic and personal, thus explaining one of the most radical conversions in the history of Latin American poetry. At this juncture we must remember that Neruda's change is indeed thematic, but it is also fundamentally formal. Resorting to the medieval tradition of epic poetry as he does, for example, requires more complex and sophisticated considerations than those thus far ascribed to the personal or the *zeitgeist*. I am interested in presenting a coherent and systematic explication of the artistic, aesthetic, and literary phenomena behind *Canto general*, particularly with regard to Mexican muralism. This book uncovers the semantics of visual imagery involved in the process of constructing and assembling the poetic text. Yet in order for us to engage in such a journey, we must first establish a basic chronological frame, and then engage in a sound theoretical discussion of the interactions of the "sister arts."

Neruda returned to Chile in 1937, after having actively supported the Spanish Republic and Spanish political exiles. The following year, after the deaths of his father and stepmother, identification with the struggle of his fellow countrymen supplanted his support of the Spanish cause, according to Emir Rodríguez Monegal. It was at this time, says Rodríguez Monegal, that Neruda conceived his first *Canto general de Chile* [*Canto General of Chile*], which evolved into *Canto general*.[5] However, this critic does not fully explain just how Neruda's new poetic expression, the shift from a purely nationalistic (i.e., Chilean) to a broader Latin American world view, came to be.

Save his native Chile, Mexico is the Latin American country which has had the greatest impact on Neruda and his work. Neruda expressed his attachment to Mexico in his memoirs:

> México vive en mi vida como una pequeña águila equivocada que circula en mis venas. Sólo la muerte le doblegará las alas sobre mi corazón de soldado dormido.

[Mexico lives on in me like a small stray eagle circulating through my veins. Only death will fold its wings over my sleeping soldier's heart.][6]

The unique characteristics of the Mexican culture embedded in the indigenous past and expressed in Mexican art captivated Neruda:

México, con su nopal y su serpiente, México florido y espinudo, seco y huracanado . . . violento de erupción y creación, me cubrió con su sortilegio y su luz sorpresiva.

[Mexico with its prickly pear and its serpent; Mexico blossoming and thorny, dry and lashed by hurricane winds . . . violent in eruption and creation, surrounded me with its magic and its extraordinary light.][7]

The ethnic theme that culminates in *Alturas de Macchu Picchu* [*Heights of Macchu Picchu*] stems not from Neruda's short two-week visit to Peru in 1943, but rather primarily from his three-year immersion in Mexican culture, history, and geography, impregnated with the pre-Hispanic. A fragment in "México florido y espinudo" [Mexico, Blossoming and Thorny], the seventh chapter of his memoirs, provides a prelude to the theme and tone of *Alturas*. The imagery used to describe the suffering of the Incan workers of Macchu Picchu is the same used in this fragment, which describes an excursion to the Mayan ruins and the poet's impressions of the sacred *cenotes*, or sunken pools of water, where he believed that young virgins were drowned: "Me parecía oír en los extraños graznidos de los pájaros la ronca agonía de las vírgenes" [In the (strange) shrieks of the birds I seemed to hear the hoarse anguish of the virgins].[8] Neruda gained a new awareness of his American identity in Mexico at this Mayan site. The passage begins in straightforward fashion and changes to subtly evoke the image of a dove perched on the hand of a Mayan statue:

La miré porque venía de otro mundo, de un mundo medido y armónico, de una columna pitagórica o de un número mediterráneo. Se detuvo en el margen de las tinieblas, acató mi silencio cuando yo mismo ya pertenecía a ese mundo original, americano, sangriento y antiguo, y voló frente a mis ojos hasta perderse en el cielo.

[I gazed at her because she came from another world, from a measured and harmonious world, from a Pythagorean column or a Mediterranean round number. She had stopped on the edge of the darkness, she respected my silence, for I had become part of this original American, blood-stained, ancient world, and my eyes followed her flight until they lost her in the sky.][9]

Neruda's description of the scene symbolizes his new thematics and his fondness for Mexico as an extension of his Chilean roots. Furthermore, the image of the dove flying away from the poet mirrors Neruda's attempt to detach himself from the aesthetic "harmony" of the European world (the "columna pitagórica" or the "número mediterráneo"). In a lecture titled "Algo sobre mi poesía y mi vida" [Some comments about my poetry and my life], Neruda clearly affirms his new Latin American identity:

> las raíces de todos los chilenos se extendían debajo de la tierra y salían en otros territorios. O'Higgins tenía raíces en Miranda. Lautaro se emparentaba con Cuauhtémoc. La alfarería de Oaxaca tenía el mismo fulgor negro de las gredas de Chillán.
>
> [the roots of all Chileans extended below the earth and surfaced in other territories. O'Higgins had roots in Miranda. Lautaro was related to Cuauhtémoc. The ceramics of Oaxaca had the same black brilliance as the clay of Chillán.][10]

Neruda had found a new imagery that somehow was at the same time familiar, and this familiarity was precisely the key that opened the way to the continental view. The ethnic theme, therefore, was the fundamental link. For this reason, it became increasingly important, even surfacing in the first journal that Neruda established as Chilean consul. Its title, *Araucanía*, provoked immediate condemnation by the Chilean government: "Cámbiele de título o suspéndala. No somos un país de indios" [Change the title or cancel it. We are not a nation of Indians].[11] Consequently, the title of the magazine was changed to *Noticias de Chile* [News from Chile]. Later, in 1943, Neruda, along with Wilberto Cantón, Juan Rejano, and others, planned a literary journal which would incorporate both poetry and politics; they intended to title it "La sangre y la letra" [Blood and Letters], but it was never published.[12]

At the time of Neruda's tenure as consul, intellectual life in Mexico was dominated by three mural painters: José Clemente Orozco, Diego Rivera, and David Alfaro Siqueiros. According to Neruda, "Estos pintores cubrían la ciudad con historia y geografía, con incursiones civiles, con polémicas ferruginosas" [Mexican painters covered the city with history and geography, with civil strife, with fierce controversies].[13] Cardona Peña was the first of several critics to recognize that *Canto general* was the literary equivalent of the Mexican muralist phenomenon.[14] Neruda maintained close contact with the Mexican mural painters, especially with David Alfaro Siqueiros, who had fought in both the Mexican Revolution and the defense of the Republic during the Spanish Civil War. Furthermore, under the supervision of Miguel Prieto, the first edition of *Canto general* was published privately in Mexico in 1950 and included illustrations by Rivera and Siqueiros. Even on the surface the titles of a number of the poems of the fourth section, *Los libertadores,* clearly indicate ekphrastic interpretations of murals by Siqueiros and Rivera (e.g., "Cuauhtémoc" and "Zapata"). "Muerte al invasor" [Death to the Invader], the title of Neruda's introduction to the Spanish translation of the war chronicles of Soviet novelist Ehrenburg, published in Mexico, is also taken from a Siqueiros mural in Chillán, Chile. Of course, Neruda's poetry and its relationship to mural art goes beyond titles, as will become clear.

Naturally, Neruda's contact with Mexican aesthetic trends was not limited to his acquaintance with mural painters; he was also closely associated with a number of writers. We know that his political stance and personal concept of poetry generated open debate among several Mexican poets, most notably Octavio Paz and José Luis Martínez, and divided them into two opposing groups: *nerudistas* and *antinerudistas*.[15] In an interview with Alardo Pratts, published in *Revista Hoy* in 1943, Neruda condemns "poetas celestes" [celestial poets], whose poetry ignores social concerns, and praises the young novelists José Revueltas (to whose family Neruda dedicated various poems), Juan de la Cabada, Ermilo Abreu Gómez, and Andrés Henestrosa.[16] Neruda's assertions provoked a furious response from Paz and Martínez, who felt personally attacked. In "Respuesta a un Cónsul" [Response to a Consul], an article published shortly before Neruda's departure from Mexico, Paz refutes the Chilean's charges and concludes:

[l]o que nos separa de su persona [de Neruda] no son las convicciones políticas, sino, simplemente, la vanidad . . . y el sueldo. La vanidad que lo obliga a aceptar cada seis meses, banquetes y homenajes de esas mismas personas que llama "carentes de moral cívica"; y el sueldo, que le permite ofrecer mesa y cantina libre a una jauría que adula su resentimiento injuriando a todos aquellos que aún creen que la república de las letras nada tiene que ver con las viejas satrapías de Oriente.

[What sets us apart from Neruda is not political convictions, but simply vanity . . . and his salary. The vanity that obliges him every six months to accept banquets and homages from the same people that he says are "lacking in civic morals"; and the salary, that permits him to offer an open bar and full table to a horde that worships his resentment, insulting all those who still believe that the Republic of Letters has nothing to do with the old satrapies of the East.][17]

While residing in Mexico, Neruda also lived in the house that had belonged to Ramón López Velarde, one of the nationalistic poets at that time, and one who had rejected *modernista* poetry.[18] It was there that the Chilean poet, as he recalls in *Para nacer he nacido* (*Passions and Impressions*), rediscovered and was inspired by López Velarde's poetry.

Mexico's geography, history, and art transformed Neruda's *Weltanschauung* and guided him in his search for a new poetic form of expression. Mexico's rich culture imbedded in its indigenous past and expressed through a variety of art forms—painting, literature, music, sculpture, and so on—fascinated Neruda. Growing Mexican nationalism and strong pride in its pre-Colombian past offered the Chilean an opportunity to reflect on his own American identity and helped relieve his existential malaise.

Mexican mural art was the predominant and most successful form of expression of the time. It condensed in its grandiose paintings the essence and ethos of this artistic milieu, playing a crucial role in the formation of *Canto general*. It could be argued that all cultural and artistic expressions of the time were only part of an ongoing thrust created by the reverberations of the Mexican Revolution, and that Neruda was merely, like others, part of this particular *zeitgeist*. But we must understand the role of muralism vis à vis the Revolution and the other art forms: the referent, the actual Mexican Revolution, was a situation in which historical actions were reported and known and had their effect on the emergent models and metaphors. Mural art was one of these models, along with the novel, music, and other art forms; but one that, as Neruda and many others acknowledged (including its most fierce detractor Octavio Paz), became in itself a dominant referent form, in which others found their signifiers and signifieds. Neruda is a poet moved by the artistic desire of representation, a desire to capture and transmit images that correspond to nontextual or poetic referents.[19] This is exactly the reason why Neruda was not interested in the historical referent, but rather in its visual representation throughout the walls of the city. Mexican mural art imposed a way of representing historic events that had little or nothing to do with "real" events. Among all the artistic forms of representation that favored a social/historical referent, muralism won the contest. It became the referent for other versions. It determined the basic scenes, images, figures, and topoi of which new representations could be constructed. It captured the popular and intellectual imaginations of all subsequent reflections on the Mexican Revolution. It would be a mistake to think of muralism simply as a phenomenon for art historians to study, because mural art not only played the role of an influential version of the story of history; it also was a historical event in itself, an episode in the revolution's history, as well as an interpretation of it.

I do not propose, therefore, to undertake a comprehensive study of all artistic expressions that could have contributed in some form or another to the process of poetic creation in *Canto general*. Such a task is not merely elusive; it would be speculative at best. In his 1982 study on methodology for comparison of "Literature and the Visual Arts," Ulrich Weisstein has the following recommendation, agreeing with Jean Seznec:

> In the comparative arts, even more than in the already overextended field of comparative literature, it is imperative . . . to eschew vast syntheses and brilliant generalizations and to concentrate, instead, on monographic studies "limited in their object and rigorous in their form."[20]

In the same article, Weisstein also warns against the excesses of the method known as *Geistesgeschichte*, which presupposes the notion of the "real" existence of "time spirits" in the study of literary works that, along with other artistic media, "display features of a common style."[21] There must be some specific connection other than mere coincidence of time period in order for two art forms to be fruitfully compared. Such connections exist between *Canto general* and Mexican muralism and can be elucidated by applying an interartistic approach.

One of the goals of this book is to provide an explication of what critics have perceived as the "chaotic" structure of *Canto general*.[22] Although Yurkiévich blames this characteristic in part on the poet's ill-fated attempt to fuse history and myth, I would like to draw attention to the formal and narrative structure of the text, a considered observation of which reveals the critical role played by the mural paintings in the form and shape in which *Canto general* was to be executed. A close analysis—section by section—of the first seven cantos of the book evinces clear parallels with Mexican mural art. In fact, the volume's narrative structure reflects chronologically, thematically, and iconologically the three main phases of the Mexican mural movement. I summarize *a grosso modo* my exegesis of this interplay. First, both Mexican muralism and Neruda's poetry depict in mythical terms the dimension of the American landscape and idealize (which is part of the mythic process) the origin, evolution, and development of pre-Colombian cultures up to the arrival of the Spaniards. Second, both art forms want to project a panoramic view of history and portray real historical figures in the way medieval painting and texts did. Third (also in the tradition of late medieval painting), in their attempt to achieve communion with the masses, both the mural painters and Neruda aimed at an *engagé* art that included the artist and ordinary people within the art object. This compendium is best elicited in the monumental Rivera murals at the National Palace. Finally, along with the Mexican painters, Neruda resorted to Marxist doctrine in his work.

According to Enrico Mario Santí, *Canto general* may be divided into two units with the center being section VIII, *La tierra se llama Juan:*

> Las primeras siete secciones forman entre sí una sola unidad, con un diseño histórico más o menos sostenido, desde los orígenes primigenios hasta la época de los dictadores, seguidas por un resumen lírico que culmina en el siguiente *Canto general de Chile.* En cambio, la ausencia de ese diseño en la segunda mitad del libro (secciones IX–XV) la hace más heterogénea.

> [The first seven sections form a single unit, with a historic design that is more or less maintained, from the primitive origins to the era of the dictators, followed by a lyrical summary that culminates in the next section, *Canto General of Chile.* In contrast, the absence of such a design in the second half of the book (sections IX–XV) makes it more heterogenous.][23]

My analysis of the text's structure is different from that of Santí. A comparison of the text with Mexican mural art, reading it chronologically as if it were a pictorial or visual text, clarifies and expands on the division argued by Santí. Yet, I would go even further: *Canto general* is in fact comprised of two books, rather than one divided into two units, as Santí suggests. The first book includes sections I–VIII (Santí groups sections I–VII, and labels section VIII an "axle"). The chronological, thematic, and symbolic design of this first book is closely linked to the monumental visual representations of Mexican muralism. The second book (sections IX–XV) is more heterogeneous and alludes to Neruda's own experiences in hiding and exile and to international tensions of the Cold War. Although Mexican mural art also treated the conflict between the superpowers, it only provided an indirect archetropic or ekphrastic model for the second book. In fact, the dates of publication of most of the poems reveal that the first book was written much earlier than previously thought, and covers a period beginning with Neruda's arrival in Mexico in 1940 and ending with the first years of his return to Chile (1943–45). The second book, according to our division, corresponds to the time, as related by the poet himself in his memoirs, when he had to hide from his political enemies in exile, from 1946 until the publication of *Canto general* in 1950 in Mexico. In the last chapter of this study we discuss in more detail the textual evidence for this assertion and the dates of publication.

The *narrative* character of the first book can therefore be explained through a detailed examination of the images, figures, and ideology in mural art. Neruda himself once described the text's narrative structure in prosaic terms: "debe de ser predregosa, polvorienta, lluviosa y cotidiana" [it should be stony, dusty, rainy and ordinary]. This explains why Santí views *Canto general* as a composite text, one that combines elements of a chronicle (subjective, immediate) and history (objective, distant) in a relationship he labels "narrativización de la historia" [narrativizing of history].[24] Indeed, this arbitrary relationship, which allows the poet to anachronistically fuse current and past events and to juxtapose the Chilean union leader Luis Emilio Recabarren with the last Aztec emperor Cuauhtémoc, emerges more clearly when viewed in light of the historic narrative model used in Mexican mural art and its techniques to achieve such juxtapositions. Demonstrating how Neruda closely followed the techniques, style, themes, and motifs of Rivera, Siqueiros, and Orozco, and the resulting interartistic significance of *Canto general* is the object of this book. The meaning of this relationship is of great importance, since, first, it elucidates the apparently disconnected structure of *Canto general;* second, in a broader perspective, it points toward a more crucial role in the book's conception played by Mexico and the muralist art than has been thought; and third, it explains Neruda's belated conversion to communism in 1945.

The recent publication of several books and articles on the study of the interarts question attests to the rising scholarly interest in the "sister arts." Beginning in 1986 with the pioneering work in this new theoretical frontier of W. J. T. Mitchell's *Iconology*, a steady stream of studies has appeared.[25] Building on the semiotic and structuralist approaches of the seventies and eighties, these new studies reflect the postmodern state of affairs in literary criticism and are consistent with the diversity, incongruity, and abundance of approaches, from deconstruction and feminism to new historicism and gender studies. Several journals are now devoted almost entirely to interdisciplinary studies, while *Word and Image* for several years now has been devoted specifically to interart studies. Virtually every scholarly periodical in the humanities has published articles in this field. *Poetics Today* dedicated a complete volume to the study of art and literature in the spring of 1989.[26] More recently, in the October 1996 issue of *Publications of the Modern Language Association,* an article on ekphrasis in George Eliot's *Middlemarch* appeared.[27] Yet while many of these studies that cross disciplinary boundaries typically focus on works from the United States, France, and England, only a few relate to Hispanic texts. One of the exceptions is *Painting on the Page* by Rosemary Geisdorfer Feal and Carlos Feal.[28] The present study helps to counterbalance this disparity by engaging in a series of interartistic explorations that combine new and traditional approaches in the study of the relationship between *Canto general* and Mexican mural art.

The systematic interpretation and application of such a theoretical frame to Neruda's book of poetry and the artifacts of muralism will contribute to the fields of literary criticism and art history, demonstrating how this approach can uncover new ways of analyzing poetry and painting. This book attempts to establish, beyond the simple description of a work of art, the specific case of the complex interactions of poems with pictures and vice versa; a relationship that is not apparent or perceptible at first glance. *Canto general,* the text, has as its hypotext a visual image, Mexican muralism. It is thus a palimpsest in an almost literal sense: a pictorial palimpsest.

Wendy Steiner has eloquently expressed the risks and rewards of such an approach:

> the greatest advantage of the interart comparison . . . is the very richness and wit of its juxtapositions. Though it cannot organize the arts into a structured, coherent system, nevertheless it gives aesthetic

speculation a copiousness long missed in the restrictive matrix of academic disciplines.[29]

A vast number of critics have engaged in this "richness and wit of juxtapositions." Rather than summarizing all the different versions of interarts relations, I will concentrate in the following chapter on prominent voices who represent major positions on the scholarly history of the debate over the differences between texts and images.

1

Image and Text

THE STUDY OF THE INTERPLAY BETWEEN VERBAL AND VISUAL REPRE-
sentations can be traced as far back as the early fifth or late sixth
century B.C. to the poet Simonides of Ceos, who was quoted by
Plutarch in *De Gloria Atheniensium* as saying "painting is mute
poetry and mute poetry is a speaking picture." This dictum became crucial in a debate that raged from the Renaissance to the
eighteenth century about the relationship between art forms. This
"witty antithesis," as W. G. Howard called it, reached great popu-
larity during these centuries and had the profound effect of virtually obliterating the limits of word and visual representation.[1]
Horace's ambiguous remark, *ut pictura poesis* (as is painting, so is
poetry) has also become one of the most widely used quotes in
the history of the subject, and clearly the favored expression of
many literary critics who treat the issue. Oddly, as popular as the
expression is, most scholars who use it do so to clarify that it is
a widely misunderstood and misinterpreted concept; that is, that
it must not be taken to mean that painting and poetry are literally
the same thing. Henryk Markiewicz, for instance, suggests that
the Horatian formulation has been taken out of context, since
originally it did not possess the theoretical interpretation it later
acquired. He proceeds to quote the entire passage, concluding
that "Horace's statement was therefore merely a free comparison,
an observation that the conditions for the optimal reception of
individual poems and paintings may vary."[2] For hundreds of
years, these two postulates—*ut pictura poesis* and Simonides' dictum—reigned in the arts, contributing to a certain confusion,
especially with respect to poetry and its relation to painting. Finally, in the eighteenth century the critical approaches of Johann
Winckelmann and Gotthold Lessing appeared. Until this point,
there was hardly any attempt to develop a critical theory of interartistic relationships, and the visual arts were in pursuit of what
Lessing termed the *mania for allegory*, while many poets of the

time had succumbed as well to the lure of allegorical and pictorial descriptions.[3] In his famous *Laocoön*, Lessing speaks out against the notion of inherent similarity of the arts and its indiscriminate application. Edward Allen McCormick states in the introduction to his translation of *Laocoön* that "Lessing was the first in modern times to define clearly the distinctiveness of the spheres of art and poetry and at the same time to penetrate deeply into the nature of these two arts."[4] Lessing's central argument is that literature is an art of time, and painting an art of space:

> if it is true that in its imitations painting uses completely different means or signs than does poetry, namely figures and colors in space rather than articulated sounds in time, and if these signs must indisputably bear a suitable relation to the thing signified, then signs existing in space can express only objects whose wholes or parts coexist, while signs that follow one another can express only objects whose wholes or parts are consecutive.[5]

Since it first appeared in 1766, *Laocoön* has been the subject of great debate and academic discussion. Until the present day critics have challenged his basic distinction between temporal and spatial arts. Joseph Frank's seminal essay on "Spatial Form in Modern Literature" is one the most important contributions to the debate. Frank is one of the best examples of an insightful critic who has used Lessing's ideas as instruments of analysis and inspiration for his own distinctions. "My aim," Frank said thirty years after the initial publication of his essay, "like that of Ortega y Gasset in his *Dehumanization of Art*, was to work out descriptive categories for a new literary phenomenon."[6] That phenomenon was the Modernist literary expression of the first two decades of the twentieth century. Although Frank's essay has been applied mostly to narrative works—his interest in the subject was prompted by a reading of Djuna Barnes's *Nightwood*—the basis for his theory is linguistic, and he begins by discussing modern poetry as a paradigm for narrative. In his discussion of T. S. Eliot and Ezra Pound (two poets whom Neruda knew well[7]), Frank notes that both undermine the temporality of language, allowing the reader to perceive the images in the poem, not in the linear flow of time, but as juxtaposed in space.[8]

In his remarks on the space-logic of modern poetry, Frank argues that readers are required to suspend the process of reference to temporality until the unity of internal references can be apprehended. Frank's notions have encountered some resistance. On this particular point, Walter Sutton has questioned the validity of the premise, on the basis that such "suspension" of temporality is impossible, stressing that since reading is a time-act, the spatialization of literature can never be entirely achieved.[9] In response to this criticism, Frank later refined his concepts in what he termed more precise linguistic terminology:

> that the synchronic relations *within* the text took precedence over diachronic referentiality and that it was only after the pattern of synchronic relations had been grasped as a unity that the "meaning" of the poem could be understood.[10]

He acknowledges that to perceive such synchronic relations involves the time-act of reading, but argues:

> the temporality of this act is no longer coordinated with the dominant structural elements of the text. Temporality becomes, as it were, a purely physical limit of apprehension, which conditions but does not determine the work and whose expectations are thwarted and superseded by the space-logic of synchronicity.[11]

Frank has also clarified his position regarding the old *ut pictura poesis* problem, stressing that he is not maintaining that the text can attain the spatiality of painting. He goes on to define the poetic/textual image, using the words of Pound: not as a pictorial reproduction but as a unification of disparate ideas and emotions into a complex presented spatially in a moment of time.[12]

From the standpoint of critical analysis, Frank's notions are of particular interest to the study undertaken here. His comparison of literary Modernism with the visual arts of the medieval tradition is also key to our understanding of the technical intricacies involved in the production of much of Neruda's *Canto general* and Mexican mural art, particularly in their treatment of history. Alluding to the contrast of past and present in creating a latent ahistoricity in the text that strives to transform itself into a unity, Frank states:

> The great works of Modernism are thus analogous . . . to those examples of medieval sculpture or book illustration in which some figures from the Old and New Testaments, classical antiquity, and sometimes local history are all grouped together as part of one timeless complex of significance.[13]

Also crucial to our purpose is Frank's theoretical distinction of temporal discontinuity in the process of transforming history into myth. For this critic, the juxtapositions of disparate historical images in James Joyce, Pound, and Eliot "bring the past into the present of the indicative; and in doing so they turn history into myth."[14] In his study of film form, Segei Eisenstein has explained that the juxtaposition of disparate images creates a synthesis of meaning between them, and that this predominates over any sense of temporal discontinuity.[15]

I want to stress, at this point, that while I share the critical position that calls for the tearing down of the barriers between the image and the text, I recognize with Frank, W. J. T. Mitchell, and many other contemporary critics that the text can never, in the literal sense (except perhaps in the case of concrete poetry) represent the visual in the same way as the visual arts (painting, film, sculpture). Mitchell, however, has also argued that the entire distinction of temporal and spatial arts is erroneous "insofar as it is employed to sustain an *essential* differentiation of or within the arts."[16] In opposition to Lessing, Frank, and others, Mitchell points out that the common artistic thrust to ignore the boundaries between temporal and spatial arts is not a marginal or rare occurrence, but a fundamental impulse in the history of artistic expression and criticism, and, moreover, "one which is not confined to any particular genre or period."[17] Mitchell's principal contribution to this debate is his opposition to the traditional spatial/temporal dichotomy, since for him the notion of time cannot be understood without the presence of spatial images, and, similarly, the distinction of space cannot be apprehended apart from time and motion. For this reason, he suggests that:

> Instead of Lessing's strict opposition between literature and the visual arts as pure expressions of temporality and spatiality, we should regard literature and language as the meeting ground of these two modalities.[18]

At the same time, even Lessing acknowledges the ability of poetry to create the *visual* depiction of an action in a text such as Homer's famous description in the *Iliad* of Achilles' shield. Lessing notes:

> he has made use of the happy device of substituting progression for coexistence, and thus converted the tiresome description of an object into a graphic picture of an action. We see not the shield, but the divine master-workman employed upon it.[19]

Thus, at the core of the debate is the possibility that the word or the text can create "visual" images, indicating the existence of such a thing as a "poetic picture." And while Lessing acknowledges this possibility in the passage just cited, he does so because Homer never allows the shield to become static or a mere digression, through a process of "substituting progression for coexistence."

The elements of poetry (words, text, speech), according to Lessing, are not only successive and constrained to temporal consecution, but are also arbitrary: "objects or parts of objects which follow one another are called actions," and therefore, "actions are the true subjects of poetry." The symbols of painting are "natural": conversely, "objects . . . which exist in space are called bodies," and so "bodies with their visible properties are the true subjects of painting."[20] Literary critics merely echo Lessing's distinctions when they claim that indeed the process of reading occurs in time, that words are read and uttered in a temporal sequence, and that narrated material is inscribed in time. Similarly, the medium of visual arts consists of forms displayed in space; the representation of such forms and bodies occurs in space, and its reception by the viewer takes place in a single moment, an instant of time. And although almost every literary critic will "admit that it makes sense to speak of literary space in genres like ekphrastic poetry . . . this admission is generally accompanied by elaborate strategies of denial which treat this sort of space as illusory, secondary, or 'merely figurative.'"[21] Wendy Steiner's views are a clear example of such positions. In her insightful analysis of ekphrasis in an e.e. cummings poem, with its attempt to overcome the flux of temporality, Steiner concludes, "Cummings (sic) has managed certain technical advances over the generally thematic and imagistic treatment of the topos by other poets, but his poem nevertheless accepts the boundaries of verbal art that make its surmounting of temporality virtual at best."[22] Interestingly, Steiner's position is not different from Lessing's own conclusions in later chapters.

As is the case of every critic who carefully studies the interplay of these art forms, as he or she develops arguments for the differentiation of the arts, Lessing begins to admit the possibility of poetic language overcoming the flux of time, since "the symbols of poetry are not only successive but are also arbitrary; and, as arbitrary symbols, they are of course able to represent bodies as they exist in space."[23] Homer, again, is the poet who best exemplifies Lessing's concession to language. Nevertheless, he limits this possibility to the special virtues of poetic language, denying it to any other sort of language, because the poet

> wants rather to make the ideas he awakens in us so vivid that at that moment we believe that we feel the real impressions which the objects of these ideas would produce on us. In this moment of illusion we should cease to be conscious of the means which the poet uses for this purpose, that is, his words.[24]

Lessing also has the following caveats:

> However, bodies do not exist in space only, but also in time. They persist in time, and in each moment of their duration they may assume a different appearance or stand in a different combination. Each of these momentary appearances and combinations is the result of a preceding one and can be the cause of a subsequent one, which means that it can be, as it were, the center of an action. Consequently, painting too can imitate actions, but only by suggestion through bodies.[25]

Conversely:

> actions cannot exist independently, but must be joined to certain beings or things. Insofar as these beings or things are bodies, or are treated as such, poetry also depicts bodies, but only by suggestion through actions.[26]

From these statements, one can infer that spatial art (painting) can only overcome spatiality and attain temporality indirectly, by "suggesting" it through "forms and bodies," while poetry must always be joined to certain agents and can create what are regarded as "bodies" only indirectly through the depiction of actions.

In his challenge of the distinction between visual art and language, Mitchell maintains that if the representation of time in painting, or space in poetry, occurs only at the second level or "indirectly," the "signifieds of painting and poetry become signifiers in their own right, and the boundaries between the temporal and the spatial are dissolved.[27] After describing Lessing's entire distinction as one hanging "on the slender thread of the difference between primary and secondary representation, direct or indirect expression," Mitchell then questions the very idea of a "direct" form of representation. He argues that essentially any form of representation is "indirect," since "direct" "cannot mean that the bodies or actions are simply present before us in the painting or poetry; that would be to deny that any representation occurs at all." Therefore, "the bodies represented by a painting are not directly represented in any literal sense; they are indirectly presented by means of shapes and colors—that is by certain kinds of signs."[28] The difference, therefore, is not one of kind, but one of degree, where, for painting, the description of bodies is more convenient while the representation of actions is simply "more difficult or inconvenient."[29] Inversely, the same is true for poetry. Thus, Mitchell affirms, "if it is only a matter of degree of effort that holds poetry and painting in their proper domains, then it is clear that this distinction cannot be the basis of any rigorous differentiation of *kind.*"[30]

Mitchell's systematic deconstruction of Lessing's notions of space and time in the arts has a twofold purpose: on the one hand, he attempts to establish as a fundamental theoretical premise that both painting and poetry are literally spatial-temporal constructs, and that the terms *space* and *time* are not antithetical entities. His second objective, not only in this essay on Lessing, but in his entire book, *Iconology,* is to uncover the political and ideological positions behind the notions of the "natural" differences between painting and poetry or image and text. This critic's career has been devoted to the task of studying the complex interactions of visual and verbal images, including their manipulation and effect in the history of criticism and the arts, and also in society during times of iconophilia or iconophobia. In fact, at the end of his essay on *Laocoön,* Mitchell describes Lessing as someone who exploits "the iconophobic and iconoclastic rhetoric that pervades the discourse we call "criticism" in Western culture."[31] He goes on to suggest that Lessing's language is plagued with metaphors of political expediency and international relations that defend the English and Germans against the corrupted ideas of the French, who are described as "false" and "frigid" neoclassicists. According to Mitchell, the limits or borders (*Grenzen*) imposed by Lessing on the arts correspond to the limits that in Lessing's terms should define the European cultural map. He notes, "a closer look reveals Lessing's partisanship: it is the French with their 'false delicacy,' their *difficulté vaincue* and their frigid neoclassicism who blur the genres by making poetry conform to the cold beauties of classical painting and sculpture."[32] Moreover, Mitchell finds buried in the text a correlation between the separation of genres and gender differentiation, which explains Mitchell's own selection of William Blake's line to open his chapter: "Time and Space are Real Beings. Time is a Man. Space is a Woman."

Mitchell's departure from the more conventional, conservative, methodological approach, devoted almost exclusively to aesthetics, is representative of the most recent criticism on the subject. Another such critic is Grant F. Scott, who adopts Mitchell's incisive ideological critique of *Laocoön* to further challenge the notions that underwrite the supremacy of the visual image over the verbal. Scott suggests in his article, "The Rhetoric of Dilation: Ekphrasis and Ideology," that there is a similarity between the notion of subordination and dependency of the ekphrastic process and the dynamics of power in the interplay of gender relations and sexuality.[33]

For centuries the debate over the supremacy of one or the other art form has dominated both artistic production and literary scholarship. Lessing's defense of the supremacy of language and Leonardo da Vinci's attack on the inferior quality of representation through language, with the implied hegemony of painting, have their contemporary counterparts in Jacques Derrida's "logocentrism" and Martin Jay's "oculocentrism."[34] Nevertheless, there are several critics in both the literary and the fine arts arenas, such as the previously mentioned Mitchell, Steiner, and Scott, but also Franklin Rogers, Murray Krieger, and others, who from different perspectives are interested in erasing or fusing the boundaries between word and text. These critics have revealed the political and ideological positions behind distinctions such as "natural" and "conventional" limitations and differences of various artistic media. Their fundamental premise is that text and image share the same logical space. The best articulation of this idea can be found in Mitchell's most recent work, *Picture Theory*, where he argues the following:

> Figurative labels ("blue" moods and "warm" colors) apply as firmly and consistently as literal ones and have as much to do with actual experience. That images, pictures, space and visuality may only be figuratively conjured up in a verbal discourse does not mean that the conjuring fails to occur or that the reader/listener "sees" nothing. That verbal discourse may only be figuratively or indirectly evoked in a picture does no mean that the evocation is impotent, that the viewer "hears" or "reads" nothing in the image.[35]

Taken to its ultimate consequences, this position asserts that the interaction of pictures and text is a *sine qua non* for representation and assumes that there is no such thing as "purely" visual or verbal art; that is, that all representations are heterogeneous and that every medium is mixed.[36]

As Wendy Steiner has eloquently said,

> The painting-literature analogy has followed a . . . Sisyphean pattern and is bound to continue doing so. For there can be no final consensus about whether and how the two arts resemble each other, but only a growth in our awareness of the process of comparing them, of metaphoric generation and regeneration.[37]

As influential as Lessing's *Laocoön*, and one of the most promising approaches to interartistic studies in recent years, is the discipline known as ekphrastic poetics. Just as the other notions treated earlier, this topos has received considerable scrutiny, mostly from literary critics and philosophers. Amy Golahny notes that,

> Only in the last several years has there been a concerted effort to arrive at precise limitations on the meaning of the term, and to define its function within a poetic text. Its current frequent use arises out of the necessity to refine concepts of discourse about the affinities, distinctions, and rivalries among the pictorial and literary arts.[38]

The term and its origin have also followed a "Sisyphean pattern." In its original association with the discipline of classical rhetoric, ekphrasis was understood as the description of an object (an urn, a shield), a place or a person; and according to Grant F. Scott, the first recorded use of the term by Dionysus Heicarnassus is with this connotation.[39] The word comes from the Greek verb *ekphraisien,* which meant "to speak out" or "to report in detail." In Hellenistic rhetoric, its meaning was broad and general; it was used to refer to any verbal description of any sort, either in art or rhetoric. It was normally invoked to interrupt the temporality of discourse, to suspend the argument of the speaker or the presentation of a poet, by shifting the listener's attention to a visual object, which was then described in great and vivid detail.[40]

Since its first incursion in modern literary criticism, in Jean H. Hagstrum's pioneering work, *The Sister Arts* (1958), the definitions of ekphrasis have been as diverse and broad as its applications. Hagstrum confines his use of the term to "refer to that special quality of giving voice and language to the otherwise mute art object."[41] Hagstrum, however, prefers the term *iconic poetry* to describe a certain kind of poetry that illustrates the association of verbal and graphic art, whose practice extends from Homer to

Yeats.[42] Steiner, skeptical of the ability of ekphrasis to overcome fully the limitations of temporality in order to attain what she calls "still moment," prefers to describe this process as "the concentration of action in a single moment of energy."[43] This definition reflects the influential notions of the "still movement" developed by Murray Krieger, first in his seminal article on ekphrasis (and "still movement") in 1967, and later in his most recent book, *Ekphrasis. The Illusion of the Natural Sign,* in 1992.

Krieger describes his own understanding of ekphrasis by integrating Leo Spitzer's definition: it is the "name of a literary genre, or at least a *topos,* that attempts to imitate in words an object of the plastic arts."[44] Krieger has adopted the conventional position of semioticians like Nelson Goodman, who sees all forms of representation as objects that can be read as texts and that can be reduced to a coherent system of signs, a language or system of symbols.[45] Goodman's *Languages of Art* is one of the modern attempts to produce a systematic general theory of symbols that takes into consideration not only painting and poetry but also other symbol systems, such as music, architecture, or even maps and diagrams.[46] Nevertheless, it has also been pointed out that the very title of Goodman's book suggests a certain level of supremacy of language over the other arts by intimating that language will provide the model for all the symbolic systems mentioned.[47]

Other critics have a similar approach. As Krieger, for example, has stated, "I am primarily interested here in the notion put forth by literary theorists about the capacity of language to do the work of the visual sign."[48] Thus, other arts could be described with the same theoretical terminology formerly reserved for the verbal arts. Krieger's position, like that of Mitchell, is rooted in the conviction that all artistic media are conventional and arbitrary, and that such notions as that of "natural signs" must therefore be rejected.[49]

Semiotics has thus caused the shift from natural-sign picture to picture-as-code. Central to this approach is Krieger's idea of the ekphrastic principle and his confidence in the capacity of the poem to become, through the paradoxical immediacy of ekphrasis, its own verbal emblem "that plays the role of a visual image while playing its own role."[50] In other words, it is an independent entity that is not perceived as a subsidiary form, subordinated to the superiority of the "natural signs" of visual form, as Scott argues. In fact, Krieger, like Lessing before him, believes that the apparent supremacy of the eye can "be countered by the superior access of language" to the inner visions of the intelligible world, but particularly by its capacity to represent what this critic calls the transcendentally "real."[51] Clearly, this is not far from declaring the autonomy of ekphrasis as a discipline. Such is the notion which defines the ekphrastic principle, which operates not only in the verbal rendition of the visual, "but also when the verbal object would emulate the spatial character of the painting or sculpture by trying to force its words, despite their normal way of functioning as empty signs, to take on a substantive configuration—in effect to become an emblem."[52]

Krieger's historical account of the evolution of the term, along with his specific distinctions of the ekphrastic experience, allow us to create a meaningful theoretical frame in which Neruda's poetry in *Canto general* can be inscribed and explained. Krieger traces the ekphrastic principle from the "visual epistemology" of Plato, with his call for *enargeia*, to its culmination in the verbal emblem of the Renaissance—the first major extended period of time in the history of this discipline.[53] By linking the evolution of the epigram of antiquity as a form of ekphrasis that reached its highest form of expression in the emblematic forms of the Renaissance, Krieger attempts to establish the supremacy of the word over the visual, since through the verbal emblem of poetry, language can overcome the limitations of space and time. In fact, Krieger's ideas are diametrically opposed to Plato's principle of *enargeia*, which was used to describe the particular use of words that created so vivid a description that they could place the represented object in front of the reader's inner vision, since Plato assumes a dependency of the word on the visual image.[54] For Krieger, the early epigrams in Greece not only subscribe to their primary use as a verbal inscription on sculptures or tombstones, but are "sometimes restive in this subsidiary role;" that the epigram "could use its words to challenge the primacy of the physical object it adorned."[55] Thus, the epigram could sometimes introduce temporality or give voice to the otherwise unmoving and silent stone, or it could add an interpretation or comment that could attach an unexpected, human dimension to the monument. In this way, the epigram could stand between the monument and its referent, undermining the notion of the visual object as a natural sign.[56]

It is not difficult to see that for Krieger the ekphrastic experience is not only an autonomous one, but that it can also overcome the limitations of space and time. For this critic, ekphrasis "is, in effect, an epigram without the accompanying object, indeed without any object except the one it would verbally create."[57] In this process the visual image, which has been translated into the verbal, is lost in the translation, while the verbal image, no longer leaning on the visual representation, becomes an independent, free-standing entity, seeking the same status as the visual. This distinction of ekphrasis as an autonomous entity is crucial to the study undertaken here, since it allows the critic and the reader to evaluate Neruda's ekphrastic experience in *Canto general*, free from the ill-conceived concept of ekphrastic poetry as a simple "description" of a visual work of art. For this reason, James Hefferman's definition of this phenomenon as "the verbal representation of a visual representation" is more appropriate and consistent with most recent criticism of the interarts.[58] This definition opens up the possibility that such visual representation can be *fictive* or *literary*. The perfect example of ekphrastic independence is precisely the famous Homeric description of Achilles' shield. In this case, as in many others, the ekphrastic object does not even exist in the literal sense, given that the shield is the product of a verbal description of a fictive or illusory object. This is the best known case of what Krieger calls the "illusion of ekphrasis," as opposed to literal ekphrasis.[59]

Nevertheless, the autonomy of ekphrasis does not depend on whether it is fictive or literal, but on the fact that in the example mentioned, we are given not a visual image of a golden shield, but a verbal shield. This is accomplished through the unique and superior capacity of words, as Lessing would say, to depict the visible and the invisible, or the "transcendentally real." Krieger concludes, "The ekphrastic principle has learned to do without the simple ekphrasis in order to explore more freely the illusionary powers of language."[60] Furthermore, such a position of independence and even superiority allows for a reversal of sorts. This brings us to the issue of the emblem poetry of the Renaissance, as treated by Krieger. In his view,

As visual companion to the poem, the emblem, which is no longer anything like a mimetic representation, seems cryptic and in need of explication, so that it leans upon a text whose verbal completeness now permit *it* to claim primacy. Though visual, the emblem has taken on a mysterious complexity that makes it function less as an imitation than as itself a text in need of interpretation, so that we welcome and depend on words as the literal code, spelling out as its own what is only hinted at in the opaque pictorial signs of another, figured code.[61]

We find ourselves obliged, then, as did Nelson Goodman and the semioticians, to see words as purely symbolic signs of representation, on the one hand, and, on the other, all visual representations as texts that can and must be treated as a language to be interpreted in a hermeneutic process rather than as mimetic "natural signs" of the referent or signified.

For Krieger, the "desire to shift art's responsibility from objects to be re-presented to a code to be interpreted helps turn all art into interpretable texts, even if—for a world confident of its metaphysical grounding—the interpretation was prescribed."[62] This leads Krieger to assert that, "the hieroglyphs of the Egyptians, though a language of pictures, are an emblematic code rather than a direct imitation of objects presumably being represented,"[63] and the same could be said for other pictographic-based languages.

At this point, once the shift from natural sign picture to picture-as-code has occurred, the boundaries between the visual and the verbal become blurred, united by essentially the same semiotic codes. The next step is for language to create the spatiality available in the visual arts, to seek, through the immediacy of ekphrasis, its transformation into a visual emblem. We have earlier seen Joseph Frank's distinctions of spatiality and temporality in narrative. Krieger follows Frank's distinctions in developing his theory. Ekphrasis is the process that allows the suturing of one medium to the other, and the device by which the poem achieves emblematic status.[64]

The poem-as-emblem for Krieger, like the image text for Mitchell, seeks to overthrow the traditional distinctions of temporality of language by creating spatiality or by finding in language the properties reserved traditionally for the plastic arts. In Krieger's opinion, "The poem as emblem, in effect supplanting its visual accompaniment, becomes the ultimate projection of the ekphrastic principle by representing a fixed object which is itself."[65] Yet, just how does language attain such a claim for spatiality? How can language overcome its own temporality? We find some answers to these questions in Krieger's seminal article on the "still movement," published in 1967. As we have been suggesting, one answer has to do with the poem's attaining a formal and linguistic autonomy by creating what Krieger describes as "a sense of roundedness," that is,

through all sorts of repetitions, echoes, complexes of internal relations, it converts its chronological progression into simultaneity, its temporally unrepeatable flow into eternal recurrence; through a meta-phorical bending under the pressure of aesthetic tension, it converts its linear movement into circle.[66]

The other answer has to do with Krieger's exposition of "still movement," a term inspired by T. S. Eliot's views, expressed in his poem "Burnt Norton," about the temporality of words and the paradoxical relation to "stillness," through form and pattern. It is through form and patterns that the poem reaches the poetic; that language can move "perpetually in its stillness," as Eliot sug-gests. Based on this principle, still movement can only be reached if the poem can claim a linguistic pattern of some sort, and a circularity within its own tenuous linearity, achieved by the use of ekphrasis, or, in Krieger's words, "the use of an object of spatial and plastic art to symbolize the spatiality and plasticity of litera-ture's temporality."[67] In this way, the visual referent, as spatial representation, becomes the metaphor in the verbal representa-tion. In such a relationship, therefore, "the spatial work freezes the temporal work even as the latter seeks to free it from space."[68] Ekphrasis, then, is introduced "in order to use a plastic object as a symbol of the frozen, stilled world of plastic relations which must be superimposed upon literature's turning world to 'still' it."[69] This critic later goes even further to claim for words the same properties of the spatial arts.

Sigurd Burkhardt, the theorist behind Krieger's idea of the poem-as-emblem, provides a more compelling and persuasive theory of the cogence and properties of words. Burkhardt states:

> If many key terms of literary analysis—"color," "texture," and "im-age," for example—are in fact metaphors borrowed from the other arts, this is the reason: poetry has no material cause. Words already have what the artist first wants to give them—body.
>
> I propose that the nature and primary function of the most im-portant poetic devices—especially rhyme, meter and metaphor—is to release words in some measure from their bondage to meaning, their purely referential role, and to give or restore to them the corporeality which a true medium needs.[70]

When corporeality is ascribed to words, the whole debate over the supremacy of one form over the other, or the differences be-tween the arts, turns into a self-effacing posture, losing ground as the traditional visual-verbal dichotomy is called into question. Mitchell observes, quoting lines from Blake:

> Once the desire to overcome the 'impossibility' of ekphrasis is put into play, the possibilities and the hopes for verbal representation of

visual representation become practically endless. "The ear and the eye lie / down together in the same bed," lulled by "undying accents." The estrangement of the image/text division is overcome, and a sutured, synthetic form, a verbal icon or imagetext, arises in its place.[71]

Yet, as has been repeated throughout this chapter, this does not mean that words, in the literal sense, can produce pictures. Mitchell himself has said,

> The treatment of vision and painting in the lingo of linguistics . . . is commonly understood to be metaphoric. Similarly, the "icons" we find in verbal expressions, whether formal or semantic, are (we suppose) not to be understood literally as pictures or visual spectacles. They are only likenesses of real graphic or visual images—doubly attenuated "images of images" or . . . "hypericons."[72]

This critic sees the history of the discipline in three moments of realization: The first he calls "ekphrastic indifference," which essentially describes the impossibility of words to represent what the visual arts can. This is based on common sense, and the assumption that different artistic media have different essential and inherent properties. The second phase he terms "ekphrastic hope," referring to the long-standing tradition of ekphrastic renditions that can be traced back to Homer's legendary shield of Achilles, and that ranges from classical rhetoric and poetry to postmodern poetry. Mitchell states, "This is the phase when the impossibility of ekphrasis is overcome in imagination and metaphor, when we discover a 'sense' in which language can do what so many writers have wanted it to do: 'to make us see'."[73] Yet such a desire to capture the "still movement" of poetry meets the resistance of those who sense or fear that the differences between the visual and the verbal might collapse. These critics begin to see that the possibility of *ut pictura poesis* or the figurative desire of ekphrasis could actually be realized. This "ekphrastic fear," or third stage is best exemplified, according to Mitchell, by Lessing's famous essay, with its prescription to poets and artists to adhere to the natural properties of their own art. Thus Mitchell concludes, "It is the moment in aesthetics when the difference between verbal and visual mediation becomes a moral, aesthetic imperative rather than . . . a natural fact that can be relied on."[74] In this last mode, the reciprocity between image and text is perceived as a dangerous, promiscuous relationship which needs to be regulated with clear limits between the senses, and the proper mode of representation for each medium.

The integration of these three "moments" becomes Mitchell's theoretical platform for his consideration of ekphrastic poetry as the genre whose main objective is the "overcoming of otherness," a discipline in which texts encounter their own semiotic "other," those rival, alien modes of representation called the visual, graphic, plastic or "spatial" arts.[75] On this basis, Mitchell refutes the "scientific" or "natural" grounds of the familiar semiotic oppositions between conventional and natural signs, arguing that such differences between the visual and the aural media are best understood as "ideologemes," a term borrowed from Frederic Jameson, and understood as "allegories of power and value disguised as a natural metalanguage."[76]

From this vantage point, Mitchell centers his discussion of the topos around the ideological notions of the "self" and the "other," in which the visual "otherness" may be anything from a professional competition between a poet and a painter to "a relation of political, disciplinary, or cultural domination in which the 'self' is understood to be an active, speaking, seeing subject, while the 'other' is projected as a passive, seen, and (usually) silent object."[77] As noted earlier, this critic considers all media to be mixed, and refuses to grant any special "gifts" to any of the arts. For him, painting can also tell stories or express abstract ideas, just as words can describe or embody static spatial states. He even goes so far as to suggest that if there is no essential difference between texts and images, then no gap between the media needs to be overcome by ekphrasis.[78] The confusion of ekphrasis, for Mitchell, stems from a confusion between the differences of medium and differences of meaning.[79] This confusion may have to do, he says, with the basic relationship of the self and the other, and with questions of racial and sexual "otherness." Whiteness, for example, normally is equated "with a normative subjectivity and humanity from which 'race' is a visible deviation." Whiteness, unlike blackness, is invisible, unmarked, "it has no racial identity."[80] A similar stand is behind gender relations in Western thought. Thus, concludes, Mitchell,

> The ambivalence about ekphrasis, then, is grounded in our ambivalence about other people, regarded as subjects and objects in the field of verbal and visual representation. Ekphrastic hope and fear express our anxieties about merging with others. Ekphrastic indifference maintains itself in the face of disquieting signs that ekphrasis may be far from trivial and that, if it is only a sham or illusion, it is one which like ideology itself, must be worked through.[81]

There is another dimension to the ekphrastic encounter that has been the subject of much critical attention: the relation between the poet/artist, the reader/viewer, and the artistic object. A major part of the ekphrastic encounter is the notion of the "archetrope" or "archetropic" experience," developed by Franklin Rogers. Rogers' study represents one of the most comprehensive and specialized works on the question of how the artist (poet or painter) creates and how these two different forms of artistic expression interact with each other. The "archetropic experience" is defined as the motivating force in the transformational process which produces first artistic vision and then the art object.[82] It is the active power to fix images. "The archetrope motivates the artistic vision, controls the artist's work, and emerges, finally, embodied in the art object."[83] From the point of view of purely literary criticism,

> the text describes a writer who under the impulse of the archetropic experience has become, . . . "the hub," . . . the organizing center of a cosmogenetic field which radiates in concentric circles outward from him to reach, ultimately the contour of the surreal world, the figure his writing creates.[84]

And the means by which the writer achieves such a figurative creation involves the role of metaphor, "the poet's tool corresponding to the painter's line."[85] Metaphor permits the fusion of the multiple into one; it becomes the means by which the poet delineates the contours of the figure that the poem makes.[86] The poetic mind contains a syntax of metaphors. If for Mitchell the ekphrastic hope was one way of overcoming the differences between the self and the other, for Rogers the metaphor becomes the "magic" device in the apprehension of the other; that which makes it possible. For Max Black, the metaphor could be described as "a filter in the apprehension of the other."[87] This device makes the most fundamental contribution to the process of art-object construction.[88] It is another term for transformation, and its essence is "resemblance." "The metaphoric process," concludes Rogers, "is most literally the form making process in literature."[89] It is the calligraphic unit of poetry.

We shall demonstrate in the following pages that the mural movement, as a whole, becomes the cosmogenetic point, containing and constraining the poet (Neruda) to a "logic" which governs the formulation of the entire *Canto general*. Muralism represents the "artistic vision"—the result of the perceptive and transformational process—that becomes the "archetrope," the kinesthetic force, the impulse or motivation which compels and guides Neruda to the "artistic image," and ultimately to the poem or the "art-object" itself.

Mitchell furthers Rogers's distinctions by including the reader's response to the ekphrastic poem, thus placing the poet in a middle position between the object described and the reader, "who (if ekphrastic hope is fulfilled) will be made to 'see' the object through the medium of the poet's voice."[90] Thus ekphrasis allows, on the one hand, the conversion of the visual representation into a verbal description, and on the other, the inversion or reconversion of the verbal representation back into the visual object in the reception of the reader.

Mitchell's objective here is not only to show the ekphrastic experience as a kind of "ménage à trois" or a triangular relationship "in which the relations of self and other, text and image, are triply inscribed," but also to suggest that in such a relationship, the visual object is associated with the female other, which is in turn offered by the poet's ekphrastic description as a "gift" to the "voyeuristic" reader.[91] The fundamental notion of reconversion or reciprocity between the visual and the aural/textual images behind Mitchell's insights can be found in what Rudolf Arnheim had earlier termed *conceptual space*, which is created by the juxtaposition of the poem and the visual object and its effect on the hermeneutical process of the reader/viewer. "Instead of a single scene," Arnheim says, "we are given two. They meet in what one might call conceptual space, in which they form a coordinated double image."[92] In the case of *Canto general* the juxtaposition of a poem and mural influences the hermeneutical process of the reader/spectator.

The idea of "conceptual space" or double image is similar to the concept of palimpsest, or the Borgesian concept of intertextuality presented in "Pierre Menard, autor del Quijote," where the verbatim writing of *Don Quijote* in the twentieth century not only produces a different work, but also transforms the original text. The premise here is that the poetry of *Canto general*, when compared or juxtaposed with the Mexican muralist paintings, forms a "conceptual space," a "coordinated double image," transforming the original "imagetext." This image is the artist's representation of reality, a purified, intensified, interpreted vision of the world. The poet's original archetropic experience is further filtered by the reader, creating yet another representation of the artistic object.

Another useful contribution to the study of the reader/viewer participation in the interarts relationship is Steiner's work, which also helps to contextualize Frank's comparison of literary Modernism with the visual arts of the Middle Ages. First citing Meyer Schapiro's discussions of the hierarchical, semantic organization of the picture plane, Steiner concentrates on the shift of focalization that occurred from medieval painting to the perspective of the Renaissance. In medieval painting the artist placed the most important subject at the center of the scene, and it was usually represented in a disproportionately larger size, subordinating the other figures by increasing distance from the center and by decreasing size. In the Renaissance, on the other hand, the relevance of the presented objects on the picture plane are more a function of their distance from the implicit viewer of the scene, eliminating the semantic weight given to size and centrality in the earlier art. Even more germane to our purposes here is Steiner's connection of art to literature:

> Unlike the semantic nature of medieval . . . perspective, Renaissance optical perspective implies a viewer and projects a scene from a specific standpoint. It is a way of relating the perceiver to the painting, since it posits a specific viewing position by which the scene depicted achieves its organization. Perspective, then, is an important part of the pragmatics of painting and finds its literary analogue in point of view.[93]

Later, Steiner resorts to Boris Uspenski's work to further refine this correspondence. For Steiner—as for Uspenski—in the transferral of the real multidimensional space onto the picture plane, the artist's position is the key orientation point, and the same is the case of the position of the narrator/poet with regard to the event described. Steiner explains,

> Spatially, just as the arrangement of a scene vis-à-vis the point of vision indicates that distance of the visual perceiver from the action, the narrator indicates his distance from a scene through such techniques as the birds-eye view, the silent scene (where he is close enough to see but not to hear), the fusion of his view with what a character within the scene is seeing, and so on."[94]

The important point here is to establish for both instances the congruent structural relationships between a paradigmatic perceiver and what he perceives. Yet there is a significant difference in this paradigmatic relation in Renaissance and pre-Renaissance perspectives. In the Renaissance, the artist has stayed outside the painting, and his point of view is shared or is the same as that of the viewer. In medieval painting, the painter frequently introduced himself within the work of art; the scene spreads out around the center, and the objects represented are the function of an abstract internal observer. In literature, this medieval perspective would find an equivalency in the first-person narrative, in which the narrator, like the central figure in the painting, presents us with all of what he or she sees through his or her eyes, subjectively. The Renaissance artistic stance outside the frame is the equivalent of the omniscient narrator, who, standing uninvolved outside the action, can "objectively" acquire and convey more information.

Steiner seems also to confirm Frank's comparison of literary modernism with the medieval tradition when she states:

> With modernism, the trend seems to have reversed itself. Literature became obsessed with first-person narrative and the limitations of knowledge implicit in it, whereas painting became much more intent on an omniscient perspective. Symptomatically, Marinetti's daughter claimed that futurism fought for the "interpenetration of the figure and its surroundings, insertion of the spectator into the middle of the picture."[95]

As we will discuss in detail later, this series of distinctions on point of view are very useful to our study in establishing the paradigmatic relation between the perspective favored by muralist painters and that projected by Neruda in many poems of *Canto general,* particularly those with more epic overtones.

In summary, all the approaches of reception and theory of the reader's role and participation are based on the tenet that the interpretation of a text, as Barthes, Iser, Prince, and others have argued, is a joint process in which both author and reader collaborate. The result in the interarts comparison is a fully independent emblematic poem inscribed in a multifaceted and complex dynamic of relationships between the poet, the reader/viewer, and the represented object.

The study of literature and its relation to the visual arts is a discipline that has been historically approached mainly from the field of aesthetics, and only recently by literary theorists, in approaches ranging from semiotics to gender studies. On the methodological side, however, there have been several attempts to create a systematic strategy that would regulate the intersection of different artistic media, yet most of these efforts have failed to establish a set of common criteria that would provide the literary critic with effective formulas to apply to both the visual and the verbal arts. The pioneering studies by Helmut Hatzfeld, Jean H. Hagstrum, Mario Praz, and others, while they have helped to develop critical parameters and historical surveys, have failed to provide a rigorous system of comparison. For this reason, Henryk Markiewiez, in his earlier cited article, in addition to connecting the study of word-image to the field of semiotics, also calls for precise definitions of critical terminology so that we can begin to establish a consensus regarding the relations that exist between the visual and the textual. The issue of pragmatic typification of the subject has been taken up by Ulrich Weisstein, who has proposed in his article, "Literature and the Visual Arts," sixteen types of linkage between literary and visual works of art. Departing from René Wellek's assertion that "the most central approach to comparison of the arts is based on an analysis of the actual objects, and thus on their structural relationships," Weisstein begins by naming "kinds of cohabitation and interpenetration that are manifest 'to the naked eye'."[96] In the interest of being concise, I will address only those types of approaches listed by Weisstein that most closely relate to the present study. I refer the reader to Weisstein's article for the complete list. The pertinent categories are as follows:

A) *Literary works that describe or interpret works of art.* This is closely related to the ekphrastic principle we have been discussing, and refers to the "iconic poem, derived from the ancient epigram or inscription."[97]

B) *Literary works so designed as to stimulate the reader's visual sense.* The poet's use of images, metaphors, similes, and other poetic devices, as is the case in Parnassian or imagist poetry, is a good example.

C) *Literary works seeking to reproduce movement styles in the visual arts.* Impressionism, cubism, or muralism are good examples of this category.

D) *Literary and art works that are linked with each other through manifestos and programmatic statements reflecting a common viewpoint and purpose.*

E) *Literary works in whose creation certain techniques or modes borrowed from the visual arts have been employed.* According to Weisstein, this refers to the application of collage to poems or the camera-eye technique used by Robbe-Grillet in *La jalousie.*[98]

F) *Literary works that share themes or motifs with works of art.*

G) *Literary works that, jointly with other literary works produced in a given era and civilization, or together with contemporary music, painting, philosophy, science, and so forth, display common features.*

Recent criticism, including commentaries by Weisstein, Steiner, and others, has cautioned against the imprecision or oversimplification of this last category, the so-called *Geistesgeschichte* or *zeitgeist*, to describe the belief in the existence of "spirits of the time." Wellek criticizes its excessive reliance on contraries and analogies, its simplistic presuppositions, and its assumption that there is actually such a thing as "a complete integration of all activities of man."[99] Wendy Steiner has also reacted to the concept of *zeitgeist*, or for that matter, any periodization term that tends to paint with a broad brush the different artistic manifestations of a given era.[100]

In the preceding pages, I have attempted to present a synopsis of the scholarly history of interarts study. While the parameters of the present study do not permit a complete survey of the immense number of theorists who have treated this subject, this outline of the most prominent and influential writings serves as an introduction to questions regarding *Canto general* and its relationship to Mexican muralism. We will refer to each of the points raised here in the appropriate contexts of the discussion of various aspects of *Canto general* and Neruda's particular ekphrastic experience.

2

Neruda and the Mural Phenomenon

Neruda, Painting and Painters

Saúl Yurkiévich once noted that

[Neruda] es un poeta visionario, es decir, movido por una voluntad de representación, de figuración, por un afán icónico, afán de transmitir imágenes. La poesía no constituye para él un objeto y objetivo autónomos, una entidad autosuficiente, autorreferente, sino un medio para comunicar mensajes que nos remiten a instancias no textuales.

[(Neruda) is a visionary poet, that is, motivated by a desire for representation, for figuring; by an iconic eagerness, an eagerness to transmit images. Poetry does not constitute for him an object or autonomous objective, a self-sufficient, self-reflexive entity, but rather a medium for communicating messages that transmit non-textual instances to us.][1]

In a way this book attempts to provide the theoretical and critical contexts behind this critic's intuitive generalizations. In the following pages we will explore how, when, and where Neruda developed this "afán icónico," this desire to transmit images, not merely words; we will pay particular attention to why Mexican mural art became the source of ekphrastic desire for the poet.

Pablo Neruda always had a special fascination with the plastic arts. His relationship to painting and painters was long-standing. It may have begun with his good friend Rafael Alberti, a painter as well as a poet, whose poetry is also rich in visual imagery.[2] In addition, it is likely that Neruda's inclination for the visual was strongly influenced by the various pictorial trends of the European avant-garde.

A review of Neruda's years in Europe shows that he was acquainted with many American and European poets and painters, and that he established close contacts with many of them.[3] Apollinaire, to mention one of the best known, like his Mexican counterpart José Juan Tablada, was always in search of visual representation in poetry and, like Mallarmé before him, was interested in concrete poetry. He also established a strong relationship with Picasso. According to René de Costa, the Chilean poet Vicente Huidobro and the Spanish artist Juan Gris were good friends and great admirers of each other's work.[4] Federico García Lorca, Salvador Dalí, and many others frequently exchanged their latest artistic endeavors, not to mention the long French tradition of interaction between painters and poets. As Octavio Paz noted in an interview: "Desde su nacimiento, la poesía moderna ha entablado un diálogo con las otras artes, sobre todo con la música y la pintura. Esta tradición ha sido central en la poesía francesa: Baudelaire, Mallarmé, Apollinaire, Reverdy, Breton" [Since its inception, modern poetry has engaged in a dialogue with the other arts, especially with music and painting. This tradition has been central in French poetry: Baudelaire, Mallarmé, Apollinaire, Reverdy, Breton].[5] Consequently, it is not difficult to assume that when Neruda arrived in Mexico and decided to embrace as a source of inspiration the work of the three most prolific and distinguished Mexican painters of that time, he was only following in the steps of European avant-garde writers.

Similarly, both Siqueiros and Rivera (as well as Roberto Montenegro) spent some time in France, Italy, and Spain, where they came in contact with new European trends. The indigenous theme of mural art is related to the European artistic search for the exotic at the turn of the century.[6] The ethnic theme may be linked to the rise of primitivism in France, as seen in the works of Gauguin, Picasso, or Matisse. Picasso's *Les demoiselles d'Avignon* finds its source in the African masks of the Ivory Coast; Gauguin's paintings from his years in Tahiti are also crucial in the development of the new *ism*. Henri Matisse's works from 1900–1920 clearly demonstrate a strong interest in the subject.[7]

But it is the works of the French-Peruvian painter Gauguin which most strikingly resemble some of Rivera's murals. A first glance at some of his works reveals that the use of color, composition, and motifs are in essence the same. *Ia Orana Maria* (Virgin with Child, 1891) shares the same technique used by Rivera many years later that consists of cleverly juxtaposing Christian iconography with the "native" representation of the "bon sauvage," in this instance by painting a halo around the head of a native woman carrying her child on her shoulder, as seen in *The Blood of the Martyrs* or *The Flowering of the Revolution* at the Chapingo Chapel. In this "native" version of *The Holy Family,* both mother and child have a halo formed with fine-lined circles. The composition and posture of the human figures in Gauguin's *Man with the Ax* (1891) could be the source for some of Rivera's murals in the corridors of the National Palace, specifically the panels devoted to Mexico's various autochthonous cultures. *Fragrant Earth* (1892) may have also inspired Rivera's huge expressionist feminine nudes found in the Chapingo Chapel. Finally, Rivera's *Creation* (1922) at the National Preparatory School may be viewed as a Mexican interpretation of Gauguin's *Where Do We Come From? What Are We? Where Are We Going?* (1897). It is also of note that Gauguin, like the Mexican mural painters, resorted extensively to the use of Christian iconography in many of these paintings. Furthermore, "Gauguin had long been interested in the particular problems presented by monumental compositions. He often cited examples of works by great painters such as Giotto and Rafael."[8] The painting just mentioned, *Where Do We Come From?* was later transposed into a mural, making it the largest painting produced by this artist. Rivera was thus following and furthering Gauguin's artistic vision; and in his own opinion, his art was even more closely linked to its indigenous roots.[9]

Moreover, the mural form was very much on the minds of many French painters at the turn of the century. Seurat's mural, *La Grande Jatte* (1884–86), Renoir's *Large Bathers* (1886), and Monet's series of *Waterlilies* (ca. 1918) are cases in point. Around 1890, a disciple of Gauguin, Verkade, expressed his master's desire to free himself from the limitations of easel painting:

> A battle cry rang out from one studio to another. No more easels! Down with unnecessary furniture! Painting must not usurp a liberty that isolates it from other arts . . . walls, walls for decorating! Down with perspective! The wall must remain a surface . . . There are not paintings, only decorations![10]

But despite the "European" genetic elements of Mexican muralism, the movement took on its own American character and achieved what the Europeans had only aimed at; namely, the adaptation of its original forms, the Amerindian art and fresco traditions, to the European fresco technique. The Mexican Revolution was one of two circumstances that facilitated the recovery of pre-Hispanic art and culture. According to Paz, the revolution modified profoundly the vision that Mexicans have of themselves and their past.[11] But such a change of vision would have failed if it had not been for another profound change in the artistic sensibility of the West: the search for the exotic and the "primitive" that begins with the European expansionism in the sixteenth and seventeenth centuries, and acquires a steady pace when, according to Paz,

> los románticos alemanes sufren una doble fascinación: el sánscrito y la literature de la India—y así sucesivamente hasta que la conciencia estética moderna, al despuntar nuestro siglo, descubre las artes de Africa, América y Oceanía. El arte moderno de Occidente, que nos ha enseñado a ver lo mismo una máscara negra que un fetiche polinesio, nos abrió el camino para comprender el arte antiguo de México.

> [The German Romantics experience a double fascination: with Sanskrit and with Indian literature—a trend that continued until the turn of the century when modern aesthetic consciousness discovered the arts of Africa, America and the Pacific Islands. Western modern art, which has taught us to view with the same eyes a black mask and a Polynesian fetish, opened the way for an understanding of the antique art of Mexico.][12]

Primitivism in painting is to modern art what the Renaissance was to medieval aesthetics, in the sense that the reshaping of perspective and conception of representation of reality that "primitivism" brought to modern aesthetics is equivalent to the change of perspective that took place during the Renaissance in relation to the simple, more allegorical representation of the medieval tradition. Siqueiros's second of three appeals to the new American generation of painters, published in *Vida Americana* in 1921, is of interest in this regard:

> An understanding of the admirable human content of "negro art" and the "primitive art" in general has oriented the plastic arts towards a clarity and depth lost for four centuries in an underbrush of indecision; as regards ourselves, we most have to come closer to the works of the ancient settlers of our vales, Indian painters and sculptors (Mayan, Aztec, Inca, etc., etc.)[13]

Upon his return to Mexico from Europe in that same year, Rivera expresses his own synthesis of the European avant-garde:

> The search that European artists further with such intensity ends here in Mexico, in the abundant realization of our national art. I could

tell you much concerning the progress to be made by a painter, a sculptor, an artist, if he observes, analyzes, studies Mayan, Aztec, or Toltec art, none of which falls short of any other art in my opinion.[14]

Muralism shared many precepts of the European avant-garde, and in fact furthered many of the explorations begun by avant-garde artists. Thus it is not merely casual that in Neruda's relationship to the muralists and their works we see a dynamic similar to that found in the works of poets such as Apollinaire, T. S. Eliot, Lorca, or Huidobro, who were strongly influenced by the iconoclastic characteristic of the avant-garde, a movement which tries to break once again with the barriers traditionally imposed on the arts.

Moreover, we must ask: is the return to the past and the ancient art of the Aztecs, Mayans, and Toltecs by the muralists a further reason for Neruda's radical change to the epic tradition of poetry? Was Neruda, like Rivera and Siqueiros, searching for the roots of his own trade? Is not the epic the first form of poetry, as are the fresco and murals the first expressions of painting? If we accept that Neruda is a poet driven by visual images, as Yurkiévich suggests, it is logical to assume that faced with such monumental visual representations, the poet felt compelled to express with words his special vision, to produce his own ekphrastic rendition of the same stature and size that would complement and reveal the hidden messages contained in the visual experience. Sometimes the ekphrastic and the visual experience can be found in the same artist, who allows him or herself the total freedom to reproduce both the poem and the picture or drawing, as is the case of William Blake, William Morris, Apollinaire, Huidobro, and certainly Lorca and Alberti; even Borges once attempted to draw a tiger.

Neruda, like these poets/artists, seems to believe in the conventionalist position that much of the world in which we believe is the result of a dialogue between the visual and verbal representation. In certain ways, Neruda anticipated the semioticians in their logocentric position that sees language as a required component of all other organized systems of representation or knowledge. Roland Barthes considers that the field of semiotics requires that language serve "not only as a model, but also a component." For Barthes, "it appears increasingly more difficult to conceive a system of images and objects whose signifieds can exist independently of language . . . ; there is no meaning which is not designated, and the world of signifieds is none other than that of language."[15]

Again, did Neruda realize immediately that the complex and intricate messages imbedded in mural art lacked that linguistic component, and thus needed the articulation that only language can provide? Did Neruda grasp early on that the excessive emphasis on ideology and strong reliance on the visual run the risk of being judged erroneously as Manichean or schematic? If we accept the premise that the answers to these queries are affirmative, *Canto general,* then, is the linguistic equivalent of mural art, a kind of linguistic companion that explicates and provides the deeper human dimension inscribed in the murals. This notion is consistent with the desire mentioned earlier to return to the past tradition of antiquity, both in Europe and in pre-Hispanic America. In this instance, the poems would be the equivalent of the epigrams that were included in medieval paintings, or the hieroglyphs inscribed on the *códices* or inner walls of Aztec and Mayan pyramids. As with the epigrams or glyphs, one purpose of *Canto general* is to function as an interpreter of the hidden messages contained in the unreliable visual imagery. At play here is a perception of the inadequacy of painting that is deeply rooted in a distrust of the communicative abilities of visual representations. Such an imbalance of representation was shared by Sigmund Freud, who saw in the (verbal) analysis of dreams (images) the necessary component to understand the visual, "the method for extracting the hidden verbal message from the misleading and inarticulate pictorial surface."[16] Rivera himself seems to share this same awareness of the limitations of the visual, as evidenced by his use of narrative ballad in the murals of the Ministry of Education in Mexico City.

But, perhaps the mutual affinity between painting, painters and Neruda can best be illustrated by the extraordinary celebration in Chile of the anniversary of the poet's eightieth birthday, marked by an astonishing exhibition of the work of thirty-five painters, "retratando su rostro, o interpretando pasajes de su vida y su poesía" [painting his portrait, or interpreting passages from his life and poetry].[17] Neruda wrote extensively about many painters of his native Chile as well as artists from other nations, and, of course, about Rivera, Siqueiros, and Orozco.

His relationship with these painters had a special meaning for the poet. As mentioned in the introduction, the first edition of *Canto general* was published in Mexico in 1950 and included paintings by Diego Rivera and David Alfaro Siqueiros. Three hundred copies were signed both by the painters and Neruda and distributed to private contributors who made its publication financially possible. Seven years before, in October 1943, the anthology *Cantos de Pablo Neruda* was published in Lima, Peru, with illustrations by Siqueiros and Carlos Beltrán. Neruda supervised every step of production for his initial Mexican edition of *Canto general.* The fact that its publication was delayed because the artists did not finish the paintings on time and that Neruda elected not to go on without them reflects the indispensability of these painters to the poet's work.

Canto general, therefore, was planned originally as a mixed-media work that opened and closed with visual images produced by two of the best known Mexican painters of the time. Later editions have mistakenly omitted the visual component of the text. But if we consider the original as Neruda's ekphrastic encounter with Mexican mural art, we must then reconsider the way in which the text has been approached until now. We must take into account, among other aspects of the interarts study, that when the poet insisted on placing the paintings on the covers or pages of his writings, he wanted the reader to also be engaged as a viewer, and even to become a participant creator in the joint interartistic venture. This opens up another dimension to the ekphrastic experience that is more like a triangular relationship between the speaker, the art object, and the audience or addressee of ekphrasis. This is the kind of ménage à trois that according to W. J. T. Mitchell is one in which the "ekphrastic poet typically stands in a middle position between the object described or addressed and a listening subject who (if ekphrastic hope is fulfilled) will be made to 'see' the object through the medium of the poet's voice."[18]

"Canto general" and Mexican Muralism:
A Critical Approach

A number of critics have acknowledged *Canto general*'s affinity with Mexican mural painting. Angel Valbuena Briones affirms:

> *Canto general* mantiene estrechos lazos de contacto con la pintura mejicana proletaria, representada por la obra de Diego Rivera, José Clemente Orozco y de David Alfaro Siqueiros. . . . El chileno ha tenido en cuenta los cuadros y los murales de esa escuela para su elaboración artística.

[*Canto general* maintains close ties with Mexican proletariat painting, represented by the works of Diego Rivera, José Clemente Orozco and David Alfaro Siqueiros . . . . The Chilean took into account the paintings and murals of that school in his own artistic process.][19]

This critic adds that the negative interpretation of the Spanish conquest contained in *Canto III* has an artistic precedent in Rivera's frescoes at Cortés's Palace (1930–35) in Cuernavaca, and, in part, his frescoes on the staircase of the National Palace.[20] In the wake of the publication of *Canto general* (December 1950), Alfredo Cardona Peña declared:

El *Canto general* es la divulgación amplificada del hombre sobre la tierra, más dueño y poseedor de su mundo. . . . Por eso fuimos los primeros en difundir la noticia de que esta obra resultaba el equivalente, en las letras, del fenómeno muralista mexicano: porque su gran espacio, y lo apretado de su universo expresivo, realizaba en igualdad de belleza la prédica de las masas.

[*Canto General* is the amplified spreading of man over the earth, more masterful and possessing of his world. . . . That is why we were the first to spread the word that this work was the literary equivalent of the Mexican muralist phenomenon: because its great space, and the tightness of its expressive universe, managed, with an equal degree of beauty, to instruct the masses.][21]

Luis Cardoza y Aragón, an art critic and close friend of Neruda during these years, has written about his personal acquaintance with Neruda and about his work. In one of his studies, he wonders if Neruda, after *Residencia en la tierra*, rediscovered his American identity through muralism and the musical innovations of Silvestre Revueltas.[22] Italian critic Giuseppe Bellini has also pointed out the plastic element of this poetry in his introduction to an anthology of Neruda's work:

La poesía de Neruda se rivela della stessa grandezza ciclopica de questa pittura. La sua potenzialità plastica si consustanzia di concetti, e il tutto conduce alla creazione di un'atmosfera tesa ed eroica dell'umanità, che è nello stesso tempo atmosfera carica di sottile lirismo nel rivivere dei miti e della natura, della prima creazione e delle razze perdute, della poesía immensa delle acque e delle selve, nell'accorato ricordo di dolorose odissee personali.

[Neruda's poetry proves to be of the same immense grandeur as that painting (muralism). Its plastic potentiality acquires substance from ideas, and the whole makes for the creation of a taut and heroic atmosphere of humanity; at the same time the atmosphere is charged with a subtle lyricism in the reliving of myths, nature, the initial creation, lost peoples, and the immense poetry of the water and the jungle—and in the sorrowful memory of painful personal odysseys.][23]

Roberto Fernández Retamar also finds in Neruda's poetry a parallel with the grandiosity, the revolutionary tone, and the artistic unity of Rivera's frescoes.[24] Juan Villegas elaborates further on this relationship. For him, "*Canto General* es un enorme fresco, multifacético, polidimensional, de una riqueza lírica impresionante, comparable sólo a los grandes murales mexicanos" [*Canto general* is an enormous, multifaceted, polidimensional fresco, with an impressive lyricism comparable only to the great Mexican murals].[25] Nevertheless, Villegas also accurately notes that while a number of critics have indicated affinities between *Canto general* and Mexican muralism, "No se ha examinado con cuidado, sin embargo, la relación, y las afirmaciones son bastante generales" [These have not been examined carefully, however, and the statements are quite general].[26] Indeed, no one has yet presented a systematic study that examines in detail the extent to which the visual images of the murals provided useful sources for Neruda's *Canto general*. The present study intends to fill this gap and to present a coherent theoretical and critical discussion of Neruda's ekphrastic experience.

I must add that Neruda was not the only Chilean who fell under the spell of the new aesthetic movement. Years earlier, his compatriot and fellow Nobel laureate, Gabriela Mistral—who came to Mexico at the invitation of the Mexican Secretary of Education José Vasconcelos during the late 1920s—derived new modes of expression from the frescoes of Mexican painters as well as from popular culture.[27]

Clearly, new forms were paving the way toward a new vision. Within Mexico, the genre that most matched the aesthetic values of muralism was the novel. In his study of the development of the novel in Mexico, Manuel Pedro González has underlined "la posible influencia que la escuela de pintura mural ejerció en el concepto y en la técnica de la novela que entre 1930 y 1940 se puso de moda" [the possible influence that the school of mural painting exercised on the conception and the technique of the novel that became popular between 1930 and 1940].[28] Though the impact of Mexican mural painting on other national literatures has not yet been undertaken, such a study could prove very useful. The role that this movement played in the works of Mexican writers such as Juan Rulfo, Jorge Ferretis, José Revueltas, Francisco Rojas González, Cipriano Campos Alatorre, and many others is clear.[29] Neruda's poetry in *Canto general*, like many of the narratives of these authors, seeks to emulate the mural painters' attempt to make the suffering and misery of the lower classes a theme worthy of aesthetic expression, becoming, at the same time, a voice for those silent witnesses of history, a means of articulating their despair. Manuel Pedro González distinguishes the most important characteristic of Mexican muralism and its essence:

> Hay en estos grandes frescos una tan cabal identificación del artista con el alma del pueblo, que más que obra personal diríase labor colectiva en la cual la gran masa hubiera plasmado sus angustias y sus ansias de redención.

> [In these great frescos there is such a perfect identification of the artist with the soul of the people, that more than personal works of art, they are a collective labor in which the great masses could have imprinted their anguish and anxiety for redemption.][30]

González likewise acknowledges the movement's wider impact:

> La aguda intuición de José Vasconcelos *previó el influjo que la pintura ejercería en otras formas artísticas* y en el pueblo. . . . La obra de los primeros maestros hizo prosélitos inmediatamente y en menos de tres lustros, México se enriqueció con una de las escuelas de pintura más originales y valiosas con que el mundo cuenta hoy, *cuya influencia no sólo trascendió a otras artes, como la novela, sino que se ha dejado sentir allende las fronteras, tanto en los países hermanos como en la plástica norteamericana* (emphasis added).

> [The sharp intuition of José Vasconcelos *foresaw the influence that (mural) painting would have on other art forms* and on the people. . . . The work of the first masters immediately created followers and in less than three decades, Mexico had become enriched with one of the most original and valuable schools of painting in the world today, *whose influence not only transcended the barriers of other art forms, such as the novel, but also has had influence beyond geographic borders, both in Latin American countries and in the plastic arts in North America* (emphasis added).][31]

Desmond Rochfort goes even further in his evaluation of the artistic significance of the movement: "Mexican mural painting is a phenomenon without parallel in modern art. In many senses it is also a unique continental-American contribution to twentieth-century painting."[32] Yet, Mexican mural art is at once a native and a Western phenomenon. It is part of the European avant-garde movement, like Latin American art in general at the beginning of the century; but the experiences of individual artists and the physical circumstances of life in the American continent gave it its own character. The fresco technique, part of the Amerindian artistic heritage, was key to the creation of a very original form of expression. Hence, it is not an exaggeration to suggest that Mexican mural art, with all its richness and vitality, revealed to young artists (writers, musicians, sculptors, and so on) new aesthetic possibilities, and gave rise to muralist themes in their works, including the novel of the Mexican Revolution.[33] One conspicuous exception was poets. Such being the case, in one of his final interviews before departing Mexico for Chile, Neruda declared to Alardo Pratts:

> Para mí, lo mejor de México son los agrónomos y los pintores. . . . Considero que en poesía hay una absoluta desorientación y una falta de moral civil que realmente impresiona. . . . La novela mexicana, en cuatro de sus representantes más jóvenes: Juan de la Cabada, Ermilo Abreu Gómez, José Revueltas y Andrés Henestrosa, llega a alcanzar las expresiones de un nuevo clasicismo.

> [For me, the best part of Mexico is the agronomists and the painters. . . . I believe that in poetry there is an absolute disorientation and lack of civil morals that is really quite impressive. . . . The Mexican novel, as practiced by four of the youngest novelists—Juan de la Cabada, Ermilo Abreu Gómez, José Revueltas and Andrés Henestrosa—has within its grasp the expressions of a new classicism.][34]

In his criticism of Mexican poetry, the poet was sending a final message to Mexican poets, who represented the only genre that did not succumb to the influence of the mural painters. The Mexican poet Octavio Paz, for example, opposed the subordination of poetry to politics or anything else.[35] Neruda's admiration of the younger generation of Mexican novelists stemmed from their receptiveness to the new artistic challenge that the country was discovering. They were in fact a new breed of artists, undergoing a process of aesthetic revelatior. The whole country was striving to define itself, to find its own personality, and to unearth from the past a genuine and autochthonous expression. The new iconoclasts refused to continue the servile imitation of bourgeois

European models and turned toward Mexican reality to find artistic inspiration, just as the Romantics had done a century before. As Manuel P. González has stated:

> Ahora se estudia y se ahonda en la observación de lo terrígeno. Se acude al análisis serio de lo vernacular, de las costumbres, de las tradiciones, del carácter y del folklore de cada región y de cada grupo cultural indígena, además de las zonas de vida urbana.

> [Now one studies and observes in depth that which is earthborn. One resorts to the serious analysis of the vernacular, customs, traditions, character and folklore of each region and each indigeneous cultural group, in addition to the areas of urban life.][36]

One could very well apply the same poetic criteria to *Canto general,* with the exception that Neruda's *Canto* attempts to embrace the entire North and South American continents, including the United States. As I will argue in the following pages, Mexican muralism provided the archetropic force, the cosmogenetic source, for Neruda's themes, imagery, figures, and motifs for his continental odyssey. It will be helpful, therefore, to outline some of the images, figures, and topoi that characterized the movement.

The Mural Movement

But how did the mural movement start? What made it possible for the artists to take a different approach to art? When we examine the Mexican artistic production from the Independence Movement through the Revolution (1810–1910), we find that, with few exceptions, it was frequently reduced to poor imitations of European models. National themes were considered worthless of any attention; authentic Mexican reality was systematically avoided. According to Luis Cardoza y Aragón, the dominant class

> vivía superficialmente en México, con los ojos en Europa. El pueblo, la nación, lo nuestro, se diría que le era extraño y hasta odioso. París e Italia, en sus aspectos finiseculares y decadentes, fijaban las normas de la alta burguesía que había perdido toda tradición nacional.

> [lived superficially in Mexico, with their eyes on Europe. It could be said that the people, the nation, our affairs, were strange and even odious to them. Paris and Italy, with their decadent and fin-de-siècle

aspects, set the norms for the upper bourgeoisie, which had lost all
sense of a national tradition.][37]

Although the Guatemalan critic is essentially correct, it is necessary to mention that during the nineteenth century there were
already several attempts to cultivate an American art, adapting
European models to the national character. A few examples are
the following: José María Obregón's *Discovery of Pulque;* Félix
Parra's *Episodes of the Conquest* (1877); Leandro Izaguirre's *Torture
of Cuauhtémoc* (1893); and, particularly, José María Velasco's vast
catalog of panoramic Mexican landscapes. These painters began
an authentic search for American themes.[38] As Dawn Ades has
stated: "The years of colonial rule were regarded as a savage inter-
ruption of Mexican history, and a continuity with the pre-
Conquest past was stressed"[39]—a vision clearly shared by Neruda, who puts in parentheses the word "(Intermedio)" before the
poem dedicated to "La colonia sobre nuestras tierras" [The Colony Covering Our Lands], in the XIV section of *Los libertadores,*
canto IV. Among the painters just mentioned, national unity was
considered vital and could not be achieved without a strong sense
of identity: the search for the historical roots of *mexicanidad.* During the Romantic period, as later during the mural movement,
there prevailed the shared sentiment to preserve the remnants of
ancient cultures, a retrospective move towards the roots of the
Aztecs, Mayans, and so on. Similarly, Romantic and mural painters rejected the imposition of European aesthetic models. Yet for
the most part, Mexican life and indigenous traditions did not
provide themes considered worthy of artistic attention. To show
the extremes that slavish imitation could reach, Cardoza y Aragón
humorously points out that "[h]asta las piedras del edificio de
correos fueron traídas de Europa" [even the stones of the post
office building were brought from Europe].[40]

The Mexican Revolution generated artistic renovation and inspired mural painting,which restored to Mexicans the image of
their own people:

> Out of it [the Revolution] the identity of modern Mexico was born,
> and the frescos painted by Rivera, Orozco, and Siqueiros in the years
> that followed were to become its most powerful visual expression.[41]

But prior to the three masters there were several early mural artists. Jorge Enciso painted the first twentieth-century murals with
Amerindian content at the Escuelas de la Colonia de la Bolsa in

Mexico City between December 1910 and May 1911 (the murals were later destroyed). Saturnino Herrán, in his short ill-fated life, devoted his art entirely to Mexican themes: *El rebozo* (1916) is his best known work. Roberto Montenegro was first influenced by the Decadents before discovering his *mexicanidad* in Europe in 1919; his series of etchings titled "Mexican Motifs" have been described by Silvio Lago as "a constant exhortation to American artists, a model showing why they should cultivate the milieu of their birth in preference to any other."[42] Montenegro was commissioned to paint the first government-sponsored mural. Adolfo Best Maugard in 1910 had already treated the Mexican theme in his illustrations for Franz Boas's ethnological study. Just as Rivera was to do later, Best reproduced in great detail the diversity of the ancient cultures of Mexico. Best, however, rejected the concept of art for the masses. Carlos Mérida, like Montenegro and unlike Best, became a strong defendant of national art as a departure from academicism. In the introduction to the catalog of his exhibition at the Museum of Fine Arts in 1920, Mérida wrote: "My painting is fired with an intimate conviction that it is imperative to produce a totally American art."[43]

Such is the artistic environment preceding Rivera, Siqueiros, and Orozco, and muralism as a defined movement. Mural painting after the Mexican Revolution of 1910 represented, for some critics, an iconoclastic force opposing modernist art practiced in Europe. Leonard Folgarait comments on the movement's relation to the political program launched by President Alvaro Obregón:

> In the history of twentieth-century art, the mural paintings produced in Mexico after the military phase of the Revolution of 1910 stand in deliberate opposition to the course of modernist art as practiced in Europe and the United States. This has to do with the beginnings of the mural movement in a postrevolutionary society, especially with regard to the policy makeup of the administration of Alvaro Obregón (1920–4) and its needs to involve culture in a legitimization of its ideology.[44]

Indeed, the mural movement is the result of a postrevolutionary society and of governmental patronage. Nevertheless, what Folgarait seems to overlook is that, as we argue at the beginning of this chapter, such iconoclastic behavior was very much a characteristic of the avant-garde in Europe, and that in its search for new forms, the incorporation of the exotic or the primitive gave way to direct artistic expressions, such as primitivism, cubism, and later muralism.

The movement's success could not have been achieved without the support of a prominent figure in the history of painting in Mexico, Doctor Atl (Gerardo Murillo). Mural painting, as it is now known, began with the return to Mexico of Doctor Atl in 1904, after an eight-year stay in Europe. Doctor Atl was placed in charge of the Academy of Fine Arts in Mexico, where Orozco was his apprentice and star pupil. He instilled his enthusiasm for the Italian frescos of the Renaissance in Orozco and the other students of the Academy. Jean Charlot, one of the first mural painters, recalls Atl's influence:

> [Atl] made them aware for the first time of the freedom of the great masters; how Michelangelo created muscles instead of copying them, making them bulge or sink rhythmically as a poet manipulates sound; how form was made flesh on the ceiling of the Sistine because of an ideal that strove to be born rather than a mirror held to bodies born of women.[45]

Charlot alludes here not only to Atl's prestige among the young painters, but most pertinently to his understanding of the important relationship of the "sister arts." In fact, Charlot's words ascribed to Atl, and his supposed recommendation to the younger artists to use Michelangelo as a model, are very much like Lessing's advice to poets to use Homer's description of Achilles' shield as a model to create with words the illusion of the visual: "Homer does not paint the shield as finished and complete, but as a shield that is being made."[46] He also sums up in this quote the archetropic experience that compels the artist to give form to the art object in a very specific way. By far, this was the most important insight the young muralists learned from Atl.

But it was not until 1922 that President Obregón's Minister of Education José Vasconcelos entrusted the painting of the murals in the amphitheater of the National Preparatory School mainly to the *Tres Maestros*. These would become the first murals in which Rivera, Siqueiros, Orozco, and others gave shape to the new artistic vision. It was Alvaro Obregón's administration that called back from Europe these expatriate Mexican artists in order to construct a national art form:

> These artists, such as Diego Rivera, left Europe and its avant-garde and modernist strategies, studied the styles and materials of Renaissance fresco murals, and gave form to the values of a "Revolutionary" regime by means of a pre-modernist aesthetic.[47]

Diego Rivera returned in June 1921. Soon after, David Alfaro Siqueiros was called back from Rome by José Vasconcelos, and joined Rivera and the rest of his fellow painters, including Jean Charlot, a French painter newly arrived in Mexico. Siqueiros himself had participated in the Mexican Revolution and later fought for the Republican cause in the Spanish Civil War. José Clemente Orozco was the eldest of the three, and like Doctor Atl, yearned for a Mexican Renaissance. Rivera and Siqueiros were ready to take on the new task. They had experienced the great artistic revolutions which had taken place in Europe and were beginning to understand and appreciate the richness and value of their own Mexican milieu. It is interesting to observe the image that Neruda had of each one of them. In his memoirs, the poet describes Orozco:

En cierta cima excelsa estaba situado José Clemente Orozco, titán manco y esmirriado, especie de Goya de su fantasmagórica patria. Muchas veces conversé con él. Su persona parecía carecer de la violencia que tuvo su obra. Tenía una suavidad de alfarero que ha perdido la mano en el torno y con la mano restante se siente obligado a continuar creando universos. Sus soldados y soldaderas, sus campesinos fusilados por mayorales, sus sarcófagos con terribles crucificados, son lo más inmortal de nuestra pintura americana y quedarán como la revelación de nuestra crueldad.

[José Clemente Orozco, lean, one-armed titan, has his place on an elevated peak, a sort of Goya in his phantasmagorical country. I talked to him often. The violence that haunted his work seemed alien to his personality. He had the gentleness of a potter who has lost his hand at the potter's wheel but feels he must go on creating worlds with his other hand. His soldiers and their women, his peasants gunned down by overseers, his sarcophagi with horrible crucified bodies, are immortal in our native American painting, bearing witness to our cruelty.][48]

Neruda also compares the work of Rivera with that of Siqueiros:

No hay paralelo entre la pintura de Diego Rivera y la de David Alfaro Siqueiros. Diego es un clásico lineal; con esa línea infinitamente ondulante, especie de caligrafía histórica, fue atando la historia de México y dándole relieve a hechos, costumbres y tragedias. Siqueiros es la explosión de un temperamento volcánico que combina asombrosa técnica y largas investigaciones.

[No parallel can be drawn between the painting of Diego Rivera and that of David Alfaro Siquieros. Diego has a classicist's feeling for line;

with that infinitely undulating line, a kind of historian's calligraphy, he gradually tied together Mexico's history and brought out in high relief its events, traditions, and tragedies. Siqueiros is the explosion of a volcanic temperament that combines an amazing technique and painstaking research.][49]

On different occasions Neruda dedicated poems to both artists—to Siqueiros during his imprisonment in 1961 and to Rivera in *Cien sonetos de amor*. It is also of note that the art historian Desmond Rochfort selected one of Neruda's poems from *Estravagario*, entitled "El gran mantel" [The Great Tablecloth], to accompany his commentary on Mexican muralism. The tone of this poem is similar to that of *Canto general*, returning to the conflict between those who enjoy abundance and those who lack the most basic sustenance.

At the heart of muralism is history. From the 1920s to the 1950s, the Mexican muralists produced works of vast ambition and scale in order to present a panoramic view of history. Folgarait comments upon this phase of the movement, insisting once more on the fact that it was part of a government program.

It was clear from the start that the accomplishments of radical abstractions were not to be considered as formal vehicles for the explicitly narrative qualities of a historical and nationalistic content. As long as the past and present history of Mexico could produce the heroics of a Cuauhtémoc, a Zapata, or a Cárdenas, and as long as the promises of the Revolution could keep an entire nation's hopes in progressive flux, the murals fed on a heady diet of deeply significant historical process as their subject matter, best carried by a realistic narrative style.[50]

The Mexican Renaissance was precipitated and shaped by the Mexican Revolution, which had created the possibility of a new artistic approach and expressed both the fulfillment and the suffering—the great contradictions and deficiencies—of such a revolution. The new artistic movement shed the colonial heritage of academic tradition and—like the Romantics a century earlier, partly in response to the great independence movements—rediscovered the suppressed popular culture, becoming immersed in its own surroundings. At first, Mexican mural painting emulated the primitivist trend of the European avant-garde, before taking its own course, reflecting and defining a new reality. In a 1948 lecture delivered to UNESCO in Mexico, Orozco described the impact of mural painting on Mexican artistic, intellectual, and cultural life:

> En las primeras páginas de la pintura mural mexicana de nuestro tiempo puede notarse ya cierta coherencia de expresión; podía empezarse a leer allí la transformación e inicio de un nuevo desarrollo del sentir, del pensar, de la conciencia del pueblo de México.

> [In the first stages of contemporary Mexican mural painting a certain coherence of expression is already evident; there was beginning to be read there the transformation and initiation of a new development in the sensibilities, in the thinking, of the consciousness of the Mexican people.][51]

That cohesive expression or unified vision of life was what gave Neruda the archetropic impulse to write his *Canto general* and is one of the objectives of this study. While attempting to exclude general speculation and without undue emphasis on the personal relations between poet and painters, I have placed side by side specific examples of *Canto general*'s poetry and murals of the "Tres Maestros" from 1922 to 1950 approximately, and have drawn such parallels between them as seem pertinent and appropriate. Also, I am cognizant of a certain simplification of the artistic phenomenon. The differences of technique and style among Rivera, Orozco, and Siqueiros are immense. While taking into account the painters' individual traits, this study focuses on the movement as a whole in order to compare its main themes and narrative configuration to *Canto general*, since the theoretical premise is that it is the movement and not a particular artist that provided the cosmogenetic experience for the poet.

We shall further argue in the following pages that the mural movement, as a whole, becomes the cosmogenetic point constraining the poet to a "logic" which governs the formulation of the entire *Canto*. Muralism represents the "artistic vision," the archetropic experience, which compels and guides Neruda to a particular iconic perception of the world and to a specific narrative configuration of his book.

Salient Trends in Mexican Muralism

The salient trends that gave form to the mural movement were defined by Orozco in a text prepared for the catalogue of his retrospective exhibition held in 1947 in the Palace Museum of Fine Arts in Mexico.

> Having studied the themes in modern Mexican mural paintings, we find the following facts: all the painters began with subjects derived from traditional iconography, either Christian or Frankish, and often literally copied them.[52]

After the first period, three well-defined trends appeared. The first of these is the Indian trend with its two variants: the archaic and the colorfully folkloric—the Olympian, Toltec, or Aztec and the types and traditions of the present Indian artists with their magnificent richness of color. That is, the mythical dimension and cosmogony of pre-Hispanic cultures and its perpetuation in the present Mexican popular culture. The second trend has a historical content in which Mexican history, typically the Spanish Conquest, is represented. In Orozco's words, "history is shown from contradictory and opposing viewpoints. Those who are heroes in one mural are villains in another."[53] And lastly, there is the trend of revolutionary socialist propaganda, in which there continues to appear, with surprising persistency, Christian iconography.[54]

The best example of the sequence of these trends, as stated by Orozco, would be Rivera's murals in the National Palace (staircase, 1929–1930; left wall, 1935, corridors, 1942–1951); the series starts with the pre-Hispanic cultures, followed by the juxtaposition of heroes and villains of Mexican history, and ends with Karl Marx, like Moses, proclaiming the new order. Continuing with his survey, Orozco describes the muralists' imagery with its great richness of expression, its iconic codes and its semantics:

> To all this outdated religious imagery very 19th century liberal symbols are added. Freedom with its Phrygian cap and the indispensable broken chains; Democracy; Peace; Blindfolded Justice carrying its sword and scales; The Nation; torches, stars, palms, olives and nopals; heraldic or symbolic animals, including eagles, lions, tigers, horses and serpents. Very ancient symbols of the "Bourgeoisie, enemy of progress" type, still play a prominent part in murals, represented by pot-bellied toffs in top hats, or by pigs, jackals, dragons or other monsters, so well-known and familiar that they are as inoffensive as the plumed serpent.[55]

A native of Jalisco, Orozco seems to be describing his own work in Guadalajara (1938–42) and that of Siqueiros's grandiose and expressive murals at the Electrical Trade Union Institute in Mexico City. The argument is valid and a generalization can be made, since most of the painters discussed here share the same iconic codes.

The importance of Orozco's own survey of the movement is not only to roughly provide a compendium of themes and trends, but also to direct close attention to *Canto general*'s structure. If we compare its formal arrangement with the main thrust of the mural movement—as described by Orozco—and the historical perspective contained within it, we find that the first book or unit of the text—formed by the first eight sections, as proposed earlier— follow, to a large extent, a similar narrative development.[56] That is, it begins with the "Creation," described through the extensive use of Christian iconographic symbols. To use Nathaniel Tarn's words, "[t]he work begins with a kind of seven-day Genesis."[57] What follows, just as in Orozco's description of the mural movement, is pre-Columbian culture, epitomized by Macchu Picchu, and the *Conquista* as the theme of the whole *Canto III*.[58] Within this historical pattern, muralism took on different aspects. As Orozco stated it, "history is shown from contradictory and opposing viewpoints." Both heroes and villains are depicted in the same mural, or, sometimes "those who are heroes in one mural are villains in another." *Los libertadores* [*The Liberators*] (IV) and *La arena traicionada* [*The Sand Betrayed*] (V) correspond to these trends.

América, no invoco tu nombre en vano [*America, I Do Not Invoke Your Name in Vain*] (VI), published in Mexico in 1943, is, according to Fernando Alegría, "la síntesis lírico-épica de las secciones precedentes" (the lyrical-epic synthesis of the preceding sections).[59] For Santí, however, the "resumen lírico" [lyrical summary] is *Canto general de Chile* (VII).[60] What is evident is that these two sections do not seem to fit with the rest of the book, perhaps because they were written before Neruda decided to compose the more ambitious *Canto general*.[61] What critics have not taken into consideration is the fact that *Canto general de Chile* contains several poems which are full of nostalgia for his native Chile but were actually written in Mexico. Furthermore, this seventh section, also published in Mexico in 1941, contains two other important trends of muralism: the eradication of national origins and the inclusion of popular art. Here for the first time are complete poems dedicated to "Talabartería" [Saddlery], "Alfarería" [Pottery], and "Telares" [Looms], where the artist embarks on a quasi-mythic quest for the roots of a pre-Hispanic past mysteriously hidden behind the artifacts and art crafts created by artisans. *América, no invoco tu nombre en vano* is indeed a structural synthesis, for its thematic design is like a micro version of the entire book, and along with *Canto general de Chile*, it represents the original kernel, the artistic inception, Neruda's first attempt to create a unified vision of the continent.

La tierra se llama Juan [*The Earth's Name is Juan*] (*VIII*) is the culmination of the artist's effort to achieve true communion with the masses. The poetic voice disappears in the throng to become a real polyphony of voices of the people. In this way, the poet attempts to approximate the collective effort involved in the fresco technique, which requires a great deal of physical labor, and where the artist's creative process resembles that of the artisan.

The close correspondence of these first eight sections to Mexican muralism's themes and narrative design suggests that *Canto general* is in fact two books, two poetic projects, in one volume, conceived as a result of two crucially different experiences, connected only by the Marxist ideology that works as a unifying code (or device) in the entire volume. The first project (the first eight sections) is largely shaped by the Mexican experience and by the cosmogenetic visual representation of mural painting. The second book (the remaining seven sections) only resembles mural art in terms of what might be called the trend of revolutionary socialist propaganda expressed through Christian iconography.

By 1943, Neruda had not only seen the early murals at the National Preparatory School and the National Palace (1922–35); but had also witnessed the ongoing evolution and development of the phenomenon. From 1942 to 1950, for instance, in the open corridors of the National Palace Rivera was portraying the rich cultural diversity of the Mexicans before the Conquest.[62] Orozco had just finished his best murals in Guadalajara (1938–39) and was painting more at the Supreme Court of Justice (1940–41). In 1939, Siqueiros had produced some of the most powerful images of Mexican muralism on the walls of the Electrical Trade Union Institute in Mexico City, and, while in exile in Chile (1942), was working on the histories of Mexico and Chile at the Mexico School in Chillán.

It must be noted, however, that Neruda's *Canto general* is not for the most part a case of direct ekphrasis or a subordinate transposition from one art form to another. Instead, it is a fully independent ekphrastic interpretation of the unifying visual experience of Mexican mural art that became the kinetic and kinesthetic force that generated the poet's ekphrastic desire for representation.

But what are the distinctions and critical notions that would support the assertion that Neruda's verbal representation is in fact independent and autonomous from the cosmogenetic visual source? In the next chapter, I will integrate the ideas of Krieger and others regarding the poem as an emblem, along with the ekphrastic principle discussed in Chapter 1, into the discussion of how Neruda establishes a dialogue between text and image.

3

The Indigenous Theme and the Search
for Roots

"La lámpara en la tierra" and Muralism

THE FIRST STAGE OF MEXICAN MURALISM MAY BE CALLED THE EX-
pression of the origin of life and is followed by an indigenous
trend. At this stage, the mythical dimension of the continent and
the idealization of pre-Colombian cultures are essential to the
structure of the composition and the creation of what James Miller
calls a "Supreme Fiction."[1] Particularly useful in this regard are
Joseph Frank's theoretical distinctions of the temporal discontinuity in the process of transforming history into myth. This is
achieved by the poet's constant juxtaposition of seemingly disparate historical images. Frank has also stressed that such an artistic
approach is part of the Modernist literary phenomenon during
the first two decades of the twentieth century, and bases his conclusions on his reading of works by James Joyce, Ezra Pound, and
T. S. Eliot. Frank's fundamental notion here is that such a literary
practice can indeed overcome the sequential limitations of the
reading process, its temporality, which allows the reader to perceive the images in the poem, not in the linear flow of time, but
as juxtaposed (synchronically) in space, giving the poem spatiality. He calls this the space-logic of modern poetry, in which "the
synchronic relations *within* the text took precedence over diachronic referentiality and that it was only after the pattern of
synchronic relations had been grasped as a unity that the 'meaning' of the poem could be understood."[2] In this way, Pound, Eliot,
or Joyce (and for that matter, Neruda) create the suspension of
time by juxtaposing disparate images and events synchronically,
thus bringing "the past into the present of the indicative; and in
doing so . . . turn history into myth."[3]

In the next chapter we will return to Frank's ideas about Modernism and its similarity to the pictorial tradition of the Middle

68

Ages. For now, the points mentioned serve to establish a specific theoretical framework that will help us to explicate the methods by which Neruda, like the other writers mentioned by Frank, creates the mythical dimension in all of *Canto general* and particularly in the invention of a "Supreme Fiction" for the Americas.[4]

Several sections of *Canto general*, such as *América no invoco tu nombre en vano* (VI), *Canto general de Chile* (VII) and *El gran océano* [*The Great Ocean*] (XIV), form part of that mythification of the American soil and its primogenic inhabitants. Sections I, II and III, present a cohesive dialectic vision of great significance for the comprehension of *Canto general*: namely, the expression of a historic narrative associated with the violation and destruction of a pristine, uncorrupted, virgin world.

La lámpara en la tierra [*A Lamp On Earth*], the first canto, includes several important motifs. The work begins with a sort of seven-day genesis. The key image of this section, as Villegas has noted, "radica en esa mostración del mundo de América, cuyo estado de ebullición—primer poema—revela su condición inicial" [lies in that display of the American world, whose effervescent state—a first poem—reveals its initial condition].[5] The first murals painted in Mexico City at the National Preparatory School in 1921 and later on the staircases of National Palace in the 1930's present a similar conception of the American land.

Rivera painted his first mural in the Simón Bolívar amphitheater of the National Preparatory School, the same place where later in 1941 Neruda first read his poem "Un canto para Bolívar." The title of Rivera's mural is none other than *Creation* (1922). The early murals of Orozco were also largely based on the concept of *The Gifts of Nature to Man*, as he titled one of his paintings. Rochfort explains that the symbolic content of these murals treat "such themes as virginity, youth, grace, beauty, intelligence, genius, force and maternity."[6] Siqueiros, too, made his mark with a mural entitled *The Elements*. As is often the case with many of these murals, there is a confusion or, rather, the use of multiple titles to identify the same work. Jean Charlot calls this mural by Siqueiros *The Spirit of The Occident Descending upon the Americas*. This title, which we believe to be close to the original, more accurately reflects the ideas of the Secretary of Education and sponsor José Vasconcelos, who described the "Raza Cósmica" [Cosmic Race] as the perfect synthesis of European and Amerindian ethnic groups. Although Rivera's *Creation* also contains Vasconcelos's ideas, the emphatic local color added by Rivera to the classical figures depicted apparently fell short of Vasconcelos's expectations.[7]

Nonetheless, and despite the different individual interpretations, the dominant iconic symbol of this first phase in all of them is the virginal and pristine condition of the earth. A second related image is represented by the feminine metaphor of Mother Earth that gives life to all. Rivera's above-mentioned mural presents the emergence of man, animal life, and nature from the tree of life. In his book *Arte y política* Rivera explains his purpose: to paint on the walls

> la célula original, conteniendo vegetales y animales en torno al árbol de la vida, entre cuyo follage están *el toro, el querub, el león y el águila*— signos del verbo, principio de todo—y de cuya cúspide emerge *el hombre*, entidad anterior al masculino o al femenino (emphasis added).

> [the original cell, containing vegetables and animals around a tree of life; among its foliage are *the bull, the cherub, the lion and the eagle*— signs of the word, the beginning of everything—and from its top emerges *man*, an entity that precedes the masculine or the feminine (emphasis added)].[8]

The three hands in the upper portion of the painting represent the *energía* that gives birth to man from the tree of life. The nude man and woman on each side of the mural are sitting on the ground so that "se sintieran en contacto todavía en esa tierra, participando de su esencia y calidad por ser forma y estructura" [they would still feel in contact with that earth, participating in its essence and warmth by being form and structure].[9]

The interartistic association with the first poem of *Canto general*, "Amor América (1400)," is inevitable. Here Neruda appropriates the very same imagery to express a unified artistic vision. Rivera's mural thus functions as the source for ekphrastic desire. This poem also serves as a perfect example of Neruda's poetic techniques of synchronic juxtaposition of images used in the creation of this mythical dimension, as illuminated by Frank's theories discussed at the beginning of this chapter. The pristine, uncorrupted world is described before the arrival of "civilization."

> Antes de la peluca y la casaca
> fueron los ríos, ríos arteriales:
> fueron las cordilleras, en cuya onda raída
> el cóndor o la nieve parecían inmóviles
> fue la humedad y la espesura, el trueno
> sin nombre todavía, las pampas planetarias.

Diego Rivera, *Creation*, 1922–23, Anfiteatro Bolívar, National Preparatory School, Mexico City (INBA).

[Before the wig and the dress coat
there were rivers, arterial rivers:
there were cordilleras, jagged waves where
the condor and the snow seemed immutable:
there was dampness and dense growth, the thunder
as yet unnamed, the planetary pampas.][10]

The reiteration of the preterite verb forms "fueron" and "fue" creates the sensation of nostalgia for that idyllic world, but at the same time expresses a sense of loss. The second stanza draws on the same Adamic metaphor found in Rivera's *Creation:* "El hombre tierra fué, vasija, párpado / del barro trémulo, forma de la arcilla" (I, 315) [Man was dust, earthen vase, an eyelid / of tremulous loam, the shape of clay] (13). The telluric bond between man and earth that gives form and foundation to all of *Canto general* is stated here, as if the poet wanted to immediately establish the work's conceptual domain. For Nelly Santos, this first section "se imbrica en la visión telúrica del tema americano. Naturaleza y aborigen son el binomio hombre-tierra profundamente identificados" [is imbedded in the telluric vision of the American theme. Nature and the aborigen are the binomial of profoundly identified man-earth].[11] It may be added, however, that such a relationship is not limited to this section, but rather becomes a recurrent topos that permeates the entire text to underline particularly the profound dichotomy between heroes and villains.

Christian and classical iconographies are used by both artists to depict this profound and strong identification with the American soil. Rivera's cherubs and virgins are mixed with pagan figures, such as Pan playing the flute on the left side, the lion and the bull, and authentic Native Americans. What is depicted is creation, the genesis of life, not only in the orthodox Western sense of the biblical genesis, but also in terms of a mythical birth from the American continent and American man as expressed in the *Popol Vuh*.

The juxtaposition of such dissimilar images is used here by the poet to undermine the temporality of language. The second part of the poem abruptly shifts the tense from the preterite to the present indicative. The poem could be defined as the opening canto that sets the stage for the process of creation that follows. It is also a poem that starts with the mythical creation of the American world, then continues with its fall from grace when the "iniciales de la tierra" [initials of the earth] were forgotten, "las claves se perdieron / o se inundaron en silencio o sangre" (I, 315) [the keys were lost / or flooded with silence or blood (14)]. Then the speaker, as the intemporal witness of all this, erupts in the present indicative to claim his prophetic and messianic voice and presence as a chronicler: "Yo estoy aquí para cantar la historia" (I, 315) [I am here to tell the story (14)]. But he does this above all to claim his belonging to that mythical, pristine world of the earthly aborigen: "Yo, incásico del légamo" (I, 315) [I, Incan of the loam (14)]. According to Joseph Frank, this poetic device allows the reader to perceive the images in the poem, not in the normal linear sequence of time, but as juxtaposed in space.[12] The reader is required by the formal structure of the poem to suspend the process of reference to temporality until the internal references in the poem can be understood as a unified semantic whole. The fusion of time in a pattern of synchronic relations takes precedent over the diachronic referentiality, allowing the poet to bring the past to the present, to overcome the sequentiality of time, and above all, "to turn history into myth," to use Frank's phrase.[13]

The series of poems that follow—"Vegetaciones" [Vegetation], "Algunas bestias" [Some Beasts], "Vienen los pájaros" [The Birds Arrive], "Los ríos acuden" [The Rivers Come Forth], "Minerales" [Minerals] "Los hombres" [Man]—all are the actual creation of that mythical space, and as in the first poem, the reader must become an active participant in order to interpret the texts. One is required to perceive the rich and diverse corpus of imagery presented by the poet, again not in the sequential order of time, but after the pattern of juxtaposed images has been apprehended as a unit. Only at this point does the hermeneutical process of the reader complete itself.

But how can the juxtaposition of disparate images be grasped as a semantic unit? The answer lies in the use of the metaphor. This rhetorical device has made the most fundamental contribution to the creative process of ekphrastic poetry. It has been described as a "filter in the apprehension of the other."[14] In this series of poems the beginning of the world is portrayed with what I term a harmonic calligraphy of metaphors. In the second poem "Vegetaciones," such nouns as "germen" [germ], "semilla" [seed], "cuna" [cradle], "maíz" [corn], "trigo" [wheat], "útero verde" [green uterus], "sábana seminal" [seminal American savanna] and verbs like "nacer" [to be born] and "geminar" [to germinate] represent, in the ekphrastic encounter, the virtual lines with which the poet completes the figurative image of the poem. They are a series of isomorphic metaphors with which Neruda paints the contours of Mother Earth. Throughout the entire section the poet engages in the depiction of a panoramic view—a mural—of flora and fauna through a wide array of metaphors, which are, in Rogers's words, "the poet's tool correspondent to the painter's lines."[15] If the dominant image used to describe the flora is that of Mother Earth, in "Algunas bestias" [Some Beasts] Neruda resorts to a rich variety of similes and metaphors: "el guanaco" is "como el oxígeno" [as oxygen] because of its resistance to heights; "el jaguar" is "ausencia fosforecente" [phosphorescent absence], "el puma" appears as a "fuego devorador" [raging fire]. The description of the birds is particularly apt:

> Todo era vuelo en nuestra tierra
> como gotas de sangre y plumas
> los cardenales desangraban
> el amanecer de Anáhuac.
> El tucán era una adorable
> caja de frutas barnizadas.

(1:319)

> [All was flight in our land.
> The cardinal, like drops
> of blood and feathers,
> bled the dawn of Anáhuac.
> The toucan was a lovely
> box of shining fruit.]

(17)

The wings of a hummingbird are "minúsculas hogueras" [miniscule bonfires] that "ardían en el aire inmóvil" [burned in the still air]. The condor is "el talismán negro de la nieve" [black talisman of the snow].[16]

In the next poem, "Los ríos acuden" [The Rivers Come Forth], Neruda returns to the feminine figure to convey the image of a nurturing mother, who represents in this case the subterranean forces of the earth:

> De tu espesura madre recogías
> el agua como lágrimas vitales,
> y arrastrabas los cauces a la arena
> . . . .
> Cruzando ásperas piedras dilatadas
> . . . .

> cortando bosques de compactos muros,
> apartando los músculos del cuarzo.
>
> (1:321–22)
>
> [From your maternal density you gathered
> the water like vital tears,
> dredged the sandy riverbanks
>
> . . . .
>
> traversing harsh dilated stones,
>
> . . . . . . ˙. . . .
>
> cutting forests of compact walls,
> sundering the quartz's muscles.]
>
> (19)

The use of the imperfect tense allows the poet to instill in the reader's mind the recreation of a cosmogenetic image. The present participle of the last lines quoted above provides the scene with lifelike motion. Some of the sections of Rivera's murals in the Chapel of the National Autonomous University of Chapingo (1926) present very similar metaphors. Nude, mother-like women become allegorical figures of the "subterranean forces," "germination," "the virgin earth," and so on. Its ekphrastic equivalent in *Canto general* is the section devoted to "Minerales," which offers a very specific interpretation of what Neruda and Rivera might describe as the exploitation of Mother Earth.

Rivera's *The Earth Enslaved,* also in Chapingo, is "a huge nude echoing the geographic outline of Mexico . . . surrounded by her tormentors: the Church, the Army and capitalism."[17] The three dominant facets of Latin American oligarchy are described here turning their backs to the country while at the same time holding her prisoner, as suggested by the sharp knifelike bayonets in the front, "protecting" her from the outside. In "Minerales," Neruda addresses Mother Earth in a very intimate manner. His use of apostrophe gives us that impression of intimacy between mother and son:

> Madre de los metales, te quemaron
> te mordieron, te martirizaron,
> te corroyeron, te pudrieron
> más tarde, cuando los ídolos
> ya no pudieron defenderte.
>
> (1:323)
>
> [Mother of metals, they burned you,
> bit you, martyred you,

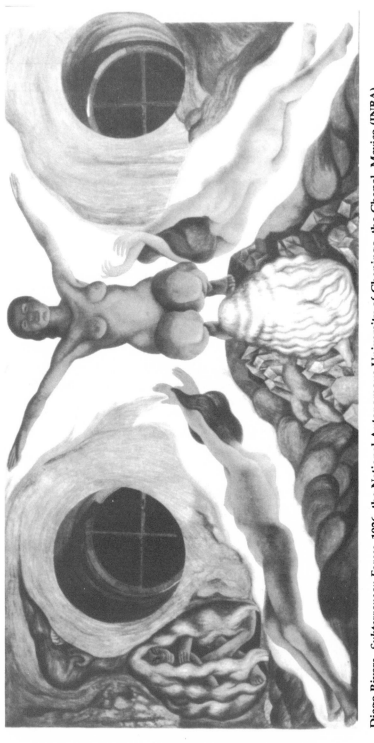

Diego Rivera, *Subterranean Forces*, 1926, the National Autonomous University of Chapingo, the Chapel, Mexico (INBA).

Diego Rivera, *The Germination*, 1926, the Chapel at Chapingo, Mexico (INBA).

> corroded you, then
> defiled you, when the idols
> could no longer defend you.]
>
> (21)

Neruda's vision is fundamentally the same as Rivera's, although the poet's intimate tone is less detached than the painter's attitude. Through the capacity of language Neruda seems to achieve a level of intimacy that the visual referent can only suggest, providing a closer, more direct human dimension to the destruction of the land. Neruda's description emphasizes the dramatic reality more than ideological denunciation. Thus, the question of who the exploiters are is not clear. He does not seem to blame any one in particular, but the accusation is implicit in the juxtaposition of elements and in the adequate literary competence of the reader.[18] The quasi-fatalistic vision pervading this section is clear

Diego Rivera, *The Earth Enslaved*, 1926, the Chapel at Chapingo, Mexico (INBA).

and is conveyed through expressions such as "cuando los ídolos / ya no pudieron defenderte" [when the idols / could no longer defend you] or in the following lines:

> Cómo podías, Colombia oral,
> saber que tus piedras descalzas
> ocultaban una tormenta
> de oro iracundo,
> cómo, patria
> de la esmeralda, ibas a ver
> que la alhaja de muerte y mar,
> el fulgor en su escalofrío
> escalaría las gargantas
> de los dinastas invasores?

(1:325)

> [How, oral Colombia, could you
> know that your barefoot stones
> concealed a tempest
> of enraged gold,
> how, homeland
> of the emerald, could you foresee

> that the jewel of death and the sea,
> the chilling splendor,
> would climb the throats
> of the invading dynasts?]

(23)

Neruda's objective to present a dialectical opposition between virginity and violation is maintained throughout the entire first section. Chile and its minerals, after all, have been the source of greed and abuse since the Europeans landed in the New World, just as in the rest of Latin America.

The constant repetition of the nasal sounds "m" and "n" in the entire section produces a nostalgic humming of despair and signals the metaphor of Mother Earth. Here the alliteration contained in the first lines of "Minerales" offers us the ultimate paradigm of this figure: "Madre de los metales, te quemaron / te mordieron, te martirizaron." Thus, the antithetical equation virginity versus violation is completed and fully expressed. The dialectic is synthesized and graphically described later in "Ahora es Cuba" [Now It's Cuba], of the third section, in which the island, like Mother Earth, is victimized by the invaders. The poetic voice is addressed to the country in the same apostrophic manner as in "Minerales":

> Cuba, mi amor, te amarraron al potro,
> te cortaron la cara,
> te apartaron las piernas de oro pálido,
> te rompieron el sexo de granada,
> te atravesaron con cuchillos,
> te dividieron, te quemaron.

(1:346)

> [Cuba, my love, they put you on the rack,
> cut your face,
> pried open your legs of pale gold,
> crushed your pomegranate sex,
> stabbed you with knives,
> dismembered you, burned you.]

(44)

It is the redeeming voice of the poet, implied in the quasi-Romantic title of *La lámpara en la tierra* and in the very first poem when the poet, after the fall of man from "heaven" ("las claves se perdieron / o se inundaron de silencio o sangre" [the keys were lost / or flooded with silence or blood]), that gives hope and comfort to his fellow inhabitants:

> No se perdió la vida, humanos pastorales.
> Pero como una rosa salvaje
> cayó una gota roja en la espesura,
> y se apagó una lámpara de tierra.
>
> Yo estoy aquí para contar la historia.

(1:315)

> [Life was not lost, pastoral brothers,
> But like a wild rose
> a red drop fell into the dense growth,
> and a lamp of earth was extinguished.
>
> I am here to tell the story.]

(14)

Though it deals with a different concern, the argument can be made that a similar dialectic and resolution can be found in *Alturas de Macchu Picchu*. As Donald Shaw has accurately concluded:

> [O]nly by meditating on Macchu Picchu both as a positive and as a negative symbolic referent, can the poet eventually reach the point (the resolution of an antithesis) at which he can present himself as possessed of the redeeming voice.[19]

From the outset, as we have been asserting, it is the poet's intention to imbed his *Canto general* in this dialectic of oppositions, to create in his work the mythical dimension, a "Supreme Fiction."[20] As Claude Levy-Strauss notes, "[m]ythical thought always progresses from the awareness of oppositions toward their resolution."[21] Needless to say, this basic binary structure was also the organizing principle of the Mexican muralist movement.

Likewise, "Minerales" represents an interesting shift, for it contains the first denunciation (by the redeeming voice) of the brutal abuse of natural resources. In the last stanza of the poem, Neruda refers to a possibly first-hand experience as a Chilean senator, when he traveled across the country visiting mines and witnessing how foreign enterprises capitalized on the naive trust of the people on the one hand, and on political corruption on the other:

> Corrí por los ciclones al peligro
> y descendí a la luz de la esmeralda,

ascendí al pámpano de los rubíes,
pero callé para siempre en la estatua
del nitrato extendido en el desierto.
Vi cómo en la ceniza
del huesoso altiplano
levantaba el estaño
sus corales ramajes de veneno
hasta extender como una selva
la niebla equinoccial, hasta cubrir el sello
de nuestras cereales monarquías.

(1:326)

[I raced through cyclones to danger
and descended to the emerald light—
I ascended to the tendril of rubies,
but I was silenced forever on the statue
of nitrate stretched out on the desert.
In the ash of the raw-boned
altiplano, I saw how
tin raised
its coral branches of poison
until it spread out, like a jungle,
the equinoctial mist, until it covered
the signet of our cereal monarchies.]

(23)

This is the "poetics of prophecy" at work. Neruda's denunciation goes beyond the condemnation of human exploitation to include an anguished outcry against the environmental destruction inflicted upon the land. The sacred telluric bond between man and earth is threatened again by the same chiliastic enemies.

The last poem of this first section, as on the last day of God's creation, describes the emergence of mankind. Neruda's main purpose, though, is to delineate a profile of the many different ethnic cultures that form American man. The first stanza recreates an image of this man that closely resembles the metaphor of man as a *cántaro*, or clay pot, developed by Siqueiros in a mural entitled *Ethnography*, painted in 1939:

Como la copa de la arcilla era
la raza mineral, el hombre
hecho de piedras y de atmósfera
limpio como los cántaros, sonoro.

(1:326)

[The mineral race was
like a cup of clay, man

David Alfaro Siqueiros, *Ethnography*, 1939, Enamel on composition board, 48⅛ × 32⅜″ (122.2 × 82.2 cm). The Museum of Modern Art, New York. Gift of Abby Aldrich Rockefeller. Photograph © 1998 Museum of Modern Art, New York.

made of stone and atmosphere,
clean as earthen jugs, sonorous.]

(24)

At this point there comes to mind the Adamic figure at the beginning of this section, which was also described as:

El hombre tierra fué, *vasija*, párpado
del *barro trémulo*, forma de la arcilla,
fué *cántaro caribe*, piedra chibcha,
copa imperial o sílice araucana.

(1:315; emphasis added)

[Man was dust, *earthen vase*, an eyelid
of *tremulous loam*, the shape of clay—
he was *Carib jug*, Chibcha stone,
imperial cup or Araucanian silica.]

(13; emphasis added)

It should be added too that the metaphor remains consistent and recurrent throughout the book. It is applied solely to what seems to be Neruda's own perception of the autochthonous or indigenous man of the continent. Benito Juárez, for instance, a pure Zapotec born in Oaxaca, who became president of Mexico at the end of the century, resembles that figure: "Tu rostro hecho de tierra americana, / . . . Tu rostro fué nacido en nuestro barro" (1:426) [Your face made of American earth, / . . . Your face was born of our clay (118–19)], but also the poetic voice that presents itself as "Yo, incásico del légamo" [I, Incan of the loam] in the first poem. It is "[L]a luna" [the moon], not God, it follows, who "amasó" [kneaded] into life all these different cultures. Here, Neruda sings of the endurance of "El Tarahumara," who "con sangre y perdernales creó el fuego" [made fire of blood and flint] of the beauty of the ceramic produced by the *Tarasco*, of the elegance of "las vestiduras" [vestments] of the Aztec clergy who, "como faisanes deslumbrantes / descendían . . . de las / escaleras aztecas" (1:327) [like dazzling pheasants / . . . descended / the Aztec steps (24)]. Yet, the beauty of the "vestiduras" contrasts here with the crude reality of human sacrifice:

y la pirámide augusta,
. . . .
en su estructura dominadora

guardaba como una almendra
un corazón sacrificado.

(1:327)

[And the august pyramid,

. . . .

within its domineering structure,
tended like an almond
a sacrificed heart.]

(24)

The same juxtaposition applies to the Mayans to whom the poet
says, "habíais derribado / el árbol del conocimiento" [you had
felled / the tree of knowledge] and now "escrutábais en los cenotes / arrojándoles novias de oro" (1:327) [you scrutinized the cenotes / casting into them golden brides (25)]. Later, in *Alturas de
Macchu Picchu* (section II), the poet would also describe the Incan
culture as one that fell from grace:

os desplomasteis como en un otoño
en una sola muerte.

. . . .

cuanto fuisteis cayó: costumbres, sílabas
raídas, máscaras de luz deslumbradora.

(1:336–337)

[you tumbled as in autumn
to a single death.

. . . . . .

all that you were has fallen: customs, frayed
syllables, masks of dazzling light.]

(35)

Here, the concept of Paradise Lost is recreated. The Mayans,
after losing "el árbol del conocimiento" [the tree of life] are now
engaged in the sacrifice of innocent victims in a desperate attempt
to recover lost knowledge. Only now, the reader is able to connect
these lines with the third stanza of the first poem of the book,
"Amor América," and decipher part of its meaning. The poet
speaks of the loss of the secret "iniciales de la tierra" [initials of
the earth]: "las claves se perdieron / o se inundaron de silencio o
sangre" (1:315) [the keys were lost / or flooded with silence or
blood (14)]. The poetic persona seems to suggest that human
sacrifice [sangre] was what Amerindian peoples had to resort to

after losing their knowledge, though the cause(s) of the rupture is (are) never explained. A different reading is possible. From the previous lines, "las claves se perdieron / o se inundaron de silencio o sangre," it might be conjectured that the poet is referring to civil war [sangre] as a possible cause or to the imposition of a kind of censorship or political repression [silencio], thus "las claves se perdieron" because they were forgotten.

These seemingly conflicting views, as it will be seen, have more to do with a comprehensive effort by the artist to describe the pre-Columbian cultures with their strengths and weaknesses, than with the resolution of the dilemma. In this effort all the Mesoamerican cultures—Tarasco, Azteca, and Maya—with the exception of the *Tarahumara* are associated with handicrafts, particularly pottery. In the "arcilla" [clay] of the "Tarasco,"

> los mitos de las tierras amorosas,
> la exuberancia húmeda de donde
> lodo sexual y frutas derretidas
> iban a ser actitud de los dioses
> o pálidas paredes de vasijas.
>
> (1:327)

> [myths of the amorous lands,
> moist exuberance whence
> sexual mud and melted fruits
> were to be the posture of the gods
> or pale walls of vessels.]
>
> (24)

Even the cruelty of the Aztecs appears to be lessened by the skillful artistry of the people in weaving, gathering crops, and coaxing jewelry out of turquoise stone. In the subtle descent to the Austral zone, special attention is focused on the Incan and Araucanian cultures. If the Mesoamerican cultures inspired earthy associations, the Incas belong to the summit, the sidereal level of the American world, while the Araucanians represent the solitude of the last corner of the earth. For the poet, the south begins with Macchu Picchu:

> Era el Sur un asombro dorado.
> Las altas soledades
> de Macchu Picchu en la puerta del cielo
> estaban llenas de aceites y cantos,

el hombre había roto las moradas
de grandes aves en la altura.

(1:328)

[The South was a golden wonder.
The towering retreats
of Macchu Picchu in the gateway to the sky
were filled with oils and songs,
man had defied the dwelling
of the great birds in the heights.]

(25)

Here Neruda sings of the famous Incan "terrazas:"

Germinaban en las terrazas
el maíz de las altas tierras
y en los volcánicos senderos
iban los vasos y los dioses.

(1:328)

[Highland corn
germinated on the terraces,
and over the volcanic pathways
traveled vases and gods.]

(25)

As the poet approaches the end of the section, a pessimistic
vision of the immediate future is foreshadowed. Talking to his
fellow Incas, the poet, as a member of the culture, implores:

Dulce raza, hija de sierras,
estirpe de torre y turquesa,
ciérrame los ojos ahora,
antes de irnos al mar
de donde vienen los dolores.

(1:328)

[Sweet race, daughter of the sierras,
lineage of tower and turquoise,
close my eyes now
before we return to the sea,
whence our sorrows come.]

(26)

Here, the sea as a traditional metaphor of death could have more
complex implications. Neruda may be alluding to a Mexican leg-

end that tells the story of a massive suicide of a group of Mayans—they all walked into the sea—just before the arrival of the Spaniards. Similar ways of "defeating" the enemy are common in both Oriental and Western cultures. In the Spanish tradition, an example is Cervantes' *El cerco de Numancia* [*The Siege of Numancia*], in which the Iberians' resistance of domination by the Roman empire took a similar form. The poet concludes the section with a return to that cosmic solitude found only at the far end of the world, in the land of the Araucanians:

> En el fondo de América sin nombre
> estaba Arauco entre las aguas
> vertiginosas, apartado
> por todo el frío del planeta.
> Mirad el gran Sur solitario.
>
> (1:329)

> [At the bottom of America without name
> was Arauco among the vertiginous
> waters, separated
> by all the planet's cold.
> Behold the great solitary South.]
>
> (26)

Solitude is all that is found in this remote part of the earth: "No busques bajo el verde espeso / el canto de la alfarería" (1:329) [Do not seek the song of pottery / beneath the dense green] (26). More than the song of the Araucanian, the poet expresses a longing for the vast riches of the Incan or Aztec heritage. The anaphora "No hay nadie" [There's no one] resounds as an empty echo throughout the poem, communicating the isolation of the Araucanians. Eight lines before the end there appears an ominous foreshadowing of the image of the *conquistador*, "Cruza el cóndor su vuelo negro" [The condor cruises its black flight].

The vision of pre-Columbian life and civilization is characterized by nostalgia in these poems. Neruda was becoming increasingly absorbed by the need to identify and imagine a reality that was fundamentally an underlying presence linking contemporary Latin American culture to its remote origins. This explains the constant shift from the past to the present and vice versa. Like Rivera in his murals painted in the corridors of the National Palace from 1942 to 1951, Neruda was summoning up a nostalgic reality, one that he could never have experienced, but one with which he nevertheless increasingly identified. Besides themes

and motifs, the images produced in these poems share the clarity
and brilliance of color found in Rivera's murals, particularly those
dedicated to Mexican cultures. Compare the following fragment
to the Huastec or Tarascan civilization murals:

> Pero muchedumbres de pueblos
> tejían la fibra, guardaban
> el porvenir de las cosechas,
> trenzaban el fulgor de la pluma,
> convencían a la turquesa,
> y en enredaderas textiles
> expresaban la luz del mundo.

(1:327)

> [(They) wove fiber, nurtured
> the promise of the crops,
> plaited feathered splendor,
> coaxed the turquoise,
> and in textile vines
> expressed the world's light.]

(24–25)

In Rivera's murals, as in these scenes, detailed emphasis is placed
on the pre-Colombian theme. "It almost appears," says Rochfort,
"as if he had intended them to be faithful historical records or
documents."[22]

The basic equation *tierra* (earth) = *barro/arcilla* (clay) = *hombre*
(man) that helps to shape the whole of *Canto general* is essential
in this section because the poet is part of the setting and a member of the cultures he describes. The poet has become, in Rogers's
terminology, "the hub," "the organizing center of a cosmogenetic
field which radiates in concentric circles outward from him, to
reach, ultimately, the contours of the surreal world, the figure his
writing creates."[23] Once we fuse these poetic images with their
visual counterparts (the murals), in other words, once "ekphrastic
hope" is put into play, in Mitchell's description "the estrangement
of the image/text division is overcome, and a sutured, synthetic
form, a verbal icon or imagetext arises in its place."[24] But the
"coordinated double image," as Arnheim calls this interaction, is
also the result of the reciprocal effect between the verbal and
the graphic.[25]

The best articulation of this relationship is Krieger's explication
of "still movement" in ekphrastic poetry. The concept describes
the ekphrastic process by which the visual referent as a spatial

representation becomes a metaphor in the verbal representation. In other words, still movement refers to the temporality of words and their paradoxical relation to "stillness," and can only be reached if the poem creates a linguistic pattern, and a circularity within its own temporal linearity, a process available in ekphrasis. According to Krieger, "the spatial work freezes the temporal work even as the latter seeks to free it from space."[26] Ekphrasis acts as the poetic device to "still" the temporal linearity of the text by superimposing upon it a plastic object as a symbol of the spatial, stilled world of plastic representation. I suggest that Neruda's *Canto general* has achieved the complete ekphrastic dimension. Its poems have taken on the "still" elements of the murals in the spatial representation normally reserved for the visual arts. The allegorical figures in the murals have been transposed in the poem as metaphoric, verbal representation. The fusion or super-imposition of a visual figure with its verbal metaphor symbolically creates spatiality in the poem by "freezing" its temporal linearity. The verbal image now possesses corporeality, a "body," as Lessing would say, that it lacked before its confrontation with its visual counterpart.[27]

When one merges these poetic images with the plastic ones, the poetic power of representation is intensified, shedding light at the same time on Rivera's murals, adding the human dimension that can be more easily expressed through language. The visual object in turn reflects back on the linguistic text. The poems provide the murals with another perspective or interpretation of the same reality, both contextualizing and evaluating them, and vice versa. But most importantly, the murals, besides explaining and justifying Neruda's choice of subject matter and specific narrative design, also facilitate the understanding of the formal, conceptual, and visual organization of *Canto general.*

The mythical dimension projected in Mexican mural art represents one of the main points of contact with *Canto general,* and particularly with this first section, which, according to Villegas, does not fit the hypothesis of the simple political intention of Neruda. In Villegas's view "no era necesario empezar tan lejos. Por lo tanto, se hace imprescindible buscar otra explicación" [it was not necessary to begin so far away. Therefore, it becomes critical to seek another explanation].[28] The critic's explanation continues: "en la imaginación mitificadora, surge como necesidad el retorno a los orígenes cuando se anuncia o se anhela un renacimiento, al comienzo de una forma de existencia" [in the mythifying imagination, a return to origins arises as a necessity when a renaissance is imminent or desired, at the beginning of a form of existence].[29] For this reason, an optimistic tone persists throughout the work. Indeed, in order to have a renaissance or regeneration, clearly a fall is necessary. Thus, the beginning of *Canto general*, like the beginning of the murals, attempts to unify its content within a frame of pristine, virgin, and uncorrupted reality, simultaneously juxtaposed with its history of exploitation and abuse. In this way the reader experiences a sense of a fatal loss, from which there is never any recovery, and, by extension, makes the arrival of the Western world—the Conquest and the *conquistador*—responsible for such destruction. This explains the use of the preterite in the first lines of the first section—*fueron, fue*—followed by the prevalence of the imperfect in the rest of the section. This is the myth-making process at work: the preterite tense in this case implies the sense of loss while the imperfect is used to recreate in the reader's mind nostalgia for a paradisiacal reality.

Angus Wilson once said that "[T]he impulse to write a novel comes from a momentary unified vision of life."[30] The "archetropic impulse" in Neruda, likewise, comes from a unified vision of the American life, prompted by the historical and thematic synthesis contained in mural art. *La lámpara en la tierra* truly embraces this holistic, almost animist approach. In fact, its main objective is to express this unified vision by linking all levels of existence: mineral, vegetable, animal, human and mythical. In "Vienen los pájaros" [The Birds Arrive], for instance, the cardinals resemble "el amanecer del Anáhuac" [the dawn of Anáhuac]. The colors of the toucan mirror those of different fruits in Nature; in a similar way, the green and yellow of the parrot serve the poet as similes for such minerals as copper and gold. The "hornero," a bird whose name derives from its nests made of clay in an oven shape, is an extension of the Adamic image and a precursor of American man. The mythical level finds its symbolic referent in the albatross, which gives form to "el orden de las soledades" [the order of the wilds] in the Araucanian land. Hence, solitude becomes its configurational element and its identification. Conversely, some minerals are linked to animal life through metaphors. "Las cordilleras antárticas" [the Antarctic cordilleras] are the "dentadura" [teeth] of a "tiburón acechante" [preying shark]. Cobalt is a "diosa serpiente vestida de plumas" [serpent goddess dressed in plumes] while sulphur recalls "un fulgor de pájaro amarillo" [the flash of a yellow bird]. Even the imagery of opposite referent is included in this first section. The condor is a "rey asesino" [murderous king] and represents such negative figures as the *conquistadores* and the clergy, "fraile solitario del cielo" [solitary monk of the sky].

"Los Conquistadores" and Muralism

The image of the condor introduces the second stage of mural painting mentioned by Orozco, in which the overriding subject of Mexican history is the Conquest. The recurrent and dominant image in the third section, *Los conquistadores*, is the condor, with its referents and synecdoches of destruction. However, in the conciliatory, apparently optimistic last poem, "A pesar de la ira" [Despite the Fury], Neruda told Cardona Peña, "se cuenta cómo, por encima de los crímenes, vinieron a nuestra América las ideas y la capacidad industrial del Renacimiento" [the story is told of how, above and beyond the crimes, ideas and the industrial capacity of the Renaissance came to our America].[31] In the same interview, he also points out: "me propuse juntar en su verdadero color la avalancha española con su superstición y su crueldad" [I decided to put together with its true colors the Spanish avalanche with its superstition and its cruelty].[32]

There are many differences among mural painters, even strong disagreements about the interpretation of a national reality. But, despite such differences, strong condemnation of the Conquest is shared by them all. Jean Charlot's best known fresco at the National Preparatory School is based on the Spanish *Massacre in the Templo Mayor* (1923). The emphasis again is on the destruction of a highly developed and sophisticated society. Its thematic and stylistic composition bring to mind, like a plastic palimpsest, Paolo Uccello's *Battle of San Romano*, particularly the section at the Uffizi Museum in Florence. The round classical linearity that is so unique to Uccello's technique was also imitated by Rivera, and more recently, by the Colombian painter Fernando Botero. Technically very different, but with the same underlying theme, Orozco's murals at the Cabañas Hospice present a sharp contrast between the metallic hardness of armor, shields, and swords and the softer, more noble condition of wood, clay, and stone. Siqueiros's murals in Chillán, Chile, like those at the Palace Museum of Fine Arts in Mexico, are also representative of this shared vision.

In *Canto general*, the opening image of the third section presents the arrival of the Spanish who are seen, as Villegas asserts, "como agentes del mal, como los dominadores, que aparecieron para perturbar la tranquilidad y la vida pacífica de los indios" [like agents of evil, like dominators, that appeared to disturb the tranquility of the peaceful life of the Indians].[33] The same interpretation of history is depicted by some of Rivera's more outstanding murals. The first series was painted between 1929 and 1935 in the staircases of the National Palace in Mexico City; the second was a commission from the ambassador of the United States in the Palace of Cortés in Cuernavaca; and the third one, describing *The Disembarkation in Veracruz*, was part of the series of murals in the corridors of the National Palace painted from 1942 to 1951. This last mural in particular bears a striking resemblance to Neruda's poem, "Llegan al mar de México (1493)" [They Reach the Gulf of Mexico].[34]

> A Veracruz va el viento asesino.
> En Veracruz desembarcaron los caballos.
> Las barcas van apretadas de garras
> y barbas rojas de Castilla.
>
> (1:347)

> [The murderous wind takes wing to Veracruz.
> In Veracruz the horses are put ashore.
> The ships are packed with claws
> and red beards from Castile.]
>
> (45)

The poet and the painter also echo that generalized viewpoint, in which all the Spaniards who accompanied Cortés and the first expeditions are considered voracious criminals and members of the lowest ranks of society:

> Son Arias, Reyes, Rojas, Maldonados,
> hijos del desamparo castellano,
> conocedores del hambre en invierno
> y de los piojos en los mesones.
>
> (1:347)

> [Arias, Reyes, Rojas, Maldonados,
> the foundlings of Castilian abandonment,
> veterans of hunger in winter
> and of lice in the roadside inns.]
>
> (45)

And three stanzas later, Neruda writes: "El hambre antigua de Europa, hambre como la cola / de un planeta mortal, poblaba el buque" (1:347) [The ancient hunger of Europe, hunger like the tail / of a dying comet, filled the ship (45)].

Referring to Rivera's mural, Rochfort comments: "The mural is not an episodic or journalistic unfolding of events; it is the creation and propagation of an idea."[35] The negative interpretation of this historical event that is the subject of section III was the result of the triumph of the Mexican Revolution and the reemergence of the same anti-Spanish sentiment that characterized the Independence period. There was a growing perception and conviction that the struggle for freedom and sovereignty had not yet been concluded. This facilitated the creation of a new renaissance, in which Europe and the Western culture were now perceived as alien and brutal. We might note that Octavio Paz, in his study *Los privilegios de la vista*, prefers the term "foundation" rather than renaissance, since the former corresponds better to the creation of a "Supreme Fiction."[36] The Revolution gave Mexicans the opportunity to see and understand their history in a way that would have been impossible before. As Paz puts it,

> La historia de México, sobre todo en sus dos grandes episodios: la Conquista y la Independencia, puede verse como una doble ruptura: la primera con el pasado indio, la segunda con el novohispano. La Revolución Mexicana fue una tentativa, realizada en parte, por reanudar los lazos rotos por la Conquista y la Independencia. Descubrimos de pronto que éramos, como dice el poeta López Velarde, "una tierra castellana y morisca, rayada de azteca."

> [The history of Mexico, especially in its two great episodes—the Conquest and Independence—can be seen as a double rupture: first with the Indian past, and secondly with the neo-Hispanic past. The Mexican Revolution was an attempt, partly successful, to reconnect the links broken by the Conquest and Independence. We suddenly discovered, as the poet López Velarde says, "a Castilian and Moorish land, with Aztec stripes."][37]

The powerful visual description of the murals contributed to an analogous interpretation in other artistic forms of expression such as the novel, music, and sculpture.[38] Neruda's immersion in Mexican history and cultural life provided him with the possibility of defending the past not only of Mexico, Peru, or Chile, but of the whole continent. Yet his purpose also involves the propagation of an idea for the future. Thus, the last poem of the canto, "A pesar de la ira," points toward the realization of such an idea—that of a better society under the auspices of socialism.

The anti-Spanish attitude is more contradictory and significant than it first appears. In 1939 Neruda still viewed Spain as the progenitor of all Latin Americans. This was the same year in which the poet was organizing the rescue of many Spaniards exiled in Paris. In a lecture (*Neruda entre nosotros* [*Neruda Among Us*]) delivered in Montevideo, he refers to Spain as "la desangrada madre de nuestra sangre" [the bleeding mother of our race], "la madre inmensa" [the immense mother].[39] Rodríguez Monegal comments:

> Muchos años más tarde, al escribir el *Canto general* y evocar la conquista española, Neruda olvidará este sentimiento y estas palabras; entonces sólo sentirá la cólera del indígena contra el conquistador rapaz; entonces sólo verá en España, no la madre desangrada, no la madre del idioma, sino el duro padre imperialista.

> [Many years later, when he was writing *Canto general* and evoking the Spanish Conquest, Neruda was to forget this sentiment and these words; then he would only feel the outrage of the indigenous people against the rapacious *conquistador:* then he would see in Spain, not the bleeding mother, not the mother of the language, but rather only the imperialist father.][40]

The fact is that Neruda's shift takes place not "many years later," as Monegal implies, but soon after his arrival in Mexico. In 1942, Neruda published "El corazón magallánico (1519)" [The Magellanic Heart (1519)], probably written at the end of 1941 and published in *Cuadernos Americanos* the following year.[41] In this poem— unlike the poem to "Almagro," written in 1938, before Neruda visited Mexico—the poetic persona adopts a confrontational tone for the first time, taking a strong stand against the *descubridores*. The discourse used to describe Magellan is consistent with the sentiment expressed throughout this third section of *Canto general*. This is how the Portuguese sailor is described:

> Cuál es el dios que pasa? Mirad su barba llena de gusanos
> y sus calzones en que la espesa atmósfera
> se pega y muerde como un perro náufrago:
> . . . .
> . . . viejo señor de luto litoral, aguilero

sin estirpe, manchado manantial, el estiércol
del Estrecho te manda.

(1:371)

[Which is the passing god? Behold his beard
    crawling with maggots
and his breeches in which the dense atmosphere
clings and snaps like a shipwrecked dog:
. . . .
old master of coastal mourning, baton
of the bastardy, tainted fountainhead, the dung
of the Strait sends you.]

(67)

Extremely important in these years is the process of rediscovery of the native land, of himself, and of his new vision that was still in a state of flux. In the search for a Latin American identity the poet goes through a vacillating process of formulation and personal confusion; the poem begins: "De dónde soy, me pregunto a veces, de dónde diablos / vengo, qué día es hoy, qué pasa" [Where am I from, I sometimes ask myself, where in the devil / do I come from, what day's today, what's happening (65)]. The existential quest seems to find redirection, if not definition, in the anti–imperialistic, anti-Spanish, ideological vision promulgated by Mexican mural art.

In *Canto general* this vision is projected—although softened in some cases—throughout the history of Latin America because Neruda interprets, like the muralists, the historical present as an extension and continuation of a traumatic birth. The poet himself elucidates this point:

En Chile, y en general, en la América del Sur, tenemos pedestales injustos, como el de Valdivia; una gran avenida lleva su nombre. . . . Se debe a que inmediatamente después de la conquista, una casta se apoderó del movimiento de liberación, implantando una nueva forma de dominio sobre nuestras poblaciones.

[In Chile, and in South America in general, we have unfair pedestals, like the one for Valdivia; a grand avenue bears his name. . . . This is because immediately after the Conquest, a caste took over the liberation movement, imposing a new form of domination over our peoples.][42]

In contrast, Neruda adds later, Lautaro is completely ignored. If the history of Latin America is perceived as a continuous process of domination since the arrival of the Spaniards, the indigenous people of the continent are seen both literally and metaphorically as the base or substrata on which this entire history of exploitation is sustained. The colossal mural by Rivera at the staircase of the National Palace is the visual representation of this perception of history. At the bottom of the central mural, the indigenous cultures are seen graphically struggling throughout Mexico's history. The historic narrative, as is the case in *Canto general*, does not follow a chronological sequence of events. Instead, it is presented as a synchronic, simultaneous phenomenon equally interchangeable with any given historical period, in the same manner of the pictorial techniques and perspective of the medieval tradition. That is why after the mythic origin of the world (right wall), what follows is the French War of 1862, or why Porfirio Díaz is at the center before the Mexican-American War of 1848, and so on. It is only at the beginning and end of these murals (right and left walls) that the history of oppression of this people is not present because an ideological parallel is drawn between the pre-Hispanic social system and the new order under Marxist ideology. This is what fundamentally distinguishes Neruda's and the Mexican muralist's artistic search for identity in the ancient cultures from the Romantic era. In the same way, the first three sections of *Canto general* concentrate almost exclusively on the ethnic theme, establishing from the very beginning a *dialectical base* for the entire book.

Oppressed and oppressors are divided along clear lines. The clergy, strongly associated with the *Conquista*, becomes a favorite target for attack in all mural painters, but in Orozco the motif reaches paroxysmic levels. In *Canto general*, the same connection is evident from the opening poem of the third section, "Vienen por las islas (1493)" [They Come Through the Islands (1493)]. As in Orozco's murals, anticlericalism is portrayed here in an overtly ironic fashion. After the destruction, murder, and torture of many Indians:

> sólo quedaban huesos
> rígidamente colocados
> en forma de cruz, para mayor
> gloria de Dios y de los hombres.
> . . . .
> Aquí la cruz, aquí el rosario,
> aquí la Virgen del Garrote.

(1:345)

> [Nothing remained but bones
> rigidly arranged

in the form of a cross, to the greater
glory of God and mankind.
        . . . .

Here the cross, there the rosary
here the Virgin of the Cudgel.]

(44)

The short poem, "Un obispo" [A Bishop], depicts the annihilation
of the indigenous culture by a representative of the church as he
burns irreplaceable *códices*. Again, the discourse is meant to in-
duce in the reader's mind a sensation of despair and loss. Another
representative of the clergy in "Las agonías" [The Agonies] is a
"corazón traidor, chacal podrido" [treacherous heart, rotten
jackal]: "Muerte, / venganza, matad, que os absuelvo; / grita el
chacal de la cruz asesina" (1:358) [Death, / vengance, kill, for I
absolve you all; / shouts the jackal with the murderous cross (55)].
    Neruda's iconic poems in this section, like Orozco's murals,
delineate the contours of the narrative with a strong series of
verbal images, recreating the devastating scene of the Conquest.[43]
In "Vienen por las islas (1493)," Neruda illustrates the destruction
of innocence with very powerful images:

Los hijos de la arcilla vieron rota
su sonrisa, golpeada
su frágil estatura de venados
y aún en la muerte no entendían.
Fueron amarrados y heridos,
fueron mordidos y enterrados.

(1:345)

[The children of clay saw their smile
shattered, beaten
their fragile stature of deer,
and even in death they did not understand.
They were bound and tortured,
burned and branded,
bitten and buried.]

(43)

The "arcilla," a metaphor of a pure and uncorrupted race and its
idyllic world [sonrisa] is broken by the deadly claw of the "buitre
rosado" [rosy vulture].
    As mentioned earlier, the image and similes of the *buitre* are
associated with Cortés, the *conquistadores*, and the clergy. In the
first sections of the book, the condor and all other birds of prey
except the eagle become the trope that shapes the configuration

of the *conquistador* and the Church. The metaphoric paradigm is established from the first mention of birds:

> El cóndor, el rey asesino,
> fraile, solitario del cielo,
> talismán negro de la nieve,
> huracán de la cetrería.

> (1:320)

> [(T)he condor, murderous king,
> solitary monk of the sky,
> black talisman of the snow,
> hurricane of falconry.]

> (18)

The same image is found in section XI of *Alturas de Macchu Picchu*. Here the "cóndor furibundo" [frenzied condor] is an "huracán de plumas carniceras" [hurricane of cruel feathers]. A foreshadowing of death for the Araucanians in "Los hombres" is expressed as "cruza el cóndor su vuelo negro" [the condor cruises its black flight]. In *Los conquistadores* almost every poem contains a synecdoche or a reference to this metaphor. Pedro de Alvarado, according to Bernal Díaz del Castillo, was Cortés's second lieutenant who ordered the genocide of the Aztecs that ended with the retreat of the Spanish forces during the ill-fated *Noche Triste*. Neruda probably alludes to this event when he describes Alvarado: "con garras y cuchillos / cayó sobre las chozas" [(he) fell upon the huts / with claws and knives]. The poet calls him "el halcón clandestino de la muerte" [the clandestine falcon of death]. Vasco Núñez de Balboa, another *conquistador*, is subtly indicated by the synecdoche "muerte y garra" [death and claw].

In "Homenaje a Balboa" [Homage to Balboa] Neruda condemns the excessive greed that blinded the invaders and led them to betrayal and treason among themselves. The image used is again that of the falcon, here devouring its own nest: "el halcón devoraba / su nido, y se reunían las serpientes / atacándose con lenguas de oro" (1:353) [the falcon has devoured its nest, and the serpents have assembled, / striking one another with tongues of gold (51)]. Later, the image is applied equally to the forces of Nazism and imperialism, which are seen as the present extension of the Conquest and the Church. The same atemporal, synchronic association of history, as well as the same metaphor attached to a similar interpretation of events and characters are common to all the mural painters, but special emphasis is given by Siqueiros at the

Electrical Trade Union Institute. While Orozco's interpretation focuses on the *buitre* image that feeds on death and carrion, Siqueiros goes even further to contemporalize it, in order to directly associate it with excessive militarization vis-à-vis ethnic conflicts in the world. It can also be noted that Mexican muralism was one of the first artistic movements in America openly opposed to the spread of Fascism and Nazism from its inception.

At this juncture, it is now possible to engage in a discussion to elucidate and analyze how Neruda's ekphrastic encounter or dialogue between text and image takes place: that is, the form and manner in which the archetropic experience transposes the visual into the verbal. To this effect we must consider the different ways in which the artist approaches the ekphrastic occurrence. In essence, the visual representation or referent of the ekphrastic version can be "fictive" or "literary." In fictive ekphrasis (or "notional" as John Hollander prefers to term it) the visual image's existence depends upon the verbal, the ekphrastic object, as in the case of Homer's description of Achilles' shield, and is the construct of a verbal description of a fictive and illusory object, rather than a "real" one. In literary ekphrasis (or "actual" in Hollander's diction) the visual image and/or referent exists independently of the verbal description. What is important to establish now is that Neruda's methodology, like Homer's, favors his own version of ekphrasis that moves between the fictive or notional and the literary or actual.

As it happens, Neruda's ekphrastic effort could also be described, using Weisstein's typology, as a literary work that seeks to reproduce movement styles in the visual arts; in this case, sharing images, themes, and motifs with Mexican mural art. Yet this does not mean that an "actual" form of ekphrasis is necessarily at work. In other words, the real existence of such murals does not preclude the poet from engaging—through the mediation of the archetropic experience—in a sort of fictive ekphrasis, reproducing, instead of a single, particular panel or painting, a unified vision of a series of murals and paintings which are linked only by similar iconic codes, as is the case in most of the poems with visual referents discussed thus far.

Of course, in some instances, Neruda has also engaged in a more "direct" form of ekphrastic encounter. The best example of this is the series of images, motifs, and symbols contained in the murals of the Ministry of Education, which we will discuss at length later. Yet, even in this instance, the ekphrastic poem seems to take on a life of its own. Thus, the distinction between the

José Clemente Orozco, *Political Junkheap*, 1924, National Preparatory School, Mexico City. Photograph by Marcos Méndez.

David Alfaro Siqueiros, *Portrait of the Bourgeoisie*, 1939, Electrical Trade Union Institute, Mexico City (INBA).

fictive and the literary forms of ekphrasis allows us to see Neruda's poetry in a quite different light, and we begin to understand
that the ekphrastic relationship with the graphic image has another complementing facet that has to do with the traditional
debate over the supremacy of one form of artistic expression over
the other. Pertinent to Neruda's work is Francoise Metzer's comment that "Ekphrasis may in fact be the attempt of writing to
overcome the power of the image in a mimetically oriented culture
of images."[44]

As the reader will recall, Krieger's notion of the ekphrastic principle, closely associated with the concept of "still movement," is
central to this supremacy debate. Krieger claims the capacity of
the poem to become, through the immediacy of ekphrasis, its
own independent verbal emblem "that plays the role of a visual
image while playing its own role."[45] This idea is crucial in our
discussion and understanding of Neruda's ekphrastic encounter
with murals, since it reverses the traditional position that perceived the ekphrastic poem as subsidiary and subordinated to the
superiority of the "natural signs" or the plastic arts. For Krieger,
as for Lessing before him, the apparent supremacy of the eye
(oculocentrism) can be countered by language's ability to access
the inner visions of the intelligible world, and its capacity to represent the transcendentally "real."[46] The ekphrastic principle for
Krieger goes beyond the verbal version of the visual; it implies
the appropriation by the poem of the spatial character of the
visual arts "by trying to force its words . . . to take on a substantive configuration—in effect to become an emblem."[47] Tracing the
evolution of the poem as emblem to the early expressions of the
epigram in antiquity, Krieger attempts to demonstrate, not only
the ability of language to overcome the limitations of space and
time, but also the autonomy of the ekphrastic poem. For this
critic, the epigrams in Greece were more than mere verbal inscription on sculptures or tombstones; they were "sometimes restive
in this subsidiary role," and "could use . . . words to challenge
the primacy of the physical object [they] adorned."[48] The epigram
could sometimes include an interpretation or comment that
would add a more complex human dimension to the monument.
For Krieger, therefore, ekphrasis is an epigram that has tran-
scended the visual referent and created its own verbal image. In
Neruda's ekphrastic experience, the visual image (the mural or
series of murals) which has been translated into the verbal (the
poem) is lost in the translation, while the verbal image, no longer

leaning on the visual representation, becomes an independent, free-standing entity, seeking the same status as the visual.

It is the contention of this study that Neruda was aware of the ability of his poetry to give voice to the otherwise unmoving and silent walls and was trying to capture the intelligible, the transcendentally "real"; that he was aware of the capacity of the poems to add the human dimension that the murals can only suggest. Neruda, like Homer in the *Iliad*, but inspired by the Mexican murals, was attempting to immortalize, to capture for posterity, the historical epic and the mythical dimension of his continent.

Including the Other Side

Having established the autonomous character of Neruda's work, we can now proceed to discuss the thematic unity of *Canto general* that relates ekphrastically to muralism, and also in general terms to the Mexican experience. The last poem of the third *canto*, "A pesar de la ira" [Despite the Fury], attempts to present the promise of hope and opens the possibility of reconciliation with the past:

> Así, con el sangriento
> titán de piedra,
> halcón encarnizado,
> no sólo llegó sangre sino trigo.
>
> La luz vino a pesar de los puñales.

(1:373)

> [So with the cruel
> titan of stone,
> the death-dealing falcon,
> not only blood but wheat arrived.
>
> The light came despite the daggers.]

(69)

As noted earlier, Neruda explained that the purpose of this poem is to point out that in addition to crime, the Conquest brought the ideas and mechanical capabilities of the Renaissance to the American continent.[49] In this final poem Neruda falls short in trying to reconcile American history or to convince the reader of his neutrality. This judgment is based solely on this third section. Here it seems that Neruda is trying to confront one of the deepest atavistic conflicts of Latin Americans, especially Mexicans, Peruvians, and Chileans: that is, between their indigenous heritage on the one hand, and on the other, Spanish language and culture. Paradoxically, this contradiction becomes an essential driving force in the structure of *Canto general*.

The utopia of that pristine world and of *Alturas de Macchu Picchu* is based on the mythification of the past in contrast with the pedestrian oppression of the present. The idyllic world, however, is undermined by the human suffering stated early on in "Los hombres" (first section), when Neruda describes the Aztecs' human sacrifices, laments the loss of Mayan knowledge so that they now have to resort to the drowning of damsels, or wonders about the cruelty among the Incas in *Alturas de Macchu Picchu*. As Giuseppe Bellini has put it,

> el grandioso comienzo del *canto,* donde se contempla la extensión toda en potencia, de las tierras "sin nombre y sin número" . . . mundo de idílica paz en el que se repite el clima de la creación, propio del *Popol-Vuh,* ve desmentida su aparente atmósfera feliz por el dolor humano.

> [the grandiose beginning of the *canto,* which contemplates in all its promise the extension of the lands "without name and without number" . . . a world of idyllic peace in which the climate of creation is repeated, as though it were taken from the *Popol-Vuh,* sees its apparently happy atmosphere belied by human pain.][50]

The Italian critic then asks: "¿Qué mucho que luego intervenga la negativa historia de la conquista, más tarde la de los dictadores, si todo es continuación de una injusticia de los orígenes?" [Is it therefore so noteworthy that the negative history of the Conquest, and later that of the dictators, would appear, if everything is a continuation of an injustice from the very origins?][51] With this argument, Bellini pretends to undermine the effectiveness of the mythic level of the canto, and by referring to *Fin de mundo* [*World's End*], he also intends to demonstrate that Neruda's vision is, in fact, pessimistic. Juan Villegas, on the other hand, sees the canto as one of the poet's most optimistic works and concludes that its mythical configuration supports and justifies the positive character of the book.[52] After citing Neruda's own comments on the hopeful nature of his book, this critic concludes: "La tristeza viene de las circunstancias personales en que fue creado" [The sadness arises from the personal circumstances in which it was created].[53] Bellini's reading, based solely on the fact that Neruda also presents the dark side of pre-Columbian civilization and of the present day, is therefore unconvincing. But it is also questionable whether the sadness in the book, as argued by Villegas, corresponds only to the poet's personal circumstances.

If the Mexican visual experience was crucial to Neruda's ekphrastic formulation of *Canto general*, it is logical to assume that the work's somber aspect can be explained in terms of the prevailing trend of Mexican postrevolutionary art that rejects traditional European models and engages in a search for roots in its own soil and its own people. Mexican painters and novelists were aiming, above all, to capture *all aspects*, both positive and negative, of their people. Hugo Rodríguez-Alcalá, in his article on the influence of Mexican muralism in *El llano en llamas*, has pointed out that Rulfo's work

descuella en la tradición del gran arte surgido de la Revolución Mexicana por más de una razón y, especialmente, *por el acercamiento espiritual al pueblo para interpretarlo en su realidad más íntima sin evitar los aspectos sombríos y crueles* (emphasis added).

[stands out in the tradition of the great art that came out of the Mexican Revolution for more than one reason, and especially *because of its spiritual connection with the people in order to interpret their most intimate reality without avoiding the most somber and cruel aspects* (emphasis added).][54]

This spiritual rapport with the people present in muralism and in Rulfo's novel raises the critical question, when interpreting *Canto general* as a whole, of the origins of a similar impulse in Neruda's poem.

By the time Neruda arrived in Mexico, mural painting had long been established as a school or movement. The Three Masters—Rivera, Siqueiros, and Orozco—more than anyone else had managed to create a collective art in which the masses become the protagonist and are described in all aspects of life. It was Orozco, however, who focused, not only on the idyllic past but also on the cruelty present in the two realities of pre-Colombian cultures. Rochfort notes that, "[i]n the 1932 mural at Dartmouth College, New Hampshire, USA, and the later mural cycle of 1938 at the Hospicio Cabañas in Guadalajara, Orozco depicted the Indian world as being both civilized and cultured as well as despotic and cruel."[55] The art critic is referring to *Ancient Human Sacrifice* at

Dartmouth and *Ancient Mexican Religion* in the Cabañas Hospice. These two series together explain why in his memoirs Neruda referred to Orozco as an "especie de Goya de su fantasmagórica patria" [sort of Goya in his phantasmagorical country], whose works, filled with violent scenes, "quedarán como la revelación de nuestra crueldad" [are immortal . . . , bearing witness to our cruelty].[56]

Orozco's attitude toward the subject, as Neruda's in "Los hombres" and *Alturas de Macchu Picchu,* is nothing less than ambivalent. In those murals, Orozco closely follows an ancient tradition deeply rooted in the national spirit. Part of the aesthetic values of pre-Hispanic artists was to describe the horror and pain of human suffering, which diametrically contrasts with the Western artistic search for beauty. Jean Charlot maintains that to understand the contemporary Mexican artist,

> one must realize that, as he tests for strong roots in his cultural subsoil, he finds that his own classics enshrined horror over beauty and reserved for the representations of physical pain and death the glamour that the Greek had allotted to lust.[57]

Orozco, like his ancestors, did not have any problem confronting and painting the harsh reality of the past and the present. This is precisely the reason for his attacks on Rivera's treatment of the indigenous theme, which, in his opinion, was better suited for export:

> What he does by putting a profusion of Indians in his pictures is to make hay while the Indian smallpox rages, a disease that is making our politicians itch. . . . As art for export it is understandable, but there is no excuse for painting it in Mexico.[58]

And when asked if he followed the indigenous tendencies of Diego Rivera, he replied:

> I would rather do it first hand, contact the original sources in the National Museum, the codices and other remains of aboriginal art that Rivera reproduces.[59]

Ironically, that is exactly what he did. Orozco, points out Charlot, "realized another masterly fusion of ancient and present plastics and emotions in the Indian squatting before a blood-soaked teocally, frescoed in 1926, in the main staircase of the Preparatoria."[60]

José Clemente Orozco, Mexican, 1883–1949. *The Epic of American Civilization: Ancient Human Sacrifice* (Panel 3), 1932–34, Fresco. Commissioned by the trustees of Dartmouth College, Hanover, New Hampshire, USA.

José Clemente Orozco, *Ancient Mexican Religion*, 1938–39, Cabañas Hospice, Guadalajara, Mexico. Photograph by Marcos Méndez.

Rivera also stated many times that his art and technique followed those of pre-Colombian murals. But unlike Orozco, Rivera's vision of the indigenous world, with its myth, superstition, and violence, in his hands becomes, according to Rochfort,

> a strange and timeless place, in which conflict and culture, agriculture or slavery are treated with equal importance and assume no rank or hierarchy. . . . He did not wish to judge the ancient Indian world by the standards of a European, Christian culture which had acted as an alien and brutal usurper.[61]

In both instances, though, their paintings reflect in different ways the perennial conflict with Western tradition and the attempt to break with traditional aesthetic values.

Canto general is part of this polemic. It synthesizes these apparently contradictory positions, which form part of the inner contradiction of the "mestizo" who shares both cultures. Neruda's purpose, like that of the muralists, is to capture the American world in its vast reality. In order to create an American myth, of course, the poet cannot avoid being part of a continental struggle for identity.[62] Octavio Paz has said that "American literature, which is rootless and cosmopolitan, is both a return and a search for tradition. In searching for it, it invents it. But invention and discovery are not terms that best describe its purest creations. A desire for encarnation, a literature of foundations."[63]

Commenting on his own *Canto general*, Neruda provides a clue for the interpretation put forward here: the attempt to embrace both the idyllic and the cruel natures of Latin America's past and present.

> Este libro fue la coronación de mi tentativa ambiciosa. Es extenso como un buen fragmento del tiempo y *en él hay sombra y luz a la vez, porque me proponía que abarcara el espacio mayor en que se mueren, crean, trabajan y perecen las vidas y los pueblos* (emphasis added).

> [This book was the culmination of my ambitious effort. It is extensive like a good fragment of time and *in it there is light and shadow at the same time, because I wanted to have it encompass the greater space in which lives and peoples die, create, work and perish* (emphasis added).][64]

Clearly, Neruda did not have in mind a black and white picture. On the contrary, his objectives include a comprehensive approach that considers all the elements available to the poet at the moment of creation of the art-object. Structurally, every section includes, as in the third canto just mentioned, at least one element or poem that functions as a counterpoint to the rest, a subversive element that threatens to deconstruct its cohesiveness. Yet the framework does not lie in a particular poem or element within the section, but also in the inner structure of the sections. Thus, the antithetical configuration of the book, its symmetry, is present within and among sections. The ninth section, *Que despierte el leñador* [*Let the Woodcutter Awaken*], for instance, contains a poem of the same name in which Neruda exhorts the autochthonous American to resist the economic, political, and cultural imperialism launched by the United States at the end of the 1940s; this represents the poet's effort to constantly establish a balance by overcoming his negative attitude toward the United States and find something positive about the North Americans, just as he did about the Spaniards in the last poem of the third section, "A pesar de la ira." Here, the giant, as Nelly Santos has stated,

> aparece arropado de un sentimiento ambivalente de admonición y desprecio, de amor y de odio, de miedo y desafío. . . . Neruda admira y ama al pueblo norteamericano simbolizado por Lincoln "el leñador"; pero . . . odia, desprecia y teme el capitalismo . . . , el imperialismo.

> [appears to be wrapped in an ambivalent sentiment of admonition and disdain, of love and hate, of fear and defiance. . . . Neruda admires and loves the North American people symbolized by the "woodcutter" Lincoln; but he hates, despises and fears capitalism . . . , imperialism.][65]

Pablo Neruda's *ars poetica* in *Canto general* and his later literary production can be defined as that of a "spiritual rapport" with the people without ignoring or overlooking the sad and somber reality of the history of the Latin American continent. In the first three sections, Neruda consistently includes his poetic persona in the art-object as the means of achieving this "acercamiento" to the masses. From Diego Velázquez's *Las meninas* to Diego Rivera's *Dream of a Sunday Afternoon in the Alameda* and Fernando Botero's *The Presidential Family*, the insertion of the artist in his own work has been, in Hispanic art, a way of expressing both protest and the collective spirit of the people. The result in *Canto general* is successful, and its effect is twofold: on the one hand, the artist acts somewhat like a firsthand chronicler, a participant in the events depicted; and on the other, he attempts to establish himself as the redeeming voice. Paradoxically, Neruda's voice and pres-

Diego Rivera, *Dream of a Sunday Afternoon in the Alameda*, 1947, The Alameda
Park, Mexico City (INBA).

ence in this book are as monumental as the Mexican murals that inspired it; so much so that the voice of the people he strives so hard to enunciate is barely heard.[66] The exception, of course, is the last section of the first book, *La tierra se llama Juan*, in which the poetic voice emanates from ordinary people.

The Indigenous Theme in Latin American Literature

There is another aspect to be considered before reaching further conclusions. It must be taken into account that the indigenous trend in postrevolutionary Mexican art was part of a worldwide movement, in which almost every nation turned to its people and traditions to find its roots. The Mexican and Bolshevik revolutions as well as World War I were the main historical events behind the shift from aristocratic to popular values and culture.

There are also other important artistic antecedents to consider. We have mentioned, for example, the widespread European interest in the search for primitive and exotic art. Yet, we must stress that this European quest was perceived by Mexican muralists, from a formal and thematic standpoint, as a limited, even futile, artistic exercise in contrast with the richness and authenticity to be found in Amerindian art.[67] That is why for Rivera the search, he said, ended in Mexico. Paradoxically, following the iconoclastic tendencies of the avant-garde, the new objective implied a rejection of the very same European art which had been compelled by the radical abstractions of Cubism to recognize the value of pre-Hispanic art. In other words, only after Cubism put forward such a radical conception of reality and opened the minds of artists to new ways of perceiving and representing the world, did the complex intricacies of pre-Hispanic art and aesthetics become apparent.[68]

The influence in Latin America of three important figures— Oswald Spengler, Herman Keyserling, and D. H. Lawrence—is well documented. Spengler's *The Decline of the West* (1918) helped to undermine the Eurocentric sense of superiority by affirming the ability of Amerindian cultures to equal or surpass the white cultures. The image of the earth as a mother figure and the vision of American soil as a purely telluric force that dominates Mexican mural art and part of *Canto general* can also be found in Keyserling's *The Travel Diary of a Philosopher* published in 1925. Lawrence's novel, *The Plumed Serpent* (1926), was also significant in the artistic search for indigenous roots.[69]

Seymour Menton, in his excellent study of the trends associated with this theme within Latin American literary history, points out that,

> [E]n cuanto cayó el castillo de los naipes de la sociedad victoriana con todas sus ilusiones frente a los torbellinos de la Revolución Mexicana, de la Primera Guerra Mundial y de la Revolución bolchevique, los autores latinoamericanos comenzaron a buscar su propia identidad y a analizar los problemas nacionales. El tema indígena volvió a ser cultivado por primera vez desde la época romántica, pero ya con mayor profundidad y con mayores pretensiones artísticas.

> [As soon as Victorian society's house of cards fell, with all its illusions about the whirlwinds of the Mexican Revolution, the first World War and the Bolshevik Revolution, Latin American writers began to search for their own identity and to analyze nation problems. The indigenous theme was cultivated again for the first time since the romantic era, but this time with greater depth and greater artistic pretensions.][70]

Canto general belongs to that major tradition of Latin American literature in which can be seen, as Rodríguez Monegal has said, "una genealogía poética que incluye a don Andrés Bello, a Rubén Darío, a Santos Chocano, los autores de la grandeza del Nuevo Mundo independiente" [a poetic genealogy that includes Andrés Bello, Rubén Darío, Santos Chocano, the authors of the greatness of the independent New World].[71] But what must be underlined here is that the indigenous theme, particularly in the first three sections, and Neruda's own vision of the American Indian differ significantly from that of Darío or Santos Chocano, or, needless to say, that of Bello. Menton clarifies:

> Aunque el indio aparece retratado en algunos poemas de Rubén Darío o en la fase postmodernista de Santos Chocano . . . en realidad no era el tema predilecto de los estetas modernistas con las manos del marqués y los bigotes tipo Napoleón III.

> [Although the Indian is described in some poems by Rubén Darío or in the post-*modernista* phase of Santos Chocano . . . in fact it was not the theme of choice of the *modernista* aesthetes with their marquis hands and their Napoleon III mustaches.][72]

For this reason Phyllis Rodríguez-Peralta compares Santos Chocano with the conqueror who "uses the Indian to provide richness and color for his poetic empire."[73] She adds that for Chocano,

"the Indian is a picturesque legend, and his last empire, a dazzling vision."[74] Roberto González Echevarría has persuasively set-
tled the issue: "[T]here are really no antecedents in Spanish for
this kind of poem, or even book, except perhaps in those colonial
histories mentioned, or in Bello. But Bello's neoclassical rhetoric
gets in the way too often."[75] The forerunner, of course, is not
literary but pictorial; it is Mexican muralism's panoramic vision,
with its epic narrative of history. By effectively dissociating *Canto
general* from an immediate literary antecedent, the way is cleared
to see that its indigenous theme has no other spacial context than
that of Mexico and mural art.

The Longing for a Rich Indigenous Culture

Neruda's poetry during these years (1920–30) and even as late
as 1938, does not include America as a theme, and the indigenous
theme is even less visible. It is interesting to observe that a tone
of nostalgia continued in "La copa de sangre" [The Chalice of
Blood], a singular statement in prose published for the first time
in 1943,[76] which represents an intuitive foreshadowing of *Canto
general de Chile*, published the same year in Mexico. Yet the indigenous theme is still not present at all. Without engaging in a detailed discussion of publication dates, it should be stated that
Canto general de Chile (1943), part of which is said to have been
written in 1939, does not include the pre-Colombian theme.[77] The
fact that the ethnic theme did not appear at all in Neruda's poetry
before his stay in Mexico is further evidence of the vital impulse
toward the indigenous movement that the Mexican experience
provided.

Canto general de Chile does, however, initiate Neruda's search
for roots. The first lines of "Himno y regreso (1939)" [Hymn and
Homecoming (1939)] express Neruda's feelings regarding his return to his homeland. But in the second stanza he gives us a clue
as to his real sentiments: "Acoge / esta guitarra ciega / y esta
frente perdida" (1:529) [Welcome / this blind guitar, / this lost
brow (214)]. Then, in the fourth stanza he writes: "Patria mía:
quiero mudar de sombra" (1:529) [My country: I want to change
shadows (215)]. An analysis of these lines from a purely biographical perspective leads to the conclusion that Neruda, after
his experience abroad and stay in Spain, finds himself confused
("frente perdida") and lost ("guitarra ciega") in his own country.
The sense of alienation is translated into a plea to a "madre" to

whom he appeals for shelter ("Acoge"). The inquiry continues in "El corazón magallánico" (1942), where the poet desperately asks himself: "De dónde soy, me pregunto a veces, de dónde diablos / vengo, qué día es hoy, qué pasa" [Where am I from, I sometimes ask myself, where in the devil / do I come from, what day's today, what's happening (65)]. This same perception of turmoil, related to a "desarraigo" [uprooting] is later reiterated by the poet in his memoirs:

> Pienso que el hombre debe vivir en su patria y creo que el desarraigo de los seres humanos es una frustración que de alguna manera u otra entorpece la claridad del alma.

> [I believe that a man should live in his country and I think that the deracination of human beings leads to frustration, in one way or another obstructing the light of the soul.][78]

The first line of the fourth stanza mentioned above ("Patria mía: quiero mudar de sombra") implies the desire of the poet to turn his poetry toward his roots. The geographic greatness and magnificence of Chile find no parallel in the pre-Columbian past. The Araucanians were a culture that Neruda admires for their fierceness and courage, but he laments the lack of a rich tradition seen in other cultures such as the Incan or Aztec civilizations.[79] Such a distinction, though, becomes especially vivid during and after his stay in Mexico. Mexico was like the first mirror in which Neruda could see the reflection of himself and his past vis-à-vis other Americans.

In several instances, the poet expresses his yearning for a rich indigenous past. The second stanza of the poem "Se unen la tierra y el hombre" [Land and Man Unite] (section III) illustrates the austerity of the Araucanians as compared to other cultures:

> No tuvieron mis padres araucanos
> cimeras de plumaje luminoso,
> no descansaron en flores nupciales,
> no hilaron oro para el sacerdote:
> eran piedra y árbol, raíces
> de los breñales sacudidos,
> hojas con forma de lanza,
> cabezas de metal guerrero.
>
> (1:364)

> [My Araucanian ancestors had no
> crests of luminous plumes,

they didn't rest on nuptial flowers,
they spun no gold for the priest:
they were stone and tree, roots
of the intractable brambles,
lance-shaped leaves,
heads of militant metal.]

(61)

A certain irony could be read into these lines, but the fact is that while the poet's description reflects his knowledge of the Aztec and Incan cultures, the above stanza does not really contain a value judgment of these societies. Yet Neruda was not alone in his nostalgia for a highly developed autochthonous culture. Similar views are shared by other Latin Americans lacking a rich indigenous heritage. Another Chilean, Gabriela Mistral, was even harsher in comparing the Araucanians to the Aztecs or Incas:

El indio araucano caminaba, combatía, cazaba. No edificaba como el azteca, no tejía maravillosamente como el quechua-aimará, no cantaba, no tenía don de organización como ellos.

[The Araucanian Indian walked, fought, hunted. He did not build structures like the Aztec, he did not weave marvelously like the Quechua-Aimara, nor did he sing, or have their gift of organization.][80]

In 1941, in one of his many lectures delivered in Mexico, Neruda seems to agree with Mistral, underscoring the differences in the area of artistic skills:

Mientras grandes razas de sacerdotes y guerreros, entre vosotros, escogían la turquesa, el jade y el oro para levantarlos a la altura de la flor, y las estructuras de los templos y pirámides de un imperio gigantesco llenaban vuestro territorio, era entre nosotros la sombra de la prehistoria.

[While great races of priests and warriors, among you (the Mexicans), chose turquoise, jade and gold to raise these elements to the level of the flower; while the structures of the temples and pyramids of a gigantic empire filled your territory, there was shadow and prehistory among us.][81]

The line "Patria mía: quiero mudar de sombra" is again called to mind. Mexico was the first place to provide the poet with the themes and materials to bring about that shift. History, geography, and culture, expressed through muralism, became the artistic tools with which Neruda was to develop new forms, images, and motifs for *Canto general*.[82]

The new voice of *Canto general*—a messianic, telluric, American voice—emerges out of that fascinating reality. In the last stanza of "México 1941" from the last section, *Yo soy* [*I Am*], the poet describes this process of (re)acquisition, in what almost amounts to a confession:

> Y así de tierra a tierra fui tocando
> el barro americano, mi estatura,
> y subió por mis venas el olvido
> recostado en el tiempo, hasta que un día
> estremeció mi boca su lenguaje.

(1:705)

> [And so I went from land to land touching
> American clay, my stature,
> and oblivion recumbent in time
> rose through my veins, until one day
> its language shook my mouth.]

(384)

As someone who has just been awakened from a long hypnotic trance (i.e., the hidden memory of the American spirit) the poet proclaims his condition as "Gran Lengua" [Spokesman] or, in the indigenous sense, shaman, becoming the sacred interpreter of the American world.[83] "Yo soy" as the redeeming voice closes the circle of "La lámpara en la tierra," in which the poet presents himself for the first time as such: "Yo estoy aquí para contar la historia" (1:315) [I am here to tell the story (14)]. There is here undisguised symmetry with Rivera's murals on the staircases of the National Palace. On the one hand, the first section of *Canto general*, "La Lámpara en la tierra," corresponds to the pre-Colombian cultures painted on the right wall, and, on the other, Marx holding the new commandments and pointing toward the horizon on the left wall parallels Neruda's own reaffirmation of his position as spokesman, as the lamp (Marxism) to guide the American continent in "Yo soy," the last section of *Canto general*. Neruda seems to have found in mural art not only a source of artistic expression, but also the model that inspired him to adopt the voice of biblical resonance and epic proportions that González Echevarría mentioned. Critical consensus regarding this period of Mexican history agrees on the dynamic impulse toward self-

definition and definition of national character. For Henríquez
Ureña,

> [t]his Mexico is at present in one of those active periods of national
> life, a period of crisis and creation . . . Mexico is creating a new life,
> affirming its own character and declaring itself fit to found its own
> type of civilization.[84]

Once Neruda faced a culture as rich as that of Mexico, and later
that of Peru, he widened his field of vision. As Tarn explains, he
realized how foolish it is for a Latin American to limit himself to
one national reality:

> Neruda is a Chilean but his Indians are not as symbolically visible as
> the Andine Inca are. This might have provided one good reason for
> him to jump as he did from an original project of a *Canto general de
> Chile* to a *Canto general* (de América).[85]

It is not accidental that his first American poem in any real sense
was "Un canto para Bolívar" [Canto for Bolívar], read in 1940 at
the National Preparatory School. Neruda was not following Andrés Bello or Olmedo's romantic vision; rather, he was pursuing
Bolivar's continental dream: Latin American unity, but through
the search for a true American identity. While in Peru, Neruda
confirmed his early suspicions that the roots of Chile were inextri-
cably intertwined with those of Mexico, Peru, and the continent
as a whole. Again, the poet describes this revelation in his
memoirs:

> Me sentí infinitamente pequeño en el centro de aquel ombligo de
> piedra; ombligo de un mundo deshabitado, orgulloso y eminente, al
> que de algún modo ya pertenecía. Sentí que mis propias manos ha-
> bían trabajado allí en alguna etapa lejana, cavando surcos, alisando
> peñascos.
> Me sentí chileno, peruano, americano. Había encontrado en aquel-
> las alturas difíciles, entre aquellas ruinas gloriosas y dispersas, una
> profesión de fe para la continuación de mi canto.

> [I felt infinitely small in the center of that navel of rocks, the navel of
> a deserted world, proud, towering high, to which I somehow be-
> longed. I felt that my own hands had labored there at some remote
> point in time, digging furrows, polishing rocks.
> I felt Chilean, Peruvian, American. On those difficult heights,
> among those glorious, scattered ruins, I had found the principles of
> faith I needed to continue my poetry.][86]

The Indigenous Theme as a Propagandistic Device

If the indigenous presence represents the foundation that sustains the entire existence and history of America, its figure thus becomes the central icon to express that new unified vision. Yet, in order to convey that vision, the indigenous figure must be presented in a way that does not necessarily reflect Neruda's "real" vision. He becomes a mythic figure, not in the romantic sense of classical, pagan heroes, but more in the Christian interpretation of sainthood or Christ-like figures.

Seymour Menton has said that all of the so-called "literatura indigenista" of this period could be classified as works of social denunciation and protest.[87] In *Canto general* the Indian is not treated anthropologically—as is the case in the novels *El indio* (1935) by the Mexican Gregorio López y Fuentes or *Yawar fiesta* (1941) by the Peruvian José María Arguedas—but rather as a political device for the articulation of an ideology, just as in the muralist movement. As such, the indigenous figure becomes part of a sociopolitical and economic transformation. Julio Rodríguez-Luis has noted that during this period in Mexico

> la Revolución plantea desde un principio . . . la posibilidad de una tranformación socio-económica que libere al indígena de su condición de siervo . . . insiste enérgicamente en la contribución indígena al proceso de la formación de una nacionalidad mexicana resultado del mestizaje (movimiento muralista, regalo de una estatua de Cuauhtémoc al Brasil por Vasconcelos, incluso, o a pesar de sus contradicciones ideológicas, el ensayo de éste, *La raza cósmica*, de 1925).

> [the Revolution suggests from the beginning . . . the possibility of a socioeconomic transformation that would liberate the indigenous people from their condition of servant . . . it energetically insists on the indigenous contribution in the process of forming a Mexican nationality born of mestizo blood (the muralist movement; Vasconcelos' gift to Brasil of a statue of Cuauhtemoc; or even, in spite of its ideological contradictions, his 1925 essay, *The Cosmic Race*.)][88]

The indigenous masses are translated into two images. One is a silent, innocent image of pure "arcilla": the clay pot metaphor of Siqueiros in *Ethnography* mentioned earlier illustrates this. Its sound comes only from the reverberation of the clay pot when touched or tapped. The other is the image of the oppressed vic-

tims of the *conquistador*, individuals—Cuauhtémoc, Lautaro, Caupolicán, Tupac Amarú—who belong to the vast arena of *Los
libertadores*, under the imagery of the martyr, or sacrifice by death
and renewal of life. In this sense Cuauhtémoc or Caupolicán are
described as no different from Luis Emilio Recabarren or Emiliano
Zapata. But even when the poet introduces himself into the poem
in the "acercamiento" or approach to the people, it is always as
an oracle or prophet who foretells the future and offers guidance.
A good example of this is the third stanza of "Cortés," from the
third canto:

> Hermano aterrado, no tomes
> como amigo al buitre rosado:
> desde el musgo te hablo desde
> las raíces de nuestro reino.
> Va a llover sangre mañana,
> las lágrimas serán capaces
> de formar niebla, vapor, ríos,
> hasta que derritas los ojos.

(1:348)

> [Terrified brother, do not
> befriend the rosy vulture:
> I speak to you from the moss,
> from the roots of our kingdom.
> Tomorrow it's going to rain blood,
> the tears are apt
> to form mist, vapor, rivers,
> until your eyes dissolve.]

(46)

Here the poetic voice intervenes to warn the innocent *Tlaxcalteca*
against the "buitre rosado" who is plotting their genocide. Neruda's objective again was not to present an anthropological profile
of the indigenous cultures, but instead a panoramic view of the
peoples of the continent, as interpreted and represented in the
visual counterpart. Neruda was not interested in the referent,
but rather in its iconic representation, in the expressive power of
the image. In this way, the poet is able to link the Macchu Picchu
workers of the past with the present workers of America. This
explains why Tarn could state: "I get no sense of a strong interest
or personal concern on Neruda's part, for Indianity as such,"[89]
and concludes that "Neruda's interest is far more geographic than

ethnographic. . . . His ethnography as such is almost bathetic."[90] This is close but not quite accurate; Neruda is more concerned with indigenous civilization as powerful ideological metaphor, as an iconic verbal representation of the oppressed masses of the continent, than with specific individuals or cultures.

Neruda develops in these first three sections of *Canto general,* through a series of iconic representations, one of its most significant dichotomies, that is, the dialectic opposition of virginity and violation, and thus sets the basic design of the work. Later, the same dichotomy evolves into several other polarities that share the same iconic code: rich/poor, *libertador/traidor,* oppressor/ oppressed, and so on. Additionally, I would argue that these sections form a cohesive unit. The dominant feminine image of cosmic dimensions in the first section represents a contrast to the antithetical symbol of the condor as the destructive element of a pristine world. The ethnic theme becomes prominent since from that uncorrupted world indigenous man emerges as the unblemished "arcilla" or "barro" and along with Mother Earth, also becomes the first victim of the invader. Only by presenting such a clash of opposites can Neruda establish himself as a *lámpara en la tierra.* These three sections also posit the notion that the indigenous peoples are the human base that has sustained for centuries the entire story (text) of Latin America—as is the case in Rivera's murals on the staircase of the National Palace. Thus, the indigenous theme becomes an ideological instrument to further argue that in certain ways the fundamental principles of communism in Latin America are not new, since their existence in America predates the European presence. It is known that the Incan and the Aztec cultures practiced some form of communism, and Neruda believed—rightly or wrongly—that Marxist doctrine would bring the cycle to an end and that lost unity and harmony would be restored. Once the grace whose loss led pre-Colombian civilizations to the abominable practice of human sacrifice was recovered, there would be no need for more "sacrifice" among Latin Americans. This explains, in part, the inordinate emphasis on the violent aspect of Mexican history expressed in many of the murals of Orozco, Rivera, and Siqueiros. It also explains the inclusion of the dark side of the Incan culture in *Alturas de Macchu Picchu* since only by confronting the antithetical aspects of the culture can the poet eventually reach a resolution and then emerge as the redeeming voice. In this way Neruda, like the Mexican muralists, attempts to justify and legitimize a socialist ideal for the New World. But most importantly, the ekphrastic encounter with mural art allows him to articulate what Krieger calls the transcendentally "real," the intelligible part of the visual referent, the human dimension that can be more easily expressed through language, shedding light on and giving voice to the silent walls, while interpreting their symbols and allegories.

4

The Panoramic View

THE HISTORICAL COMPONENT OF MURAL PAINTING IS CHARACTER-
ized by a synthetic approach to the recreation of historic events
and figures. Along the staircase of the National Palace a whole
universe is condensed into a single panoramic view. Likewise, the
poetry of *Canto general* seeks to express this historical synthesis,
conceived always in very general terms and with broad interpretations. The purpose is the same and the narrative very similar;
what differs is the scope and the means by which the synthesis
is transmitted. In Rochfort's view,

> Rivera had attempted in these murals to communicate over the heads
> of a philistine bourgeoisie, beyond its narrowly exclusive literary cul-
> ture, to a largely illiterate public. In doing this, he had built an intellec-
> tual and artistic base on which he could now construct, through epic
> panorama, a vision of the historical process of Mexico's evolution.[1]

Despite the fact that poetry is not as immediately accessible to
the general public as are the murals, Neruda's objective parallels
that of the Mexican painter. Reading Neruda's book is in many
ways similar to viewing the Mexican murals. The poet's original
impulse, as stated previously, was directed toward the search for
and discovery of his own national heritage. As he himself has
explained in an unpublished lecture, he felt the need to reach his
people, to "extenderme en la geografía, en la humanidad de mi
país, definir sus hombres y sus productos, la naturaleza viviente"
[extend myself in the geography, in the humanity of my country,
to define its people and its products, its vibrant nature].[2] But after
his stay in Mexico, and after his two-week visit to Macchu Picchu
in Peru, Neruda experienced a breakthrough in his conception
of the historical process in Latin America. He found that the
roots of the American histories were intertwined, in his words,
"confundidas y como debajo de la tierra" [confused and as if they
were under the earth].[3] "Cambié entonces el plan" [So I changed

the plan], he told Cardona Peña, just before the publication of *Canto general* in 1950, "y lo transformé en un *Canto general* llevando el propósito de arquitecturar un poema a toda nuestra América" [and I transformed it into a *Canto General* with the idea of structuring a poem for all our America].[4] Four years later, in 1954, Neruda insisted that the roots of all Chileans could be found under the ground of other territories, that heroes of Chilean history were related to other Latin American figures (O'Higgins's roots were in the Venezuelan Miranda; Lautaro was somehow connected to Cuauhtémoc) and that the handicrafts of Oaxaca had "el mismo fulgor negro de las gredas de Chillán" [the same black brilliance as the clay of Chillán].[5]

It can be argued that the shift from local to continental concerns is the result of two related personal experiences in two nations and cultures both possessing a strong indigenous heritage, Mexico and Peru. But Mexican muralism can be shown to be the structural foundation of *Canto general*. The book's configuration, with its epic panorama, is one of the strongest arguments in this regard. As has been stated, the emphasis on the ethnic theme, especially in the first sections, is an effort to establish a kind of foundation—both mythical and real—for the volume, based on the notion that indigenous peoples are the human substrata that has sustained and endured the Sysiphean history of Latin America. It is followed, in general terms, by the themes of colonial Latin America and the Independence movements, and by contemporary political conflicts. How these themes are particularly presented in painting and how they are translated into ekphrastic poetics is the focus of this chapter. To this end, we must first direct our attention to the kind of artistic/poetic tradition evoked here; then we will turn to the specific techniques and narrative perspectives with which both the mural artists and the poet present historical matter.

Mexican mural painting and *Canto general* have both been described as works of epic proportions. The assertion refers not only to their monumental size, but also to the encompassing, ambitious intention of the artists and the poet, and, of course, to the particular characteristics of their genre. *Canto general*'s association with the epic form is in many ways relevant to our study, particularly when we remember that the very origin of ekphrasis as a discipline is closely associated with this genre. Grant F. Scott, in his comprehensive study of the subject, states that ekphrasis as a literary topos "originates with Homer and his contemporaries," then adds,

> ekphrasis begins as a special aspect of the epic, as a type of featured inset which nominally digresses from the primary narrative line. Only later, with Ovid, does it become a separate endeavour altogether, a form adopted as an end in itself.[6]

Moreover, the first ekphrases, according to Scott, "concern utilitarian objects—shields, cups, garments, architecture—rather than collectibles and museum pieces . . . which are meant to communicate to an absent audience the sheer visual appearance of a thing."[7] In the next chapter we will examine Neruda's own ekphrastic rendition, in *La tierra se llama Juan* (section VIII), of several "utilitarian objects." But even without that discussion, the connection is clear: the muralists search for the mythical origins of Mexico, and their panoramic depictions of history from before the Conquest to the present, have striking parallels with Neruda's own search for a literature of foundations and his desire to create a verbal representation of the vast American reality, to be captured in a volume of biblical ambitions.

The other aspect of the epic that must be singled out has to do with the definition of the topos. According to Marchese and Forradellas, the concept of life contained in the Homeric epics reveals the central value of the myth treated therein, not merely in its literary aspect, but more importantly as an ethical norm— an exemplary narrative—in which historical events are lost in an undefined, fabulous, and admirable past: gods and heroes are mixed, confronted, and linked by similar passions with no distinction between one and the other.[8] Our objective here goes beyond linking *Canto general* with the epic tradition in poetry— that has been done by Guillermo Araya, Alfredo Cardona Peña, Giuseppe Bellini, and others. We are interested in inscribing Neruda's work within a corpus of great works by great poets, from Homer and Dante to T. S. Eliot and Ezra Pound, that have been driven by a desire for iconic representation of reality and the mythical dimension of history. In other words, we are also concerned here with the complex process of ekphrasis, its ability to translate from the visual—either real or fictive—to the verbal image, and its capacity to capture (or appropriate) the "other." In this case, the "other" is the mythical representation of history in mural art. Indeed, the strongest evidence of *Canto general*'s relation to mural art lies, not only in the epic configuration common to both, but in the affinity of techniques utilized by the mural artists and the poet, and in the particular point of view with which they attempt to recreate the mythical dimension of history.

While it is not difficult to establish links between muralism and the European fresco tradition of the Renaissance, it is not quite so obvious that the form and perspective of composition and execution in Mexican mural art belong to the medieval tradition in painting more than to the Renaissance. Medieval paintings favored the juxtaposition in the same frame of multiple events and figures (multiple from our twentieth-century vantage point) seemingly in no particular chronological order, and was dominated by a point of view that depicted its hierarchical world order by the size and centrality of the figures.

One wonders, of course, why the muralists did not adopt the more modern techniques and perspective of the Renaissance, when fresco painting flourished? One of the answers has to do with the fact that the medieval tradition in painting dominated much of colonial art in Mexico; it remained present in the popular arts, and in the religious paintings or ex–votos tradition. One should also take into consideration the similar pre-Hispanic techniques with which anonymous artists elaborated the pictograms of the *codices,* as well as José Guadalupe Posada's turn-of-the-century popular graphic art.[9]

There is another aspect, however, that until recently has not been given adequate consideration by art historians, due to the mistaken notion that mural art is a rejection of Modernist aesthetics (see Folgerait, for example), on the one hand; and the theory of an adoption of a "social realist" style by the muralists on the other. Nothing could be further from the truth, particularly for Siqueiros and Orozco, but also for Rivera. In her study of *Art in Latin America,* Dawn Ades opens her chapter titled "Modernism and the Search for Roots" with the following statement:

> The radical artistic developments that transformed the visual arts in Europe in the first decades of this century—Fauvism, Expressionism, Cubism, Dada, Purism, Constructivism—entered Latin America as part of a "vigorous current of renovations" during the 1920's.[10]

A few pages later, she adds an important distinction that allows us to better understand the ideology of aesthetics behind much of Mexican mural art—and for that matter, *Canto general.* Ades notes: "It was the idea of an art for the people, rather than the adoption of a 'social realist' style that, on the whole, mattered."[11]

This is precisely the argument that we have presented in chapters 1 and 2 of this study regarding Neruda: that he subscribed to the aesthetic values of the European avant-garde, and that his relationship with and knowledge of Modernist poets like Eliot and Pound were key in his own work, particularly their juxtaposition of past and present, used to undermine sequential temporality. As it happens, Neruda's association with Eliot and Pound and the Modernist aesthetics helps to explicate the ekphrastic encounter with mural painting and the connection of both Neruda and the muralists with medieval art.[12] Nor does Neruda participate in a "social realist" form of art in *Canto general;* rather an idea of "art for the people," similar to the idea that dominates muralism, is present in Neruda's poetry.

Joseph Frank, who has studied Modernist aesthetics from a structural standpoint, is convinced that ever since the Renaissance, art has cultivated both the objective visual imagination (the spatial) and the objective historical imagination (the temporal); and that such a praxis of dependence on mimetic representation was abandoned by the Modernists:

> What has occurred . . . may be described as the transformation of the historical imagination into myth—an imagination for which historical time does not exist, and which sees the actions and events of a particular time only as the bodying forth of ethereal prototypes.[13]

Using Mircea Eliade's ideas expressed from a religious standpoint, Frank notes that, in modern thought,

> a resistance to history, a revolt against historical *Time,* an attempt to restore this historical time, freighted as it is with human experience, to a place in time that is cosmic, cyclical and infinite.[14]

Out of these distinctions, thirty years later Frank was to come to the realization that the great literary works of Eliot, Pound, or Joyce are analogous to those expressions of medieval book illustrations in which historical figures from different time periods are all grouped together synchronically in the same frame.[15]

Frank's remarks apply equally well to *Canto general,* where the syntactical, chronological sequence is replaced by a structure of juxtaposed images and events presented and perceived by the reader/viewer as simultaneous. This is precisely the defining artistic principle that shapes the treatment of history in *Canto general* and mural painting; and it is the source of the apparent contradiction, noted by Yurkiévich and others, between history and myth in *Canto general*.

In the previous chapter we discussed how, from the very first poem, Neruda established this principle as a guiding structure for the entire book. In sections IV and V, examined in this chapter, the practice becomes essential, since it deals with real historical figures, providing us with the opportunity to refine and expand our analysis of the ekphrastic experience.

"Los libertadores" and Muralism

In *Los libertadores* [*The Liberators*] (section IV), Neruda portrays historical figures from both the past and the present. These figures represent the archetypal hero, who assumes the task of leading his people in a struggle for liberty and who is willing to sacrifice his life in the fight against oppression. This section displays, as Juan Villegas observes, "una galería de seres humanos que representan esos valores ideales" [a gallery of human beings that represent those ideal values].[16] The panoramic portrait of heroes, as noted earlier, is comparable to Rivera's historic anthology contained mainly in the immense mural at the National Palace. Rivera's mural, however, is not limited solely to the depiction of national heroes, but also includes some antiheroic figures, as does Neruda's section V, *La arena traicionada* [*The Sand Betrayed*]. Hence, both sections IV and V form (like the previous sections) a coherent continuum that follows the narrative structure of Rivera's murals; all are based on a dialectic of opposites and the juxtaposition and contrast of disparate images, of antithetical events and characters, in the same way that sections I and II are thematically the inverse of section III.[17]

In the mural just cited, there is a simultaneous, seemingly incoherent presentation of events taking place at different times in Mexican history that provides a panoramic view. Clearly, continuity of space and time was not an integral part of the artist's perspective. The grouping of figures derives from an interpretation of history based on ideological rather than chronological terms. Simultaneously different images from various periods in Mexican history are seen, as well as the figure of Karl Marx on the west wall, pointing, like Moses holding the ten commandments, toward a future based on a proletarian revolution. Neruda's corres-

Diego Rivera, *Huastec Civilization*, 1950, The National Palace, Mexico City. Photograph by Marcos Méndez.

Diego Rivera, *Tarascan Civilization*, 1942, The National Palace, Mexico City. Photograph by Marcos Méndez.

Right wall, Diego Rivera, *The History of Mexico. From the Conquest to the Future*, 1929–30, The National Palace, Mexico City. Photograph by Marcos Méndez.

Left wall, Diego Rivera, *The History of Mexico. From the Conquest to the Future*, 1935, The National Palace, Mexico City. Photograph by Marcos Méndez.

Center, Diego Rivera, The History of Mexico. From the Conquest to the Future, 1929–30, The National Palace, Mexico City. Photograph by Marcos Méndez.

Diego Rivera, *The Disembarkation in Veracruz*, 1951, The National Palace, Mexico City. Photograph by Marcos Méndez.

Diego Rivera, *The Blood of the Martyrs*, 1926, the National Autonomous University of Chapingo, the Chapel, Mexico (INBA).

ponding technique to create the same effect of stasis in poetry is the juxtaposition of different verb tenses. The combination of preterite and imperfect, present and future, within the same poetic space serves the identical purpose as the technique of simultaneity in the fresco. It allows Neruda to unify disparate events taking place at different times into a complex presented spatially in a moment of time.

In "América Insurrecta (1880)" [Insurgent America (1880)], for example, the preterite, present, and future are combined in a dialectical discourse that only at the end of the poem achieves the desired effect in the mind of the reader: that is, the emergence of a new man ("hoy" [today]) to create a new society (future) born from the blood given by the martyrs of the past—the same prognosis expressed in several of Rivera's murals:

> Patria, *naciste* de los leñadores,
> de hijos sin bautizar, de carpinteros,
> de los que *dieron* como un ave extraña
> una gota de sangre voladora,
> y *hoy nacerás* de nuevo duramente.
>
> (Emphasis added; I:399)

> [O homeland *born* of woodcutters,
> of unbaptized children, carpenters,
> those who *gave,* like a rare bird,
> a drop of winged blood,
> *today you'll be born* harshly.]
>
> (Emphasis added; 94)

In the final line, the adverb "Hoy," used as anaphora, followed by an apostrophe, in this instance a verb conjugated in the future tense, creates the prophetic merging of present and future in the same temporal space, or "spot of time," as Wordsworth would have called it[18]:

> Hoy nacerás del pueblo como entonces.
>
> Hoy saldrás del carbón y del rocío.
> Hoy llegarás a sacudir las puertas.
>
> (1:399)

> [Today, as then, you'll be born of the people.
>
> Today you'll emerge from the coal and the dew.
> Today you'll come to shake the doors.]
>
> (94)

The use of a narrative voice in second person singular (apostrophe) reminds us of the early poem "Minerales" (first section), where the aim is to address the reader directly in a confidential, intimate fashion. Yet structurally, Neruda is trying to transcend the limitations of literal reality in order to blur time's movement.

In "A Emiliano Zapata (Con música de Tata Nacho)" [To Emiliano Zapata With Music by Tato Nacho] the equivalent of Rivera's visual effect (in addition to the actual ekphrasis) is attained in the same way, by introducing in each section (or frame) of the poem a different verb tense. The first frame depicts the oppressive situation of the peasantry and the beginning of the uprising in the preterite tense:

> Cuando *arreciaron* los dolores
> en la tierra, y los espinares desolados
> *fueron* la herencia de los campesinos,
>
> . . . .
>
> *se encabritó* en el alba transitoria
> la tierra sacudida de cuchillos.
>
> (Emphasis added; 1:433)

> [When sorrows *multiplied*
> on the land, and desolate thorns
> *were* the peasant's estate,
>
> . . . .
>
> the land rent by knives
> *reared up* in the transitory dawn.]
>
> (Emphasis added; 125)

The second frame paints a landscape of *campesinos* joining the revolutionary movement. The imperfect tense conveys the new optimism vis-à-vis the peasant struggle: "En todo el horizonte aparecía / la multitud de la semilla armada" (1:433) [On the entire horizon the multitude / of his armed seed appeared (125)]. In the next frame, the change to present tense and first person allows the poetic voice to merge now and in the immediate future with that of Zapata in a mythical expression of solidarity with the Mexican Revolution:

> Reparte el pan, la tierra:
> te acompaño
> Yo renuncio a mis párpados celestes,

Yo, Zapata, me voy con el rocío
de las caballerías matutinas.

(1:434)

[Distribute bread, land:
                    I'll follow you.
I renounce my celestial eyelids.
I, Zapata, depart with
the cavalries' morning dew.]

(126)

In the last three frames, or stanzas, the present tense is maintained, but the narrative point of view switches from third person
to first person plural and singular. The change in perspective
allows the poet to describe Zapata's ambush from multiple angles,
to create a sense of collective participation, and to inscribe the
poet's redeeming voice, respectively:

La luna duerme sobre las monturas.
La muerte amontonada y repartida
yace con los soldados de Zapata.
. . . .
Pedimos patria para el humillado.
Tu cuchillo divide el patrimonio
y tiros y corceles amedrentan
los castigos, la barba del verdugo.
. . . .
De la nieve del sur vengo a cantarte.
Déjame galopar en tu destino
y llenarme de pólvora y arados.

(1:113)

[The moon's asleep on the saddles.
Death, stacked and distributed,
lies with Zapata's soldiers.
. . . .
We asked for a homeland for the humiliated.
Your knife divides the patrimony
and gunfire and chargers put punishments
and hangman's beard to flight.
. . . .
From the snowy South I've come to sing to you.
Let me gallop in your destiny and take
my fill of gunpowder and ploughshares.]

(125–26)

The life that is narrated has been reduced to the dimensions of a series of panels or murals, which in the poem serve as constant props for vision. The literary text refers implicitly or explicitly to a visual representation, which, in turn, serves as a metaphorical mirror for the text, giving it spatiality.

The series of four poems devoted to the figure of Lautaro is another example of the literary equivalent of pictorial technique used by Neruda. The four poems are illustrations of the Araucanian hero's evolution from his initiation to vengeance against the *conquistador* Valdivia and will be discussed shortly. For now, let us take a close look at Rivera's murals in the National Palace, which clearly demonstrate the same process in the creation of the art-object. As I have suggested in this chapter, the technique of presenting various simultaneous events on the same plane was characteristic of the frescos painted during the Middle Ages, early Renaissance, and the pre-Colombian era, and was later adopted by the Mexican mural painters.[19] Their purpose was identical: to instruct a large number of people on a specific interpretation of history, including the beliefs and deeds of heroes and villains— and to implant in the viewer/reader's consciousness the sense of being part of a timeless, unceasing historical process.

In this sense, the structural configuration of the mural in the staircase of the National Palace explains the seemingly irregular structure of *Los libertadores* that critics such as María Rosa Olivera-Williams have pointed out: "Presenta esta cuarta serie una estructura bastante irregular. No sólo contiene un gran número de poemas (sesenta y ocho en total), sino que la materia histórica que cubre es vastísima" [This fourth series presents a fairly irregular structure. Not only does it contain a large number of poems (sixty-eight all together), but also the historical material that it covers is extremely vast].[20] Villegas also notes: "La sección no se limita al período de la Independencia, que podría ser lo adecuado si se piensa en la continuidad cronológica. Pero, hemos dicho, la clave de la composición la proporcionan ciertas unidades temáticas" [The section is not limited to the Independence period, which would be adequate if one were thinking in terms of chronological continuity. However, as we have said, the key to the composition is to be found in certain thematic unities].[21] I would say that these "thematic unities" in fact correspond to those which make up the thematic pattern of Mexican muralism, namely, a panoramic view of history: for example, from before the arrival of the Spaniards in the New World to the present and/or recent past, as is the case of Orozco's murals at Dartmouth College and in Guadalajara, Siquieros's murals in Chillán, Chile, and the Palace Museum of Fine Arts, and Rivera's mural in the National Palace. However, the design of both this section (and almost all others in *Canto general*) and Rivera's murals follows a certain chronological order. It encompasses history from Caupolicán and Cuauhtémoc to Luis Emilio Recabarren, Chilean union leader and one of the founders of the Communist party in Chile, who committed suicide in 1924.

We now proceed with the specific analysis of the ekphrastic experience. *Los libertadores* opens with its most salient image: intertwined roots under the American soil. The metaphor shapes the contours of this section, in which the poet expresses his concept of the *libertador* and reconstructs part of the historical process of that epic panorama which *Canto general* is meant to embrace. The complementary image with which the *libertador* accomplishes his goals is the tree, symbolizing freedom and the people: "The constant renewal of the tree, through the roots in the soil, on a natural plane is parallel to the continuity of *libertadores* on a historical plane, whose bodies feed the blood of the continent."[22] In an attempt to define Neruda's interpretation of the *libertador* Guillermo Barzuna Pérez concludes that in general it occurs in a "metaphorical process," where man as liberator is a product of the creative process of nature.[23]

This important topos of death and renewal of life through the roots of the tree is ingeniously represented in one of Rivera's series of murals of 1926 in the Chapel at Chapingo entitled *The Blood of the Martyrs*. The structure of the Chapel as a whole portrays the forces of nature on one side and of history on the other. In this particular mural the two forces are fused together. The dead body of the martyr lies on the ground while three female kneeling figures with five revolutionary *campesinos* mourn the corpse of their fellow countryman. Above the victim, an enormous tree with a thick trunk extends its roots, recycling the life of the peasant. Its branches end in star-shaped leaves, in other words the star of freedom (the star of the Revolution). Laurence E. Schmeckebier has noted the use of the traditional Christian symbols in this mural interpolated in Communist doctrine, a recurring technique in Mexican muralism. He finds in this martyr scene a departure from the Pietà scene, in which "the use of tricky halos such as the hat behind the head of the dark figure of the martyr" becomes the element with which Rivera transposes Christian doctrine into Marxist philosophy.[24] This aspect will be treated at greater length in this chapter; for now it should be added that this mural presents other possibilities of interpretation. The composition may also be construed as a Christian nativity scene. The shape and posture of the figures outlined with soft, unbroken lines are much like the clay/ceramic figures still made today by Mexican artisans and placed under the Christmas tree. The central star in the tree, then, is the star of the Annunciation while the halo around the woman's head on the left suggests an association with the Virgin Mary. In this way, the mural effectively incorporates both sacred and secular elements: nature, history, death, and birth, inscribed in a timeless circularity.

Rochfort suggests that in this mural Rivera "again returns to his theme of sacrifice of death for the revolution, this time to express it as a process of perpetual contribution and renewal."[25] Clearly, the tree is the Tree of Freedom, but it is also the Tree of the Revolution, the means by which the Mexican Revolution and freedom is nurtured. This is also the same image found in the first poem of *Los libertadores*. It has been said that the *árbol* of this poem represents freedom[26] and the *pueblo*,[27] but it also represents the prophetic and messianic call of the poet to engage in social revolution: "*Aquí viene el árbol, el árbol / de la tormenta, el árbol del pueblo*" (1:374) [*Here come the tree, the tree / of the storm, the tree of the people* (71)]. What is coming is the continental revolution, conveyed in the term "tormenta,"[28] which is fed by the sacrifice of death. "Aquí viene el árbol, el árbol / nutrido por muertos desnudos, / muertos azotados y heridos" (1:374) [Here comes the tree, the tree / nourished by naked corpses, / corpses scourged and wounded (71)]. At the outset, the ekphrastic association is not with the tree, but rather with the corn plant. In "Vegetaciones" [Vegetations] when the corn stalk emerges from the ground, it becomes the vehicle of contribution and renewal. The image described in the poem brings to mind another mural of Rivera's series on *The Blood of the Martyrs*, also in Chapingo, where the body of Zapata lies under the roots of a corn plant:

> Como una lanza terminada en fuego
> apareció el maíz, y su estatura
> se desgranó y nació de nuevo,
> diseminó su harina, tuvo
> muertos bajo sus raíces,
> y, luego, en su cuna, miró
> crecer los dioses vegetales.
>
> (1:317)

> [Like a fire-tipped spear
> corn emerged, its stature

Diego Rivera, *The Blood of the Martyrs* (Emiliano Zapata), 1926, the Chapel at Chapingo, Mexico (INBA).

was stripped and it gave forth again,
disseminated its flour, had
corpses beneath its roots,
and then, in its cradle, it watched
the vegetable gods grow.]

(15)

Like the tree in Rivera's mural, "el maíz" is nurtured by "muertos
bajo sus raíces," and from its roots will give life to the heroes,
the "dioses vegetales." Here Neruda resorts to a series of enjamb-
ments to convey in poetic form the effect of continuity and immor-
tality, of timeless circularity. Its movement from the somber tone
of the beginning toward the light of the optimistic future at the
end corresponds to Rivera's contrast of the luminous star and the
white-clothed peasants on the right with the dark brown colors
of the background. The same image, of course, is reproduced at
the end of the first poem in *Los libertadores:*

Asómate a su caballera:
toca sus rayos renovados:
hunde la mano en las usinas
donde su fruto palpitante
propaga su luz cada día.

(1:375)

[Look at its hair:
touch its renewed rays:
plunge your hands into the factories
where its pulsing fruit
propagates its light each day.]

(72–73)

It is important to underline the significance of the metaphor of
cyclical renewal contained in this fourth section. Every *libertador* is
described by a variant of this original metaphor: the cosmogenetic
point or archetropic experience that contains and constrains the
poet to a "logic" that is the basis of the entire *Canto*. For this
reason "Cuauhtémoc (1520)," the second poem of this series, is
delineated with such an iconic code. Neruda apostrophizes the
young warrior in the informal second person singular, "tú," used
when the poet wishes to insert himself into the literary scene.
He calls Cuauhtémoc "joven hermano" [young brother], and the
poet receives from his hand the gift of the revelation of the Aztec's
(i.e., Mexican's) "patria desnuda" [naked country]:

En ella nace y crece tu sonrisa
Como una línea entre la luz y el oro.

Son tus labios unidos por la muerte
el más puro silencio sepultado.

El manantial hundido
bajo todas las bocas de la tierra.

(1:376)

[On it your smile is born and grows
like a line between the light and the gold.

Your lips sealed by death are
the purest entombed silence.

The fountain submerged
beneath all the earth's mouths.]

(73)

The first distich above refers to the optimistic growth of a dynamic postrevolutionary Mexican nation. Thus, "patria" becomes the equivalent of "el árbol del pueblo" [the tree of the people] described in the first poem of this section. The second couplet is the extension of the cyclical paradigm tree-death-birth. The death of the hero becomes a "manantial hundido / bajo todas las bocas de la tierra," from which that "patria" is nourished. There follows a flashback to the persecutions of the dark days of the *conquista*, marked by a consistent shift to the past tense when referring to this topic:

Oíste, oíste, acaso,
hacia Anáhuac lejano,
un rumbo de agua, un viento
de primavera destrozada?

(1:376)

[Did you hear, did you hear, by chance,
from distant Anáhuac,
a waterway, a wind
of shattered springtime?]

(73)

In the second part of the poem the poet implies that the autochthonous people were taken by surprise, or that because of their

naïveté they did not know how to interpret events: "Era tal vez
la palabra del cedro. / Era una ola blanca de Acapulco" (1:376) [It
was perhaps the cedar's voice. / It was a white wave from Acapulco (73)]. Cuauhtémoc fails to discern the conqueror's real intentions, just as the reader fails to grasp the poet's references
to "cedro" and "ola blanca." What is certain is the uncertainty
established by the adverbial form "tal vez." The idealized vision
of the indigenous peoples as innocent victims is expressed
throughout the book by interrogative phrases, like the one above,
or as in the passage in "Minerales," in which the poet poses the
following question:

> Cómo podías, Colombia oral,
> saber que tus piedras descalzas
> ocultaban una tormenta
> de oro iracundo, . . .

(1:325)

> [How, oral Colombia, could you
> know that your barefoot stones
> concealed a tempest
> of enraged gold, . . .]

(23)

This explains in part why Lautaro is accorded special attention,
aside from the fact that he is a native of Neruda's homeland. For
the poet Lautaro represents the exception, the only pre-
Colombian figure who possessed the necessary distrust and audacity to defeat the enemy. Lautaro resisted the invaders using
their own weapons: betrayal, deceit, and deception.[29] Conversely,
in the fifth stanza, a somber and macabre night serves as the
prelude that announces the final sacrifice of the young Cuauhtémoc. "Toda la sombra preparaba sombra. / Era la tierra una
oscura cocina, / piedra y caldera, vapor negro" (1:377) [All the
shade prepared shade. / The land swas a dark kitchen, / stone
and caldron, black steam (74)].
     At this point the description reverts to the poetic present, in
which Cuauhtémoc's sacrifice gives new life to his nation: "Ha
llegado la hora señalada, / y en medio de tu pueblo / eres pan y
raíz, lanza y estrella" (1:377) [The fateful hour has arrived, / and
among your people / you're bread and root, spear and star (74)].
Like a Christ figure, Cuauhtémoc must give his life to redeem the
people. He is destined to die at an "hora señalada," as if cosmic
forces determined his fate. The metaphors of "pan" and "raíz"

stand for the Christian symbols of bread and wine; Jesus Christ's body and blood have become body and earth (*raíces*).

The last line of the apostrophe to Cuauhtémoc ("eres pan y raíz, lanza y estrella") takes up the recurrent metaphor used to designate the essential trait of the *libertador*. If this section could be reduced to one word, it would be *nourishment*. The line's binary structure defines the whole poem. "Pan" and "raíz" in the first part refer to the cycle described before, but "lanza" and "estrella" imply more than this. "Lanza," in addition to symbolizing the courage of the warrior, is the condition *sine qua non* for resisting the invader and gaining freedom; "estrella" is defined by Neruda later, in a line from *Nuevas odas elementales*, as "cereal de platino espolvoreado en la sombra" (2:264) [cereal of platinum scattered over the shadow]. Both images are metaphors of the optimism and hope generated by the Revolution, and at the same time represent the dialectic counterpart of the shadow described a few lines earlier: "Toda la sombra preparaba sombra. / Era la tierra una oscura cocina." The third part of the poem also reveals Cuauhtémoc's heroic defiance of the invader, after Moctezuma has been stoned to death by his own people:

> El invasor ha detenido el paso.
> No es Moctezuma extinto
> como una copa muerta,
> es el relámpago y su armadura,
> la pluma de Quetzal, la flor del pueblo,
> la cimera encendida entre las naves.
>
> (1:377)

> [The invader has stopped his advance.
> He (Cuauhtemoc) is not Moctezuma, extinct
> like a dead chalice,
> he is lightening and his armor,
> a Quetzal plume, the flower of the people,
> a flaming crest amid the ships.][30]

In the next stanza and despite his transformation into "relámpago," "Queztal," "la flor del pueblo," and so on, the hero succumbs to the invader's superior military skills: "Pero una mano dura como siglos de piedra / apretó tu garganta" (1:377) [But a hand hard as centuries of stone / gripped your throat (74)]. Yet the torture and punishment to which Cuauhtémoc is subjected thereafter are not enough to subdue his courage and strength:

No cerraron
tu sonrisa, no hicieron
caer los granos del secreto
maíz, y te arrastraron,
vencedor cautivo,
por las distancias de tu reino.

(1:377)

[They didn't choke
your smile, they didn't make
the secret corn's kernels
fall, but they dragged you,
captive conqueror,
through the far reaches of your kingdom.]

(74)

This "sonrisa," just before the final sacrifice, establishes the historical thread and the link with the "sonrisa" of renewal, mentioned in the second stanza of the poem. Again Christ-like, Cuauhtémoc accepts his fate, smiling as death approaches. The smile becomes both the fatalistic sign that conveys a sense of utter surrender and the symbolic gesture of the courage of Cuauhtémoc, who despite torture does not bow to his captors' covetousness and refuses to reveal the location of Aztec gold ("granos del secreto maíz").

The poem's structure is supported by what Jorge García Antezana would call a "cadena semántica de opuestos correspondientes a la naturaleza binaria del pensamiento mítico" [semantic chain of opposites that correspond to the binary nature of mythic thought].[31] The repetition of the adversative conjunction "pero" [but] throughout the poem serves to counterbalance the mythical and historical levels. In the first instance, the innocence of the young warrior is suddenly imperiled by a real threat: "Pero en la noche huía / tu corazón como un venado" [But in the night your heart fled . . . / like a bewildered deer]; conversely, the hero's somber future is overcome by the transcendence of his commitment to his people: "Pero no hay sombra en tu estandarte" [But there is no shade on your standard]; and finally, the fleeting success of Cuauhtémoc's defiance comes to a tragic end: "Pero una mano dura como siglos de piedra / apretó tu garganta" [But a hand hard as centuries of stone / gripped your throat].

The poem is not a factual description of Cuauhtémoc, but rather an ekphrastic interpretation of his sacrifice. This time the interartistic model corresponds more to Siqueiros than to Rivera

David Alafaro Siqueiros, *The Torture of Cuauhtémoc,* **1950, The Palace Museum of Fine Arts, Mexico City. Photograph by Marcos Méndez.**

because of the expressionistic elements incorporated into the poem, enveloping the figure in a more sublime quasimystical aura.

Indeed, Neruda's heroes are mythical, but they belong at the same time to the earth, not to an elusive paradise.[32] Here, as is the case in the rest of the book, the inclusion of Christian icons is only used to advance the poet's political ideology. Of course, the technique is not new or exclusive to the Chilean; it has a long literary history. In Western culture, "Christ has come constantly to symbolize man's trap *and* man's freedom."[33] Mexican muralist painters also resorted extensively to these technical devices from the outset of the movement, as is the case of Orozco's *The Trench* at the National Preparatory School (1924), or some of Rivera's murals in Chapingo.

Orozco once said that "all the painters began with subjects derived from traditional iconography, either Christian or Frankish."[34] Referring to the propagandistic aspects of the technique in Mexican muralism, Schmeckebier has noted that "[t]he interpolation of traditional Christian accessories to a quasi-Communist doctrine . . . is a characteristic means of embellishing Marxist philosophy with orthodox iconographical attributes."[35]

José Clemente Orozco, *The Trench*, 1924, National Preparatory School, Mexico City. Photograph by Marcos Méndez.

The simulation and exploitation of the Christian ideology deeply rooted in Mexican culture were considered the most effective means to communicate with the vast majority of the people. According to Jean Charlot, these artists and writers aspired to earn the sympathy and approval of the Catholic Church and its parishioners: "Mexican Marxists found it difficult not to hold to the apron strings of the Mother they kicked."[36] The purpose was to sugarcoat the pill so the people could swallow it, and to endeavor to conform to the teachings of the Church. Unlike in the Soviet Union, the Socialist movement in Mexico did not oppose the Church, as a pamphlet by Lombardo Toledano shows: "El reparto de tierras a los pobres no se opone a las enseñanzas de Nuestro Señor Jesucristo y de la Santa Madre Iglesia" [The redistribution of land to the poor is not in opposition to the teachings of Our Lord Jesus Christ and of the Holy Mother Church].[37] Charlot suggests, as we have just done, that Mexican muralism had to continue the strong influence of the colonial pictorial tradition— dominated by religious themes—and had to face the fact that purely indigenous art could have failed. "Where Aztec art had failed us in our program of plastic propaganda, colonial art shone as a supreme model. The self-contained, self-sufficient Indian form could not help us paint murals that talked to people."[38]

The figure of each *libertador* depicted in this section is outlined by means of a series of isomorphic metaphors. Fray Bartolomé de las Casas is a "luz antigua, suave y dura / como un metal" [ancient light (. . .) smooth and hard / as metal]. The contemporary oppression of the worker brings to the poet's mind the suffering of the indigenous peoples described by the Dominican priest. As de las Casas' successor, the poet considers himself a spokesperson for the masses who must continue the denunciation of such oppression: "Gracias porque tu hilo fue invencible" [Thank you, for your thread was invincible]. And like Cuauhtémoc, de las Casas also gives life and hope: "todo bajo tu sombra / renace, desde el límite / de la agonía fundas la esperanza" (1:378–79) [everything's reborn / under your shade, from the limits / of agony you engender hope (75)]. At the end of the poem the poet invites the friar to witness the present injustice and asks him for the strength to endure, by means of the same process of transubstantiation invoked to the Incan throng in Macchu Picchu; "Hablad por mis palabras y mi sangre" [Speak through my words and my blood]:

> Y para no caer, para afirmarme
> sobre la tierra, continuar luchando,
> deja en mi corazón el vino errante
> y el implacable pan de tu dulzura.
>
> (1:380)

> [And to keep me from falling, to help me plant my
> feet firmly on the ground, to continue fighting,
> bequeath to my heart the errant wine
> and the implacable bread of your sweetness.]
>
> (77)

In "América insurrecta (1800)" (1:398), Neruda calls this entire historical gallery of *libertadores* a "levadura colectiva" [collective yeast]. Caupolicán is "el árbol duro de la patria" [the homeland's hard tree] and Lautaro is born from the blood of Caupolicán after his death. "Tupac Amarú (1781)" is the seed that "germina en la tierra" [germinates in the ground], and so on.

From 1941 to 1942, Siqueiros painted *Death to the Invader* in Chile, which combines Chilean and Mexican history. Siqueiros had been accused in Mexico of an armed incursion on Trotsky's house and was sent to prison. Neruda helped him and his wife leave the country by facilitating a visa to Chile. The poet explains the circumstances under which the mural was developed:

> México había construido una escuela en la ciudad de Chillán que había sido destruida por los terremotos, y en esa «Escuela México» Siqueiros pintó uno de sus murales extraordinarios.

> [The people of Mexico had built a school in the Chilean city of Chillán, which had been destroyed by earthquakes, and in that "Mexican School" Siqueiros painted one of his extraordinary murals.][39]

The content of this mural is key to the exegeses of the next poems. On one side is represented the history of Chile, and on the other, the history of Mexico. The mural's relevance is rooted in the difference of approach to history as compared to Rivera's murals in the National Palace. Here the historical synopsis is focused on the heroic figures while the *invasor* has been reduced to an anthropomorphic figure. In Rivera, as in most of the other muralist painters, heroes and villains are juxtaposed in the same plane and are given equal historical representation.

With the exception of two poems "Fray Bartolomé de las Casas," and the series that begins with "La colonia cubre nuestras tierras" ["The Colony Covers Our Lands"]), the first half of this fourth section up to "Bernardo O'Higgins Riquelme (1810)" corresponds in theme, tone, and design to Siqueiros's murals in Chillán, particularly the panel devoted to the history of Chile. All the Mexican heroes included in the Mexican panel are also described in this section of *Canto general*, though it does not seem to follow as closely the painter's sequence.

Los libertadores reflects Neruda's conception of his national history versus the continental history. Chile and its heroes form a clearly defined unity, as one might expect, while the Mexican counterparts are seen as part of the puzzle of Latin American history; thus, the second half of the section is grouped not by national but rather by continental figures. In general, nonetheless, the section maintains the basic scenes, images, figures, and topoi of Siqueiros's murals. Siqueiros's emphasis on the heroes explains to a large extent the organization of the fourth section: why Neruda decided to follow a thematic rather than a chronological line, and why he separates heroes from villains, placing them in different sections. But, perhaps the most important element of interplay between the mural and this section, besides the affinity of composition, is their fierce and violent tone. As the

David Alfaro Siqueiros, *Death to the Invader*, 1941–42, Mexico School, Chillán, Chile (INBA).

David Alfaro Siqueiros, *Death to the Invader*, 1941–42, Mexico School, Chillán, Chile (INBA).

title of the mural indicates, it is about destroying the *invasores* and is quite a different approach from the passive, nonaggressive image of the Christ-like figures of Rivera and Orozco discussed earlier. Here, the heroes are not innocent victims of violation and death; on the contrary, these mythical heroes (Cuauhtémoc, Caupolicán, and Lautaro in particular) in the imagination of the artists succeed in resisting and defeating the invader. As is often the case, there is both a fictional and a realistic reversal of events and fortunes. The Americans, after all, have triumphed over the Spanish (invading) forces in a struggle that lasted for centuries: "Tres siglos estuvo luchando" [For three centuries the warrior . . . fought on] reads a line from "La dilatada guerra" [The Protracted War]. It is a struggle that culminated with the independence movements of the nineteenth century: "América Insurrecta (1800)" with its corresponding heroes—O'Higgins, San Martín, and so on. This section deals in general with the defeat of the Spanish invasion, not the Conquest, since conquest implies— Neruda suggests—subordination and acceptance, and America never did comply with or cede to the invaders. This was only a historical parentheses, thus explaining why the series of poems on the *colonia* are titled, in parentheses, (*INTERMEDIO*).

Describing Siqueiros's mural on the afternoon of its unveiling, one of Neruda's biographers, Velodia Teitelboim, commented:

> Como un relámpago multicolor está allí, grabada en un movimiento perpetuo la historia de ambas naciones. Una sobrecogedora interpretación pictórica de luchas, de contradicciones, vaciada en *panneaux* convulsionados.

> [Like a multicolor stroke of lightening it is there, the history of both nations recorded in perpetual movement. A moving pictorial interpretation of struggles, contradictions, spilled onto convulsed *panneaux*.][40]

The Chilean figures included in the mural are Francisco de Bilbao, Caupolicán, Lautaro, Bernardo O'Higgins, Luis Emilio Recabarren, and José Manuel Balmaceda. Neruda's ekphrastic version of "Toqui Caupolicán" [Chief Caupolican] displays striking parallels with Siqueiros's mural, particularly the association of the hero with nature and his mythical character reminiscent of a Greek god:

> Caupolicán, su máscara de lianas
> levanta frente al invasor perdido:

.   .   .   .
es un rostro del bosque
.   .   .   .   .   .
una cabeza con enredaderas.

De Caupolicán el Toqui es la mirada
hundida, de universo montañoso.

(1:383)

[Caupolicán raises his mask of lianas
in front of the lost invader:
.   .   .   .
it's a woodland face,
.   .   .   .
a head with vines.

Chief Caupolicán has the deep-set
look of a mountainous universe.]

(79)

The term "invasor" (included in the mural's title) is repeated several times throughout the poem. We now are confronted with a case of actual ekphrasis, where the literary piece is the verbal representation of an existing visual representation. Poem and image create a "conceptual space" in which they form a coordinated double image.[41] In this reciprocal effect, the mural serves the poem more than as a source of inspiration; it provides the plastic, spatial element. The mural becomes a metaphor within the poem which helps it, according to Krieger, to "still" or symbolically freeze in space its temporal and sequential limitations. The poems, on the other hand, add the human complexities only suggested in the mural, giving voice to the silent wall, articulating a different interpretation of the same reality, capturing the intelligible, the transcendentally "real," the imagination of the artist; but only to throw it back at the reader in the form of a verbal complexity of images. The "conceptual space," mentioned by Arnheim, is a synthetic way of describing the overcoming of the image/text division and the appearance in its place of a verbal icon or image-text.

An interesting ekphrastic interpretation is outlined in "Lautaro entre los invasores" (1:387) [Lautaro Among the Invaders], which narrates the death of the invader Valdivia at Lautaro's hands. "Bernardo O'Higgins Riquelme (1880)" represents for Neruda the father of the nation ("Eres Chile, entre patriarca y huaso") [You're

Chile, between patriarch and cowboy], whose only dream is "una bandera de tres colores en el sur" [a tricolored / flag in the South]. Like the other *libertadores*, O'Higgins's inherent strength inspires freedom: "Pero hemos heredado tu firmeza, / tu inalterable corazón callado, / tu indestructible posición paterna" (1:402) [But we've inherited your firmness, / your unalterable composed heart,/ your indestructible paternal position (97)]. But it is Lautaro, among all the heroes, who receives special attention. Poems VIII through XII are completely devoted to this figure. The series describes, on the mythical as well as the historical levels, a kind of developmental pattern of the hero from his emergence from Caupolicán's blood "La sangre toca un corredor de cuarzo. / Así nace Lautaro de la tierra" [1:385] [The blood touches a gallery of quartz. / . . . that's how Lautaro is born of the earth (82)] to his victory against Valdivia in the memorable battle of Tucapel in 1553.[42] Neruda associates Lautaro with metaphors of luminosity and agility. In poem 9, "Educación del cacique" [The Chief's Training], in which the poet describes his initiation, Lautaro is a "flecha delgada" [slender arrow], "viento dirigido" [driving wind], "velocidad" [velocity] or "luz repentina" [sudden light]; and, like Cuauhtémoc, he is also "relámpago" [lightening]. A series of brief, single-line statements structurally parallels the hero's dynamism, swiftness, and luminosity. Unlike Cuauhtémoc or the other indigenous characters, Lautaro knows immediately how to interpret the presence of the conquerors. Thus, he prepares himself to fight the invader.

By presenting him as the only pre-Columbian figure possessing the necessary audacity to defeat the enemy, Neruda strongly suggests that Lautaro represents the archetypal model that could have produced a different historical outcome and one that Latin Americans must emulate if they want to gain true independence. For this reason, in "El corazón de Pedro de Valdivia" [Pedro de Valdivia's Heart] the last poem of the series, the poet introduces himself into the scene which he is describing and becomes a participant in the vindication of his ancestors. He knows that in order to overcome the invader, the Araucanians will have to match his hostility and cruelty. In an image that recalls the Aztec priests, who shared in consuming the hearts of their victims as part of the rite of sacrifice, the poet proceeds to do the same with "El corazón de Pedro de Valdivia."

> Entonces repartimos el corazón sangrante.
> Yo hundí los dientes en aquella corola
> cumpliendo el rito de la tierra:

[Then we shared the bleeding heart.
I sank my teeth into that corolla,
fulfilling the rites of the earth:]

At the end, then, the voice of the poet in the plural "nosotros" [we] is fused with the "yo" [I] of Lautaro, who conjures his enemy by drinking his blood:

"Dame tu frío, extranjero malvado.
. . . .
Dame en tu sangre tu cólera.
. . . .
Dame la guerra que trajiste".

(1:390)

[Give me your coldness, evil foreigner.
. . . .
Give me your fury in your blood.
. . . .
Give me the war you brought.]

(86)

At this juncture of interartistic comparison, it seems appropriate to recall our discussions in chapter 1 of the semantic organization of the picture plane that concentrates on the shift of focalization that occurred in painting from the Middle Ages to the Renaissance.

It is important to underline here the significant difference in the paradigmatic relation between the perceiver and what is perceived in Renaissance and pre-Renaissance perspectives. In the former, the artist remains outside the picture, his point of view is the same as that of the outside viewer; in the latter, the artist frequently introduces himself into the artistic space in which the described scene radiates outward from the "center," and the objects and figures represented are the function of an internal, limited observer. For Steiner, the equivalent of the medieval perspective in literature is found in the first person narrative in which the narrator, like the central figure inside the painted frame, controls what we "see" by presenting subjectively only what is seen through his or her eyes. Conversely, according to Steiner, the omniscient narrator would be the equivalent in literature of the "outside" perspective of the Renaissance.

Thus, Neruda's fusion of the "nosotros" and Lautaro's "yo" is a good example of the poet's ekphrastic adoption of the point of view favored in medieval painting. This was also very common in mural painting, particularly in Rivera's work, where the artist insisted upon introducing himself or his wife Frida among the historical figures in the scene, therefore projecting their first-hand participation in the makings of revolutionary Mexico. In Neruda's work, as is clear in this poem and many others discussed here, the ekphrastic equivalent of this pictorial technique becomes one of the most important artistic tools in his effort to create an imagetext. Along with the superimposition of different figures, images, and times, the medieval perspective allows the poet to bring the spatiality of the plastic arts to the verbal image, and this in turn allows him to overcome the temporal limitations of the text.

In the Lautaro poem, for example, the poet's central position from the very beginning is the key orientation point from inside the scene or the event described. Spatially, the fusion of his view with that of Lautaro, along with the size and centrality given to the historic figure and to himself, reduces the distance of the viewer/reader to the action, limiting his view to only what the poet/narrator sees.

The medieval perspective utilized by Neruda furthers and complements Frank's assertion that the works of Modernist poets like Eliot and Pound are analogous to medieval visual art expressions where historical figures from the Bible or classical antiquity are sometimes grouped together with local or contemporary figures "as part of one timeless complex of significance."[43]

The interartistic association facilitates in this case a deeper understanding of the dominant perspective in the poem, which does not emanate from some objective spectator at the margins or outside the narrated action, but instead come from someone who participates directly in the world surrounding him. But to assert that this series of poems is a case of actual ekphrasis does not imply a parasitic subordination of the poem to the visual referent. To the contrary: in fact, if we look carefully, we can see that while the images, figures, and topoi correspond to those of Siqueiros, the artistic point of view—the poet in the scene—emulates Rivera's narrative technique, and the scene of the sacrifice at the end brings to mind as well the images of Aztec sacrifices depicted in the murals of Orozco. In other words, the ekphrastic poem constitutes an independent, self-sufficient iconic imagery that shares representational codes with certain works by Siqueiros, Rivera, and Orozco. The flexibility of language allows Neruda to construct a composite ekphrastic version drawn from different visual and plastic sources with the objective of producing the most powerful verbal image of the visual representation of Lautaro. The presence of the poet at the center of the scene of sacrifice is a way of achieving that power, of relating the reader to the poem, inviting, almost forcing active participation in the ritual, and by extension, in the collective struggle. For this purpose, Lautaro is the perfect icon.

Lautaro is the exception, not the norm. His awareness is at variance with the naïveté of Cuauhtémoc, Moctezuma, or the *Tlaxcaltecas*, who recognized too late the real intentions of the invaders. Only at the end does Cuauhtémoc, unsuccessfully; attempt to recover the lost city of Tenochtitlán. In contrast, the series of poems depicting Lautaro represents an ideal revolutionary model for confronting the oppressive forces of imperialism. Once more, the poet rallies the people to engage in social revolution.

On the north wall of Siqueiros's mural, the Mexican side, national heroes flank Cuauhtémoc, who has just killed the invader. José María Morelos y Pavón, Miguel Hidalgo y Costilla, and Emiliano Zapata are on the left, and Benito Juárez and Lázaro Cárdenas are on the right. The sequence of historical figures in *Los libertadores* does not correspond chronologically to Siqueiros's mural. But the poems do reflect an artistic image or a composite image related to the initial archetropic experience.

The metaphor used by Neruda to describe Benito Juárez in "Viaje por la noche de Juárez" [Journey Through the Night of Juárez] derives from the image of original man formed by "arcilla," contained in the initial poem of the first section: "tu rostro hecho de tierra americana" [your face made of American earth]. Unity, solidarity, and nourishment are associated with Juárez:

> Para nosotros eres pan y piedra
> horno y producto de la estirpe oscura.
> Tu rostro fue nacido en nuestro barro.
>
> .   .   .   .
>
> tus ojos la enterrada alfarería.
>
> (1:426)

> [For us you're bread and stone,
> oven and product of the dark race.
> Your face was born of our clay.
>
> .   .   .   .
>
> your eyes buried earthenware.]
>
> (119)

As in Siquieros's murals, history and fiction combine to create the character's mythic dimension. Juárez, though a man of the nineteenth century, is in direct contact with the most elemental essence that formed the American man:

> JUAREZ, si recogiéramos
> la íntima estrata, la materia
> de la profundidad, si cavando tocáramos
> el profundo metal de las repúblicas,
> esta unidad sería tu estructura.
>
> (1:435)

> [Juárez, if we mined
> the intimate stratum, the matter
> from the depths, if digging we could strike
> the deep metal of your republics,
> this unity would be your structure.]
>
> (118)

A pure Zapotec born in Oaxaca, Juárez became the first president of Mexico of indigenous origin. Because of Juárez's ethnic background, Neruda depicts him as more similar to Cuauhtémoc, Caupolicán, or Lautaro than to O'Higgins, Recabarren, or even Zapata.

Zapata, a mestizo, conveys all the elements of a revolutionary figure. "A Emiliano Zapata (con música de Tata Nacho)" is a poem in which Neruda returns to the same narrative structure used in "El corazón de Pedro de Valdivia." The first part of the poem presents the exploitation of the peasantry: "Cuando arreciaron los dolores" [When sorrows multiplied]. The second part corresponds to Zapata's uprising and his union with the Revolutionary forces: "Yo renuncio a mis párpados celestes. / Yo Zapata, me voy con el rocío / de las caballerías matutinas" (1:434) [I renounce my celestial eyelids. / I, Zapata, depart with / the cavalries' morning dew (126)]. As we have seen, the ambush of Zapata is foreshadowed in the third part of the poem.

> La muerte amontonada y repartida
> yace en los soldados de Zapata.
> El sueño esconde bajo los baluartes
> de la pesada noche su destino,
> su incubadora sábana sombría.
>
> (1:434)

> [Death, stacked and distributed,
> lies with Zapata's soldiers.

Beneath the heavy night's bastions
the dream hides his destiny,
his somber incubating sheet.]

(126)

The last part is a call to the peasantry to join Zapata and the
Revolution in order to obtain "tierra y libertad" [land and free-
dom]—Zapata's revolutionary motto. At the end of the poem, the
poet beseeches Zapata to entrust him with the task of continuing
the Revolution: "Déjame galopar en tu destino / y llenarme de
pólvora y arados" (1:435) [Let me gallop in your destiny and
take / my fill of gunpowder and ploughshares (127)]. Needless to
say, the poetic strokes to delineate Zapata's contours are part of
a syntaxis of isomorphic metaphors used by the poet to describe
all of the *libertadores:* Cuauhtémoc, de las Casas or Juárez. Zapata
is a "semilla armada" [armed seed] and a "férreo manantial" [fer-
rous fountainhead] that "reparte el pan, la tierra" [distributes
bread, land].

However, there is one element that distinguishes this poem
from the others in the fourth section and from the rest of the
book, and that is further evidence not just of the ekphrastic impulse, but also of the techniques and perspectives of the medieval
tradition. Neruda has inserted excerpts of popular Mexican songs
called "corridos de la revolución" [ballads of the Revolution] between the stanzas of the poem. The musical selections recount
the tale of a peasant who leaves the "rancho" and his "Borrachita"
to join the Revolution. Neruda's ekphrastic description of the hero
bears a strong resemblance to Rivera's mural painted at Cortés'
Palace in 1929 entitled *Zapata.* In this fresco, Zapata is shown next
to his white horse holding a sickle in his right hand, after having
defeated the enemy. In the background are his followers, the *za-
patistas.* Like Neruda, Rivera presents an idealized interpretation
of the figure. The white horse symbolizes freedom and the virtu-
ous goodness of Zapata's cause while the sickle clearly becomes
a propagandistic device for the new ideology. On the other hand,
the poem also corresponds to a series of arched and square
frames painted at the Ministry of Education in Mexico City in
1926–28, in which Rivera freely illustrated two political *corridos.*
The texts of these ballads are inscribed on red ribbons or scrolls
painted above the panels of the mural.

The second *corrido,* "La Revolución Mexicana," is illustrated by
a portrait of Emiliano Zapata, who holds a banner proclaiming
his revolutionary slogan: *Tierra y Libertad.* These murals embody

Diego Rivera, *Zapata. Agrarian Leader,* 1929, Cortés's Palace, Cuernavaca, Mexico (INBA).

Diego Rivera, *The Night of the Rich, The Night of the Poor,* **1926, The Ministry of Education, Mexico City (INBA).**

the archetropic experience that prompted Neruda's artistic vision, confining him to a logic that determines the poem's form. The songs inserted in the poem are intended to reproduce the musicality of the *corridos* inscribed on the ribbons above the frames. Both muralist and poet are seeking to incorporate in their works the musical tradition of the people, yet another avenue to a truly collective art. It is also useful to note here Rivera's persistent reliance on the pictorial tradition of the medieval world, where speech in the illuminated manuscript tends to be represented as a scroll, which "emanates from the gesturing hand of the speaker rather than the mouth; language seems to co-exist in the same pictive/scriptive space."[44]

The final image of this series is one of the most powerful of the whole *Canto general*. It recalls that cosmogenetic metaphor of Rivera's mural *The Blood of the Martyrs*, which opened the section, and now closes the cycle. It is the image of the seed and tassel shown at the end of "Llegará el día" (1:458) [The Day Will Come (147)]. The prophetic message concludes with an exhortation to the masses to recognize the continuity of life flowing from the deaths of the martyrs:

> No renunciéis al día que os entregan
> los muertos que lucharon. *Cada espiga*
> *nace de un grano entregado a la tierra,*
> y como el trigo, el pueblo innumerable
> junta sus raíces, acumula espigas,
> y en la tormenta desencadenada
> sube a la claridad del universo.
>
> (Emphasis added; 1:459)

> [Don't renounce the day bestowed on you
> by those who died struggling. *Every spike*
> *is born of a grain seed in the earth,*
> and like the wheat, the innumerable people
> join roots, accumulate spikes,
> and in the tempest unleashed
> they rise up to the light of the universe.]
>
> (Emphasis added; 148)

The entire poem represents the climactic point of the poet's messianic voice in *Canto general*. This prophetic desire also dominates the artistic vision of Mexican mural painters. In his book *My Life, My Art*, Diego Rivera wrote that in the murals at the Ministry of Education he aspired

> to reproduce the pure basic images of my land. I wanted my painting to reflect the social life of Mexico as I saw it, and through my vision of the truth to show the masses the outline of the future.[45]

No other poet in Spanish American letters has been more conscious of his messianic role in the historical process of Latin America than Pablo Neruda. It was this characteristic to which Bellini referred when he described Neruda as a "Gran Lengua," who, while functioning as a sacred spokesman for the people, is at the same time separate from the multitude. For González Echevarría, his "is not a voice one can hope to imitate, emulate, or compete with. Neruda's voice has biblical resonances."[46] Neruda's voice in this book is as monumental as that of the Mexican mural art that inspired it.

"La arena traicionada" and Muralism

Section V, *La arena traicionada*, represents the antithesis of *Los libertadores*. Together, they complete that panoramic view of historical figures filtered through the eyes of the poet. According to Neruda, this fifth canto "es la historia de cómo fue burlada la independencia araucana por estos mismos grupos, que describo minuciosamente en el Canto V (las fuerzas retrógradas que traicionaron nuestra arena son las tiranías, el imperialismo, la injusticia, etc.)" [is the story of how the Araucanian independence was undermined by those same groups, that I describe in minute detail in Canto V (the reactionary forces that betrayed our sand are the tyrannies, imperialism, injustice, etc.)].[47] Besides dictators and chiefs of state, the cast of characters includes lawyers, bankers, foreign companies, and members of the oligarchy. Again, the primary technique to which Neruda resorts is dialectic opposition, not only between this canto and the preceding one, but also within its own structure.

The basic dichotomy of the oppressor-oppressed relationship is underlined throughout the section. According to Villegas, "En la imaginación de Neruda, la antítesis opresión-libertad se manifiesta en la forma de héroes frente a seres monstruosos" [In Neruda's imagination, the oppression-liberty antithesis occurs in the form of heroes confronting monstrous beings].[48] Such a dichotomy is not exclusive to this canto; it forms part of the basic configuration of the book. Yet *La arena traicionada* represents the strongest denunciation of the systematic oppression of the American continent by both local and foreign elements. If continuity in *Los libertadores* was maintained through the sacrifice of the martyrs, greed and corruption are the forces that assure the reappearance of the tyrannical figures in *La arena traicionada*. It all stems from the original sin, the violation of the American soil by the *conquistadores*, combined with the betrayal that starts with Malinche, Cortés's indigenous mistress. González Echevarría has argued that betrayal is the foundational story of *Canto general*:

> Betrayal is not original sin, it is an evil act committed by men in full knowledge of their own doings. Like the flood in Vico's system, which provides a second beginning after which history is man-made (as

opposed to Genesis) . . . [i]t is also violence committed against a given communal text, which sets up a rupture in history and in the interpretation of words, the shared words of the community.[49]

María Rosa Olivera-Williams considers that Los conquistadores "[s]on lo que no es árbol. No 'pertenecen' a la naturaleza y tampoco pueden relacionarse con ella. No tienen fundamento ni raíces. Su vocación, su necesidad así, es el aniquilamiento" [are whatever is not the tree. They do not 'belong' to nature, nor are they able to relate to her. They have no foundation or roots. Their vocation, thus their necessity, is annihilation].[50] The nature of the "vocación" and "necesidad" of "aniquilamiento" is problematic, but Olivera-Williams has pointed out the very essence that distinguishes the libertador from the traidor. The latter's rootlessness is indicated as early as the fourth poem of Los conquistadores (section III), where Cortés is invested with the following features: "Cortés no tiene pueblo, es rayo frío, / corazón muerto en la armadura" (1:348) [Cortés has no country, he's chilling thunderbolt, a cold heart clad in armor (46)]. The implication is that Cortés and the other conquistadores did not settle down anywhere, including in Spain, because they were moved only by greed and ambition. For Neruda, the development of these figures throughout history:

se debe a que inmediatamente después de la conquista, una casta se apoderó del movimiento de liberación implantando una nueva forma de dominio sobre nuestras poblaciones.

[is due to the fact that immediately after the Conquest, a caste took control of the liberation movement, imposing a new form of domination on our peoples.][51]

This new "casta" emerges in the middle of Los libertadores in an "intermedio" referring to the colonial period. Because of its thematic content, this "intermedio" would have been better placed in La arena traicionada, but apparently Neruda did not want to alter the historical dialectic that the section traces. Was Neruda following the murals at the National Palace, where simultaneous historical events are juxtaposed on the same plane, or did he want to underline the negative aspects of colonial Latin America by drawing a line between pre- and postcolonialism because he cannot identify a single hero? The answer will be that perhaps both intentions are present. As stated earlier, Neruda's aim in this parenthesis is to present the Colonia as an extension of the Conquista. It is an intermezzo because, in the poet's interpretation, La

Colonia represents merely a continuation of what the *conquistado-res* had begun. From the revolutionary perspective the colonial period is an interlude between the Conquest and the Independence movements. Therefore, in the fifth section the objective would be to present another interlude which must come to an end, following the model of postrevolutionary Mexico. The first poem, "La colonia cubre nuestras tierras," describes how the new "casta" replaced the *conquistador*: "llegó la ley al mundo de los ríos / y vino el mercader con su bolsita" (1:392) [law came to the world of rivers / and the merchant arrived with his little purse (88)]. Like the *conquistador*, this "mercader" rationalizes his crimes; the righteous endeavor of Christianizing the Indian justifies in his mind all sorts of abuses and enslavement:

> En las sombras del día tenebroso
> el mercader hizo su reino
>
> .   .   .   .
>
> en que el hereje, retorcido,
> hecho pavesa, recibía
> su cucharadita de Cristo.

(1:393)

> [In the sinister day's shadows
> the merchant built his empire,
>
> .   .   .   .
>
> in which the writhing heretic,
> reduced to ash, received
> his little spoon of Christ.]

(89)

The second poem, "Las haciendas" [The Haciendas], describes the development of the feudal society based on the *encomienda*, a sophisticated Spanish disguise of slavery, the original purpose of which was to provide Christian education to the indigenous people:

> La tierra andaba entre los mayorazgos
> de doblón en doblón, desconocida,
>
> .   .   .   .
>
> hasta que toda la azul geografía
> se dividió en haciendas y encomiendas.
> Por el espacio muerto iba la llaga

del mestizo y el látigo
del chapetón y del negrero.

(1:394)

[The land passed between the entailed estates,
doubloon to doubloon, dispossessed,

. . . .

until the entire blue geography was
divided into haciendas and encomiendas.
The mestizo's ulcer, the overseer's
and slaver's whip
moved through the lifeless space.]

(89)

The scene brings to mind some of the images, symbols, and themes of Rivera's murals at the Chapingo Chapel. One title sums it up: "The Exploiters." This work, painted in 1926, narrates how the Mexican peasants were made the object of the white man's exploitation.

The "intermedio" is more than a prelude to *La arena traicionada*, where, as has been indicated, the dichotomy *libertador-conquistador/colonizador* evolves into the form of a conflict between the rich and the poor or the oppressor and the oppressed. The gallery of tyrants is as wide-ranging or more so than that of the *libertadores*. The section is roughly arranged in chronological order from 1800 to approximately 1950: Doctor José Gaspar Rodríguez de Francia in Paraguay, Juan Manuel Ortiz de Rosas in Argentina, Gabriel García Moreno in Ecuador, Manuel Estrada in Guatemala, Juan Vicente Gómez in Venezuela, Gerardo Machado y Morales in Cuba, Mariano Melgarejo in Bolivia, Anastasio Somoza in Nicaragua, and so on. All of the dictators of Latin America are not described with the objectivity of a historian, but rather with the subjectivity of a chronicler[52]—and, I would add, with the sensitivity of an artist dominated by the visual representation of history imbedded in mural art. There follows a section in which Neruda resorts to one of the most common and effective rhetorical devices used by all the Mexican muralists: the contrast of two conflicting elements on the same plane. Two antithetical images are combined to generate dramatic tension. "Las oligarquías" [The Oligarchies] seems to reiterate the presence of the new "casta" mentioned earlier in the "intermedio" of *Los libertadores*. However, Neruda is here referring to the oligarchy created after the independence movements. The poem presents the whole spectrum of this oligarchy. The first stanza introduces this new breed of

"nuevos ricos con escudo / con policía y con prisiones" [nouveaux
riches with coats of arms / with police and with prisons]. The
second and third stanzas create the poem's internal dissonance,
and the second characterizes some of these "nuevos ricos":

> Hicieron una línea negra:
> "Aquí nosotros, porfiristas
> de México, "caballeros"
> de Chile, pitucos
> del Jockey Club de Buenos Aires,"
>
> . . . .
>
> "Allá vosotros, rotos, cholos,
> pelados de México, gauchos,
> amontonados en pocilgas,
>
> . . . .
>
> desbaratados, miserables,
> sucios, perezosos, pueblo."
>
> (2:473)

> [They drew a black line:
> "Here on our side, Mexico's
> Porfiristas, Chile's
> "gentlemen," gentry from
> the Jockey Club of Buenos Aires,"
>
> . . . .
>
> "There on your side, rabble, half-breeds,
> Mexico's down-and-outers, gauchos
> heaped together in pigsties,
>
> . . . .
>
> derelicts, miserable scum,
> filthy, shiftless, masses."]
>
> (161–62)

The next stanzas denounce the intervention of the Church for
its protection and active support of the privileged classes; the
repression of the poor by the police and the army; and finally,
the systematic brutalization of the masses by dictators, aristo-
crats, the Church, and other oppressive forces.

> En México produjeron pulque
> para él, en Chile
> vino litriado de color violeta,
> lo envenenaron, le rasparon
> el alma pedacito a pedacito,
> le negaron el libro y la luz,

.   .   .   .
y entonces no tuvo entierro
litúrgico: su ceremonia
fue meterlo desnudo entre otras
carroñas que no tienen nombre.

(1:474)

[In Mexico they produced pulque
for him, in Chile
violet-colored rotgut wine:
they poisoned him, scraped
his soul, bit by bit,
denied him books and light,

.   .   .   .
and then he had no church
burial: his ceremony consisted of
casting him naked amid the rest
of the nameless carrion.]

(162–63)

In "Promulgación de la ley del embudo" [Promulgation of the Funnel Law] Neruda describes how these false patriots designed a legal system to safeguard their dictatorial regimes. In alternating lines in the middle of the poem, the poet emphasizes the contrast between rich and poor:

Para el rico la buena mesa.
La basura para los pobres.
El dinero para los ricos.
Para los pobres el trabajo.
Para los ricos la casa grande.
El tugurio para los pobres.
El fuero para el gran ladrón.
La cárcel al que roba un pan.
París, París, para los señoritos.
El pobre a la mina, al desierto.

(1:475)

[For the rich, square meals.
Garbage for the poor.
Money for the rich.
For the poor, work.
For the rich, mansions.
Hovels for the poor.
Exemptions for the robber baron.
Jail for the man who steals a loaf.

Paris, Paris for the dandies.
The poor to the mines, the desert.]

(164–65)

These clashing images in the poem recreate the themes and images of some of the murals painted on the walls of the Ministry of Education by Rivera in 1926. Several alternating frames or panels contrast the affluent elite and the indigent masses: for example, *The Night of the Rich* in one frame and *The Night of the Poor* in another. The alternating lines in the stanza above, which are the equivalent of segments of murals, allow the reader's visualization of the theme and serve as "virtual lines," in the pictorial sense, to create the imaginary picture that the poet intends the reader to perceive. The content of the two mural scenes mentioned above is limited to what is strictly relevant to the rich and the poor and their opposite life-styles. Despite the propagandistic feature of both artistic forms of expression, painting and poetry, it may be argued that what is uppermost in the artist's concern is the artistic vision, the archetropic force that creates in the mind of the reader the conceptual space. This is the purpose of the poet who has in mind a particular group of paintings.

While a study of Mexican mural painting reveals to a considerable extent the narrative structure of *Canto general*, it also helps to explain Neruda's conception of and relationship with history. Criticism regarding this aspect of the poet's work is generally confusing and contradictory. Scholars have normally taken a position based primarily on biographical information.

Alain Sicard, for example, is of the opinion that "[e]n España descubre Pablo Neruda la Historia y, al mismo tiempo, que la Historia es, según frase de Marx, 'historia de la lucha de clases'" [in Spain Pablo Neruda discovers History and, at the same time, that History is, as Marx says, "the history of the struggle of the classes"].[53] Neruda does not "discover" History or the history of class struggle in Spain, or Mexico, or anywhere else except in his native Chile. Sicard seems to forget that Neruda's father was a railroad worker and that later Neruda came in direct contact with the extreme poverty in the Far East. Sicard's position is not completely unfounded; however, it lacks precision, for Neruda finds in Spain "poets of the people," like Rafael Alberti, Federico García Lorca, or Miguel Hernández. But to say that he discovers "History" in Spain is an overstatement. Villegas has noted that committed poetry has always been a recurrent motif in Neruda's work. "En la infancia" [In his early childhood], says this critic, "ya aparece una de sus primeras inquietudes con respecto a los problemas sociales. Recuerda cuando los ferroviarios llegaron de visita a casa del padre y entonces siente la proximidad de la pobreza" [there was already present his first uneasiness with regard to social problems. He remembered when the railroad workers came to visit his father's house, and he felt the proximity of poverty].[54] Villegas then cites the last stanza of poem III, "La casa" [The House] of *Yo soy* [*I Am*]:

> Y hasta mí, de los seres, como una separada
> barrera, en que vivían los dolores,
> llegaron las congojas, las ceñudas
> cicatrices, los hombres sin dinero,
> la garra mineral de la pobreza.
>
> (1:696)

> [and from those beings to me, like a separate
> barrier, inhabited by sorrow,
> anguish arrived, sullen
> scars, men without money,
> the mineral claw of poverty.]
>
> (376)

According to Eugenia Neves, *Canto general* "es la primera obra que entrega una visión y una interpretación histórica de América Latina, una visión organizada del pasado y del presente en torno a una lucha continuada por conseguir su libertad" [is the first work that offers a vision and a historical interpretation of Latin America, a vision organized according to the past and the present around a continuous struggle to obtain freedom].[55] Saúl Yurkiévich, on the contrary, considers that *Canto general* "carece de articulación rigurosa, de ordenamiento simétrico que disponga el material (cronológico, anecdótico o temático), de un desarrollo, de un despliegue progresivo, de un continuo lógico" [lacks rigorous articulation and a reasonably articulated, chronological, anecdoctic or thematic symmetrical order, a development, a progressive unfolding, a logical continuum].[56] Others attempt to limit the book's content to a specific historical context. Neves, for example, states that *Canto general* was created in response to the effect of the Cold War in Latin America during the late 1940s. Villegas draws a different conclusion: "la antítesis dominante de la época no era *capitalismo* versus *socialismo* o *burgueses* contra el *proletariado*, sino *fascismo-antifascismo*, lo que en el *Canto* se actualiza en forma de *opresión* versus *libertad*" [the dominant antithesis of the era was not *capitalism* versus *socialism* or the *bourgeois* against the *proletariat*, but rather *fascism-antifascism*, which in *Canto general* becomes *oppression* versus *freedom*].[57] Both critics ignore the fact that *Canto general* was produced during a span of ten years (1939–49). Thus the book was affected by countless different experiences, including those mentioned and many more.

Also controversial is the perspective from which Neruda wrote *Canto general*. Olivera-Williams, after examining the content of the introductory poem of *La arena traicionada*, concludes that this particular poem "es de gran importancia para la interpretación de todo el *Canto general,* ya que da cuenta de la perspectiva histórica y no mítica que Neruda asume al componer este libro" [is of particular importance in the interpretation of all of *Canto general,* since it attests to the historical, not mythical, perspective that Neruda assumed when he composed this book].[58] Villegas, on the other hand, defends the notion that myth is the cosmogenetic principle that structures *Canto general.*[59] There is a third position held by Yurkiévich. As expounded in his essay "Mito e historia: Dos generadores del *Canto general,*" both myth and history shaped *Canto general,* although this critic reaches the conclusion that the two principles are mutually exclusive: "La densidad metafórica . . . de los mitemas básicos hace que el texto no pueda leerse como relación de hechos, como crónica o epopeya históricas" [The metaphorical density . . . of the basic *mitemas* makes it impossible to read the text as a narration of facts, like a historical chronicle or epic poem].[60] Finally, Rafael Bosch, after ten pages dedicated to refuting Yurkiévich's study, devotes two paragraphs to the proposition that Neruda, as a historian, belongs to the great tradition of nineteenth-century revolutionary poets. According to him, poets such as Heine and Lenar, Herwegh and Wierth, Pushkin and Nekrásov, Mazzini and Carducci, and Espronceda are among the premier historical analysts of their societies.[61] The only difference, maintains Bosch, is that Neruda "ha podido y sabido aplicar las herramientas histórico-críticas a toda la Historia de América Latina" [has been able to apply historical-critical tools to all the History of Latin America], although Bosch does not specify what these "tools" might be.[62]

The core of the problem lies in the critics' tendency to overlook the fact that Neruda is a poet driven by the visual, by a fondness for iconic representation. There is also a failure to understand that *Canto general* was, on the whole, motivated, like mural art, by the idea of creating an art for the people, rather than by a "social realist" style. As has been shown, the presentation of history in *Canto general* was determined by its artistic visual expression in Mexican muralism, especially in the frescoes of Diego Rivera in the National Palace. The apparent lack of rigorous articulation, of a logical sequence of events, as argued by some critics, can be explained by the panoramic display of history and historical figures in the frescoes of the National Palace, the complete title of which reads, "The History of Mexico: From the Conquest to the Future." In the painting, as stated earlier, there is a simultaneous, ostensibly incoherent presentation of events taking place at different times in Mexican history, in the same way in which pre-Colombian and medieval painting and frescoes were constructed. The purpose is to make their own history available to the masses in condensed, synthetic form. History is shown, in Orozco's words, "from contradictory and opposing viewpoints."[63] In other words, the mythical and historical dimensions of reality are both embraced and intertwined.

Orozco also accepted socialist propaganda as one of the trends of Mexican muralism, "in which there continues to appear, with surprising persistency, Christian iconography."[64] The context in which *Canto general* is conceived and partially written encompasses not only the rise of fascism but also the Mexican intellectual and cultural postrevolutionary movement initiated by Vasconcelos in the 1920s, as well as President Cárdenas' (1934–40) efforts to institute Zapata's promises of the agrarian reform. Mexican cultural nationalism, displayed on the walls of public buildings, inspired Neruda to create and give a particular structure to *Canto general*. The program of cultural nationalism was shaped by Vasconcelos; he considered art, aesthetic appreciation and creativity mankind's most precious values. As Jean Franco comments, Vasconcelos "developed a theory of human and social evolution" in his essays, *La raza cósmica* [*The Cosmic Race*] (1925) and *Indiología* [*Indiology*] (1927).[65] His quasi-mythical theories were interpreted in the murals of Rivera, Orozco, and Siqueiros. In all of the Mexican frescoes history and myth merge in time and space. This should come as no surprise, since Mexican history, like Latin American history in general, has always been intertwined with myth, and the Mexican mural painters were only interpreters of this cultural reality. Above all, in *Canto general*, as in Rivera's frescoes, both myth and history are its cosmogenetic structuring principle and aesthetic objective. Jean Pierre Feber has accurately noted that [Neruda interprète l'histoire en modelant un matériau historique parcellisé, trié, altéré, voire falsifié, pour donner à entendre l'Histoire" [Neruda interprets history by modeling an historical material that is fragmented, selected, altered, even falsified, in order to facilitate the understanding of History].[66] As Feber accurately points out, Neruda's aim is not to present a precise documentary account (after all, the poet is not a historian), but rather to explain certain events in terms of the history of class struggle:

> [L]'histoire telle qu'il [Neruda] la voit et la présente dans la *Canto General* est une histoire élaborée, recomposée et stylisée selon des normes et dans un but précis, ou dates, faits et personnages historiques fonctionnent comme des signes.

> [History as he (Neruda) sees it and presents it in *Canto General* is a history elaborated, rewritten and stylized according to certain norms and with a precise objective, where dates, facts and historical characters function as signs.][67]

For this reason, Sarandy Cabrera has suggested that even the poet's persecution by Videla is equated to the oppression of conquered Native Americans or the martyrdom of the leaders of the Independence movement.[68]

While certain critical interpretations regarding the historical aspect of *Canto general*, especially those of Sicard, Yurkievich, Olivera-Williams, and Bosch may be challenged, the objective here has been to present another angle in the discussion, one which may provide a deeper understanding of *Canto general*. Mexican muralism not only provided a source of thematic and technical inspiration, but also helps to explain Neruda's conception of history. History in *Canto general* has been transformed into myth, in the very same way as in the murals. The artist is not concerned with accuracy or the chronological description of events.[69] History is treated as a simultaneous, synchronic rather than sequential or diachronic phenomenon in order to undermine the rational Western conception of cause and effect and to present Latin American history as a recurrent, never-ending story of deceit and deception.

5

The Poet and the People

"La tierra se llama Juan" and Communion with the Oppressed

Perhaps the most important aspect of Mexican mural art and *Canto general* is the inclusion of the common people as a historical character. The artist's purpose is to achieve authentic fusion with the soul and heart of the people to produce a work with collective impact, capable of communicating with the vast majority. The average person may become a motif, a character, or the emblematic allegorical representation of a theme, with aesthetic implications. According to Ades in her book on art in Latin America,

> The emergence of the muralists in Mexico after 1921 was an important factor in the debates of the 1920s and '30s concerning art's engagement in social and political issues. It was the idea of an art for the people, rather than the adoption of a "social realist" style that, on the whole, mattered.[1]

Clearly, we, like Ades, are generalizing the movement as a whole. But as she points out, "There was considerable divergence, not to say opposition, among the mural painters . . . and Siqueiros especially pushed for the use of modern materials, experimental techniques and a dynamic expressionist style built partly on the principle of montage."[2] We have contended from the outset that Neruda's ekphrastic encounter with mural art is mainly an aesthetic endeavor, with ideological overtones, that belongs to the Modernist and avant-garde movements. Social realism, as it was practiced in Mexico particularly by novelists, was not compatible with Neruda's style or convictions about art and poetics. Muralism, on the other hand, was.

In 1929 in Paris, Rivera had proclaimed the end of bourgeois art and the emergence of a new era of collective art.[3] Neruda

169

made similar ideological pronouncements on several occasions, condemning those artists who did not commit to the social task. In "Poetas celestes" [Celestial Poets] Neruda indirectly attacked Octavio Paz and his followers for turning their back on political *engagement*. The artist must emerge as a redeeming voice or as the vehicle through which the oppressed masses can express their suffering. "Speak through my words and my blood," says the poet at the end of *Alturas de Macchu Picchu*. The same idea is repeated at the beginning and end of *Canto general*. This is, we could say, the central purpose, or the poet's utopia.

Accordingly, of all the themes that conform the narrative structure of Mexican muralism, the integration of the lower classes as a historical character represents the best artistic effort to interpret Marxist ideology, which functions as the unifying device for all aspects of muralism. In this kind of approach, the artist's goal is to identify completely with the spirit of the masses in order to create, not a personal art object, but rather a work with collective impact. Thus the poet is trying to liberate his art from himself, his persona, and his individuality. *Canto general* can be defined in such terms, and it may be argued that Neruda's aim in this book is indistinguishable from that of the Mexican painters, although of course the methods used to achieve this goal differ from one form of artistic expression to another. Several topoi in *Canto general* correspond to Mexican muralism's aspiration and commitment to reach the masses, thus establishing a direct ideological parallel with the Mexican painters, particularly Rivera. But while they may differ in the medium they use, the muralists and Neruda share the same ideological standpoint, and a strikingly similar array of imagery. They also correspond in their iconoclastic efforts to overturn the values and precepts of European art, and in their inversion and transgression of the images of Christian iconography. Thus, from an interartistic point of view, our interest in this chapter now centers around the notion of ideology and its historical relationship with images.

According to Mitchell, such a relationship starts off with the etymological origin of the word "ideology." "'Idea' comes from the Greek verb 'to see' and is frequently linked with the concept of 'eidolon,' the 'visible image' that is fundamental to ancient optics and theories of perception."[4] Based on their linguistic association, Mitchell moves to the philosophical connection, arguing that the concept

> is grounded, as the word suggests, in the notion of mental activities or "ideas" that provide the materials of thought. Insofar as these ideas

are understood as images—as pictorial, graphic signs imprinted or projected on the medium of consciousness—then ideology, the science of ideas, is really an iconology, a theory of imagery.[5]

Mitchell's aim is clear. He wants to show how the notion of "imagery serves as a kind of relay connecting theories of art, language and the mind with the conception of social, cultural, and political value."[6] And as one could expect from the conventionalist that Mitchell is, his premise is based on the conviction that "vision" is always conditioned by subjectivity (sexual, racial, class or cultural differences, etc.); that "there is no vision without purpose";[7] therefore to look is always to interpret, to involve the body and the mind and to block something out, whether or not one is aware of this process. It is from this concept of selective "seeing," of vision as a product of experience and acculturation, that Mitchell formulates his arguments and conclusion: that "the notion of ideology is rooted in the concept of imagery, and reenacts the ancient struggles of iconoclasm, idolatry and fetishism."[8] In fact, this conclusion encapsulates Mitchell's ultimate goal imbedded in his book title, *Iconology: Image, Text, Ideology,* and serves as the conceptual framework for this chapter's exploration of Neruda's total ekphrastic experience. In other words, by establishing the etymological and conceptual links between ideology and imagery, we seek to eliminate the differences between images and words in order to analyze systems of power and values. "Eye and ear," says Mitchell, "are in this respect no different from other figures of difference between words and images: they are categories of power and value, ways of enlisting nature in our causes and crusades."[9] Given this perspective, we can now see that Neruda was a poet not just driven by the visual desire aesthetically, but that through mural art he discovered the power of the image and thus engaged in the kind of ekphrastic experience that would shape all of his future poetry. *Odas elementales,* for example, is nothing more than a collection of ekphrastic vignettes of ordinary instruments of life: socks, tomatoes, onions, and so on.

In other words, muralism, like all avant-garde movements, was a form of iconoclastic art, and the key to its wide success was its appropriation of the dialectics of orthodox Christian iconology, on the one hand, and, on the other, the application of iconoclastic rhetoric that subverted traditional semantics of its iconography by superimposing new visual models of interpretation on the old "idols" or images of religious worship. Iconoclastic movements will generally attempt to use a new or repackaged image to attack an earlier one. In this regard, Mitchell remarks:

> the repudiated image is stigmatized by notions such as artifice, illusion, vulgarity, irrationality; and the new image (which is often declared not to be an image at all) is honored by the titles of nature, reason, and enlightenment.[10]

Exactly this dynamic appears in *Canto general* and in mural art. The images of the *campesino*, the indigeneous people, or the worker, or their historical representative national figures, are always associated with elements of nature and nourishment (light, clay, earth, tree, bread, star, and so on), while the *conquistador*, the Catholic priest, and other re-interpreted figures of history are consistently presented as unrooted from their soil, or as human aberrations in a land to which they do not belong, and are associated with images of death, darkness, ignorance, violence, and destruction. A condor made out of metal, for example, is one of Siqueiros's more clear metaphors of this.

The iconoclastic movement, therefore, always pretends to be the true ideology, free from the illusory idols of prejudice, while the repudiated ideology is always presented as idolatry or fetishism. There is a cyclical pattern of the historical practice of iconoclastic rhetoric that ends always by turning ideology into a form of idolatry, but within the cycle, the iconoclastic movement does not perceive itself as a creator of idolatry. In the same way, a person who believes black cats bring bad luck does not see that belief as superstition, but rather as true reality. In other words, the imposition of Christian ideology and imagery by the Spaniards was an iconoclastic effort against the "idolatry" of the imagery of pre-Hispanic civilizations. Ironically, the iconoclastic rhetoric of Neruda and the muralist painters has as its object not merely the subversion of religious iconology imposed by the Western Europeans, but more radically, to reverse the systematic process of destruction of the images and signs that belonged to pre-Colombian cultures.

At this point, however, we must note an interesting paradox of Neruda's and the muralists' iconoclastic efforts. Ironically, the subversion of the old iconography through the forms and methods favored by the avant-garde movements, mostly European in their origins, is at the very least ambiguous. Taken to its ultimate consequences this ambiguity about European iconography reveals this subversion as in fact deconstructive of its own structure, since while it rejects what they termed "bourgeois" aesthetics, it also eschews a form of "social realism" in favor of a Modernist conception of reality that emphasized the non-representational notion of image, and spatial paradigms such as formalism and structuralism.

The simultaneous juxtaposition of multiple figures and images in many of Rivera's murals is clearly the technical product of his Cubist years in Europe, and the same can be said of Siqueiros's expressionist style that characterizes most of his work. Orozco is the exception in many ways, but nor could he be described as a "social realist." The question, then, is why Neruda and the mural painters did not succumb to the "social realism" that dominated other forms of artistic expression. The answer, of course, has to do with the inevitable influence of the avant-garde movements, but also with the relation between the concept of ideology and imagery and their iconoclastic association with idolatry and fetishism. Neruda, like the muralists, engages in a battle of images to destroy the old idols of the mind. That is to say, Neruda is not only a poet dominated by a desire of iconic representation— which would imply a certain kind of dependence or subjection of the poet to the visual image—but more importantly he is a poet who seeks to create new and independent images.

From all the above, we contend that the correspondence of the ideology and imagery in *Canto general* with that of Mexican mural art represents one of the strongest arguments of the close relationship between Neruda's masterpiece and the muralist movement. Clearly, the affinity of ideology alone does not make the argument completely, since it could be explained in terms of the "spirit of the times." But affinity of ideology along with shared imagery does make a conclusive case. This is where the interartistic approach, with all its applications seen thus far, becomes crucial, for it establishes the strong connection between text and image above and beyond the imprecise notion of *zeitgeist*.

We will now explore the process by which *Canto general* and mural art fuse ideology and images in order to create a coherent vision of the world. We will begin with the political and ideological context.

The ideological and iconic impact of the muralist painters on Neruda's concept of the collective work has not received adequate critical attention, in part because of the tendency to overlook the strong anti-Spanish stance and the marked American nature of the book.[11] The few scholars who have taken a glance at Neruda's Mexican experience usually refer to it in an aside, either in a note or tangentially in a passing comment. For instance, in her study of the collective nature of *Canto general*, Jean Franco, sums up the poet's friendship with the Mexican painters in one sentence:

> No hay que descontar tampoco la amistad de Neruda con los pintores muralistas mexicanos, sobre todo con Siqueiros, que también querían un arte capaz de comunicarse con el pueblo.

> [Nor can we discount Neruda's friendship with the Mexican mural painters, especially Siqueiros, who also sought an art capable of communicating with the people.][12]

Neruda's experience in Mexico was more decisive than previously thought. He arrived at the height of a national cultural program launched by Vasconcelos, in which painters dominated the intellectual life of the country. As we saw earlier, for Manuel Pedro González the poetic vision of the Mexican muralist movement and their relationship to the people was such that the murals almost seemed to be collective rather than individual works of art, where the pain and misery of the masses plays an integral role.[13] These are indeed the basic poetic principles that Neruda attempts to incorporate into *Canto general:* that is, the masses as a motif, character, and metaphor of the collective nature of the art-object. In 1929, Diego Rivera, already a member of the Mexican communist party, gave several lectures in Paris on the new role of art in Latin America, in which he called for the end of art as we knew it, and the emergence of a new art for the ordinary citizen. Siqueiros, in a manuscript entitled "La fundación del Sindicato" [The Founding of the Union], established the premise that was to guide the new artistic approach:

> The syndicate of painters is the party of collective work. It wants to destroy all ego individualism. . . . To practice these postulates the syndicate will create a cooperative [which] will also elaborate a collective plan for the application of the principle of work in common.[14]

This claim seems to confirm another by the muralists that their frescoes were related technically and conceptually to pre-Columbian art, in which the artistic object was subordinated to the will of the people, and the artist eschewed in his work any trace of individuality.[15]

As a result of such identification with the American masses, Neruda, like the muralist painters before him, adopted an iconoclastic rhetoric that rejected the European or Western culture as the primary source for artistic inspiration or subject matter:

> (Poeta, buscas en tu libro
> los antiguos dolores griegos,
> los orbes encadenados
> por las antiguas maldiciones,
> corren tus párpados torcidos
> por los tormentos inventados,
> y no ves en tu propia puerta
> los océanos que golpean
> el oscuro pecho del pueblo).

(1:452)

> [(Poet, in your book you seek
> ancient Greek sorrows,
> the orbs oppressed
> by ancient maledictions,
> your twisted eyelids
> pursue invented torments,
> and you don't see at your own doorstep
> the oceans that pound
> the people's dark breast.)]

(142)

The same conflict is behind Neruda's attack on the "poetas celestes" (1:479) in *La arena traicionada*. In fact, the term "poetas celestes" implicitly alludes to Octavio Paz and his followers. In an interview with Alardo Pratts in 1943, Neruda condemned the evasiveness of contemporary Mexican poetry:

> Para mí, lo mejor de México son los agrónomos y los pintores. . . . Considero que en poesía hay una absoluta desorientación y una falta de moral civil que realmente impresiona.

> [For me, the best thing about Mexico are the agronomists and the painters. . . . I believe that in poetry there is an absolute disorientation and a lack of civic morals that is really quite impressive.][16]

This statement provoked the wrath of José Luis Martínez and Octavio Paz, who replied with a diatribe in *Letras de México* just before Neruda's departure.[17] Neruda's attack was clearly based on his strong new conviction regarding the role of poetry in Latin

America. For this reason, upon his arrival in Chile in November 1943, he would again declare:

> Toda reacción que no esté al servicio de la libertad en estos días de amenaza total, es una traición. Todo libro debe ser una bala contra el eje; toda pintura debe ser propaganda; toda obra científica debe ser instrumento y arma para la victoria.

> [Any reaction that is not at the service of freedom in these days of total threat, is a betrayal. Every book should be a deadly bullet; every painting should be propaganda; every scientific work should be an instrument and arm for victory.][18]

In view of this, the poet determined to become the mouthpiece of the people, the vehicle through which the masses and the oppressed could express their suffering: "Hablad por mis palabras y mi sangre" (1:344) [Speak through my words and my blood (42)]. His is the opposite of the Orphic voice that is only available to a few extraordinary beings.[19] The messianic mission that will advance the victory,

> implica en el pensamiento socialista y comunista, la tendencia de ver el arte como el modelo del trabajo no enajenado y también al artista como una especie destinada a ser absorbida por la colectividad.

> [implies that in socialist and communist thinking there is the tendency to see art as the model of work that is not contaminated, and also the artist as a species destined to be absorbed by the masses.][20]

The Mexican frescoes are an iconoclastic movement against the imagery of bourgeois art and are literally the result of a true collective effort. Rivera was always aided by a team of "assistants,"[21] and, in many instances, he used common people as models to represent ordinary people in his murals. To achieve the same effect in poetry, as a form of ekphrasis, the particular limitations of the medium force the poet to resort to other, poetic devices, such as the transfer of the poetic voice to a member of the collective throng. This is the case in *La tierra se llama Juan*, which in Neruda's words, "está escrito con las mismas palabras del pueblo, con sus faltas y su modo de decir las cosas. Son vidas de trabajadores contadas por ellos mismos" [is written with the very words of the people, with their mistakes and their way of saying things. It is lives of workers recounted by they themselves].[22] In a 1953 lecture delivered in Mexico, Neruda tells how "esa crónica poética había sido hecha por todos" [that poetic chronicle had been made by everyone], and then adds, "no hay material antipoético si se trata de nuestras realidades" [there is not antipoetic material if we are talking about our realities].[23] Neruda also revealed in a 1964 conference his desire to be considered a "poeta cíclico que pasara de la emoción o de la visión de un momento a una unidad más amplia" [a cyclical poet that could go beyond the emotion or the vision of the moment to a more encompassing unity].[24] The concept, according to Enrico M. Santí, can be traced to Giambattista Vico (1688–1744) who, in his *New Science*, used the phrase to describe the nature of homeric poems:

> El "poeta cíclico" no podía ser el individuo genial que la modernidad erige en la figura del Autor, sino una fuente popular anónima existente en los festivales, ferias y mercados de la Grecia antigua.

> [The "cyclical poet" could not be the individual genius that modernity erects in the figure of the Author; he could only be a popular anonymous source existing in the festival, fairs and markets of ancient Greece.][25]

Once again, the connection with Homer and the epic is made, but this time from a different angle: Santí, through Vico, sees the epic poems of Homer as the encyclopedia of Greek antiquity and Homer himself as a "poeta cíclico." However, while Santí posits this encyclopedic parallel mainly from the didactic nature of *Canto general* and Homer's epics, there is a further connection to be made with Homer and his association with ekphrastic descriptions, not only because of the famous shield passage, but also because of the frequent depictions of ordinary people and objects, all of which strongly suggests an effort to become a true "poeta cíclico."

This vision of Homer as the "people's poet" is not new. Long before Vico, Dionysius Cassius Longinus (213–273 AD), a platonic philosopher and historian, seems to argue in favor of this interpretation in his treatise *On the Sublime*. Longinus was translated by Boileau in 1674 and was quite popular in Lessing's time. Lessing, in his *Laocoön*, quotes Longinus as saying that "it seemed to him . . . that Homer raised men to gods and reduced gods to men."[26] Lessing himself later acknowledged that the Greeks "placed special value on excellence in all the arts and on labor, and that the best worker in even the smallest things might succeed in immortalizing his name,"[27] and quotes a passage from the *Iliad* in which Homer describes Tychios, the worker who made the leather shield for Ajax, and who, according to Lessing, is none other than the name of a saddler of Homer's acquaintance to whom Homer wanted to express friendship and gratitude by mentioning his name.[28] Whether this was actually the case is certainly a matter of debate, but the point is that at least from Lessing onward, the idea of inclusion of the working and popular classes in the epic is noted. This kind of inclusion is clearly one of Neruda's strong endeavors in *Canto general*, and the eighth section best illustrates this artistic effort; the poetic voice disappears among a polyphony of voices from ordinary people.

The poem "Jesús Gutiérrez (Agrarista)" [Jesús Gutiérrez (Agrarian)] narrates in first person the title character's adherence to the Mexican revolutionary movement, continuing what his father began when he joined Zapata's forces: the fight for freedom. The poem is divided into three parts. The first recounts Gutiérrez's father's death during the Revolution: "En Monterrey murió mi padre, / Genovevo Gutiérrez, se fue / con Zapata" (1: 554) [My father Genovevo Gutiérrez, / died in Monterrey. He left / with Zapata . . . (238)]. The second section is a panegyric to Lázaro Cárdenas, who implemented many of Zapata's commitments: "Aquí está mi casa, mi tierra / pequeña, el certificado / firmado por mi general / Cárdenas . . ." (1:554) [Here's my house, / my little / parcel of land, the certificate / signed by my general / Cárdenas . . . (238)]. In the last part of the poem the narrator reiterates his willingness to continue the fight in order to defend the gains made by the Mexican Revolution. The structure of the piece is similar to that of Rivera's mural, Ballads of the Revolution, at the Ministry of Education, and the generating metaphor is the same one used to describe *Los libertadores* (Cuauhtémoc, Lautaro, Zapata, Recabarren, and so on). Jesús Gutiérrez represents the renaissance of his father's sacrifice and struggle for freedom. Common, ordinary people are thus equated with those historical figures who fought for freedom. Hand in hand, both have always supported each other: "Detrás de los libertadores, estaba Juan / trabajando, pescando y combatiendo, / en su trabajo de carpintería o en su mina mojada" ("La tierra se llama Juan" 1:571) [Juan followed upon the liberators / working, fishing and fighting, / in his carpentry work or in his damp mine (253)].

As in the homeric poems, ordinary people are also portrayed in mythical terms, as in the case of "Abraham Jesús Brito (Poeta popular)" [Abraham Jesús Brito (People's Poet)]. Brito, as the poet's alter ego, is the true "poeta cíclico" of the common folk and like Lautaro or Caupolicán is deeply rooted in American soil:

> Jesús Brito es su nombre, Jesús Parrón o pueblo,
> y fue haciéndose agua por los ojos,
> y por las manos se fue haciendo raíces,
> hasta que lo plantaron de nuevo donde estuvo
> antes de ser, antes de que brotara
> del territorio, entre las piedras pobres.
>
> (1:558)

> [His name is Jesús Brito, Jesús Parrón or People,
> and he kept turning into water through his eyes,
> and through his hands he kept turning into roots,
> until they planted him again where he was
> before he came to be, before he rose
> from the territory, amid the poor stones.]
>
> (242)

The key line is "hasta que lo plantaron de nuevo donde estuvo," which recalls these lines from "México 1941" of the last section: "y subió por mis venas el olvido / recostado en el tiempo" [and oblivion recumbent in time / rose through my veins (384)]. This line summarizes from another perspective the poet's own return to his roots in a rather metaphysical, almost Borgesian way.

This communion completes the equation poet = people = nature established from the very beginning of the book. As in mural art, the people, historical heroes and pre-Colombian figures are all mythified or altered—some are transformed into martyrs and others into redeemers—to become symbols of emancipation and freedom.

Villegas convincingly outlines the binary nature of the book and sets forth the following distinctions:

> A nuestro juicio, dos son los tipos predominantes en esta nueva galería heroica. Por una parte está el redentor o portador del mensaje de redención social. Por otra, el miembro del pueblo que ha sido explotado, una especie de "pharmakos" en un mundo hostil y cruel.

> [In our view, there are two predominant types in this new heroic gallery. On the one had is the redeemer or bearer of the message of social redemption. On the other is the individual of the people who has been exploited, a kind of "pharmakos" in a hostile and cruel world.][29]

Diego Rivera, *The Flowering of the Revolution,* 1926, the Chapel at Chapingo, Mexico (INBA).

Such mythical stereotypes are extremely common in Rivera's murals as well. *The Flowering of the Revolution,* also identified as *Benediction* by Schmeckebier,[30] is a good example of the first type mentioned by Villegas: the redeemer. The fresco was painted in 1926 at the Chapel of the Autonomous University of Chapingo. The three figures at the top of the frame resemble Catholic priests sharing Communion bread during the celebration of mass with their fellow peasants. The wheel of the threshing machine in the background forms a sort of halo behind the worker's head. The worker on the left, a priest-like figure, offers his fellow peasants the sacred bread of life and freedom. Rather than benediction, this mural portrays the communion of the proletariat, since the scene depicts the moment in the mass when the Catholic priest offers the sacrament to the parishioners.

In one of the frescoes of the Ministry of Education, the concept of communion transcends Mexico's boundaries to embrace all

Diego Rivera, *Our Bread,* 1928, The Ministry of Education, Mexico City (INBA).

races. In *Our Bread,* painted in 1928, Rivera resorts once more to
Christian iconography to express his world view. On this occasion
he offers a Marxist interpretation of the Last Supper and the Eu-
charist, in which the Mexican peasant at the center [the cosmic
race] with the red star on his chest shares his bread (in communion) with the peoples of five continents. Both types—redeemer
and *pharmakos*—are depicted in a mural titled *The Exploiters* at the
Chapingo Chapel. The figure on the left, a redeemer, is searched
by the American foreman after leaving the mine (the allusion here
is to one of the strikes against a U.S.-owned mine that ended in
a massacre in 1906, which eventually contributed to the outburst
of the Revolution in 1910). Meanwhile, the peasants on the right
are harvesting wheat under tight surveillance and with the threat
of punishment. The gallery of people contained in these murals,
as in *Canto general,* includes peasants, soldiers, factory workers,
miners, weavers, and, of course, the artists themselves.

We see at work one of the most important aspects of both *Canto
general* and Mexican muralism: their didactic purpose. These artists had a strong commitment to create a kind of art that would
be accessible to everyone, especially to those with very little or
no education. Like the muralists, Neruda seeks to communicate
to all Latin Americans his own interpretation of history, which is
different from the official history, but above all, he aims to educate
and raise the consciousness of an entire continent. *Canto general,*
in Cabrera's opinion,

> lleva al lector a un mundo de cosas y acontecimientos que lo compren-
> den, lo nutren de historia poética, de cosas y hombres que existen,
> con lo que cumple un verdadero milagro poético.
>
> [leads the reader to a world of things and events that shape him, that
> nurture him with a poetic history, of things and men that exist, with
> which process he accomplishes a true poetic miracle.][31]

Santí even compares the didactic purpose of *Canto general* with
such encyclopedic works as the Bible, the Mayan *Popol Vuh,* Homer's *Iliad,* and more recent works such as Andrés Bello's *Silvas
americanas,* Walt Whitman's *Leaves of Grass,* and Ezra Pound's
Cantos.[32] It is precisely this form of encyclopedic instruction that
also corroborates *Canto general's* interrelation with Mexican mural art.

As previously observed, Rochfort expresses a similar view regarding Rivera's murals in the National Palace, where the artist

attempts to communicate with a largely illiterate public by recreating, through an epic panorama, a vision of Mexican history through the centuries. The "epic" and oral aspects of *Canto general* are not unintentional. They correspond to the heroic tableau of the murals, displaying the trajectory of Mexican history. Nor is it simply by chance that both artists resort to medieval techniques, as noted earlier. During the Middle Ages artists also aimed their works at a largely illiterate public that required oral and visual representation of their heroes and history. The poem's "epic" or oral quality is analogous to the visual element of the murals. González notes, "En tal sentido, la pintura mural mexicana se asemeja a la suprema expresión artística del medioevo, la catedral gótica, obra colectiva y expresión fiel del anhelo místico de la época" [In this sense, Mexican mural painting is similar to the supreme expression of medieval art, the gothic cathedral, a collective work and a faithful expression of the mystic desire of the era].[33] Jean Franco uses the same parallel to describe Neruda's attempt to reach a collective form of art:

La posibilidad de una nueva forma de poesía épica se le presenta como un acercamiento a un arte colectivo, parecido al de la edad media. Su admiración por un arte que fuera liberado del pecado original del individualismo queda patente en un discurso de 1960 en que habla de "las agujas de las pagodas y las flechas góticas de las basílicas [que] querían alcanzar a Dios sin que nadie les firmara con nombre y apellidos."

[The possibility of a new form of epic poetry occurs to him as an approach to a collective art, similar to that of the Middles Ages. His admiration for an art that would be free of the original sin of individualism is patent in a 1960 speech in which he speaks of "the pagoda needles and the gothic arrows of the basilicas that yearned to reach God without anyone signing his name.][34]

Franco has demonstrated Neruda's attempt in *Canto general* to create poetry similar to the oral verse of epic song:

El *Canto general* nunca puede alcanzar a este tipo de arte colectivo, pero se acerca a la poesía oral, y de allá a una poesía producida por la colectividad, mediante el uso de ciertas fórmulas que pertenecen a la literatura oral o al hablar en voz alta, a la oratoria y a la polémica. Estos códigos sugieren una poesía oral con tanta fuerza que ciertos críticos hablan de lo épico o de la "oralidad" del *Canto general*.

[*Canto General* can never be this kind of collective art, but it approaches oral poetry—and thereby a poetry produced by the collective people—through the use of certain formulas that derive from oral literature or the spoken voice, from oratory and polemics. These codes suggest an oral poetry with such power that certain critics speak of the epic quality or the "orality" of *Canto General*.][35]

In this case, *Canto general*'s link to the oral poetic tradition of the Middle Ages confirms that Mexican muralism, with its own epic narrative largely based on the collective nature of art in the medieval world, provided Neruda with the perfect artistic solution to express his new political doctrine. On several occasions the poet himself reiterates that his poetry is addressed to the common person on the street:

> No escribo para que otros libros me aprisionen
> ni para encarnizados aprendices de lirio,
> sino para sencillos habitantes que piden
> agua y luna, elementos del orden inmutable,
> escuelas, pan y vino, guitarras y herramientas.

(1:714–15)

> [I don't write so that other books can imprison me
> or for passionate apprentices of lilies,
> but for simple inhabitants who request
> water and moon, elements of the immutable order,
> schools, bread and wine, guitars and tools.]

(393)

Poem XII of *El fugitivo* [*The Fugitive*] represents the climactic point of the poet's communion with the oppressed. The poem is the poet's ultimate attempt to abandon his individualism, a prerequisite to truly embracing and belonging to a collective entity. Throughout the poem, prepositional phrases such as "A todos" [To all], "A vosotros" [To you (plural)], "a ti" [to you (singular)] and "a ti mismo" [to you yourself] serve as apostrophes to the people and as a means of establishing a direct contact between the poetic voice and his audience. Yet the poet wishes to go beyond language and become one with the masses:

> Solamente
> pienso
> que he sido tal vez digno de tanta
> sencillez, de flor tan pura,
> que tal vez soy vosotros, eso mismo,

esa miga de tierra, harina y canto,
ese amasijo natural que sabe
de dónde sale y dónde pertenece.

(1:604)

[I only
think
that I've perhaps been worthy of so much
simplicity, of a flower so pure,
that perhaps I'm you, that's right,
that bit of earth, flour and song,
that natural batch that knows
whence it comes and where it belongs.]

(285)

Yet, as Santí has also noted, the poet lacks the ability to achieve total integration with the pueblo. The poet, says Santí in a parenthetical note,

> no ha de ser ni el "Homero" de Vico ni las voces desmembradas de Pound; en cambio, sí irá y vendrá, en relación dialéctica, entre sí mismo y la masa, lo que en términos formales equivale al vaivén constante entre la meditación lírica y la narración épica.

> [it is not to be the "Homer" of Vico nor the dismembered voices of Pound; rather, it will go and it will come, in a dialectical relationship between itself and the masses; what in formal terms is the equivalent of the constant switching between lyrical meditation and epic narration.][36]

Indeed, other scholars, including Franco, have pointed out this flaw in the book. In the poems just mentioned, for example, the apostrophes establish a direct connection with the people, but not a melding of identity. For every "a ti" [to you] there is an implicit "de mí" [from me] and "soy vosotros" [I am you] is still the voice of individualism, or at least dualism ("tal vez soy vosotros" [perhaps I am you]). The same inconsistency is shared by the Mexican mural painters, whose artistic size and prominence in the intellectual life of Mexico made such integration impossible.

Popular Art

The different techniques used by Neruda to make his poetry a work for the masses have been summarized in the studies of

Yurkiévich, Franco, Villegas, Riess, and others mentioned in this chapter. Those formulas and aesthetic principles pertinent to Mexican mural art will be highlighted here. Riess has indicated one of these: "The mundane, everyday actions of work and labor are given a profound and resonant dimension far beyond the particular context of the event."[37]

In poem V of *Canto general de Chile,* various handmade objects embody all manner of traditional crafts and reflect, like Macchu Picchu, the human life, the hands that produced them. In the first section of the poem, "Talabartería" [Saddlery], the poet finds in an old saddle the unified vision of the equation saddle = artisan = nature. Multiple elements converge on the same object to give rise to the poetic vision. The saddle becomes a representation of the work of men through time:

> Cada recorte es una mano, cada
> costura es una vida, en ella vive
> la unidad de las vidas forestales,
> una cadena de ojos y caballos.
>
> (1:535)

> [Every cut is a hand, every
> stitch a life in which the unity
> of forest lives, a chain of eyes
> and horses, lives on.]
>
> (220)

"Alfarería" [Pottery Shop], the next section of the poem, possesses mythical dimension. The ceramic piece contains a profound secret, and the poet perceives in it a subtle sign that helps to decipher its arcane mystery: "Torpe paloma, alcancía de greda, / en tu lomo de luto un signo, apenas / algo que te descifra . . ." (1:535) [Crude dove, clay piggy bank, / on your grieving back a sign, something / that barely deciphers you . . . (220)] But the poet cannot understand how the people, despite their suffering, continue to develop the great artistic tradition:

> Pueblo mío,
> cómo con tus dolores a la espalda,
> apaleado y rendido, cómo fuiste
> acumulando ciencia deshojada?
>
> (1:535)

> [My people,
> how—shouldering your sorrows,

beaten and subdued—how did you manage
to accumulate naked science?]

(220)

Again, Neruda credits the people with a sense of fortitude and
self-denial that makes them stoically plod on, regardless of the
oppression to which they are subjected. The ceramic objects are
the bridge that connects the soil and pristine, uncorrupted man
with the artisan and poet of the present:

> Prodigio negro, mágica materia
>
> . . . .
>
> cántaro de Pomaire en cuyo beso
> tierra y piel se congregan, infinitas
> formas del barro, luz de las vasijas,
> la forma de una mano que fue mía.

(1:535)

> [Black prodigy, magic matter
>
> . . . .
>
> Pomaire's earthen pitcher in whose kiss
> earth and skin congregate, infinite
> forms of clay, vessels' light,
> shape of a hand that was mine.]

(220)

In "Telares" [Looms], the last section, the poet again beholds
the stoic nature of the other artisans, who altruistically devote
their lives to produce beauty:

> Manos del pueblo mío en los telares,
> manos pobres que tejen, uno a uno,
> los plumajes de estrella que faltaron
> a tu piel, Patria de color oscuro,
> substituyendo hebra por hebra el cielo
> para que cante el hombre sus amores
> y galope encendiendo cereales!

(1:536)

> [My people's hands on the looms,
> poor hands that weave, one by one,
> the starry feather that your
> skin lacked, dark-colored Country,
> substituting the sky fiber by fiber

so that man may sing his loves
and kindle grain on the gallop!]

(221)

The poet finds in these artifacts the "iniciales de la tierra" [initials
of the earth] ("Amor América [1400]"), which "[n]adie pudo /
recordarlos después . . . / . . . las claves se perdieron" (1:315) [no
one could / remember . . . afterward . . . / . . . the keys were lost
(13–14)]. The sign found in the piece of ceramic corresponds to
these "iniciales," a cabalistic emblem for the future. For the poet,
the object becomes a kind of oracle which assists him in deci-
phering its secret "iniciales," which he now needs to become the
messianic voice that will redeem the oppressed. We must also
stress that it is part of the expression of a unified vision which
contains the notion of harmonious continuity and perfect communion among all levels of life (human, animal, vegetable, and
mineral) as mentioned in chapter 3.

Here we must note yet another association with Homer, connected to the idea of "poeta cíclico." Neruda's ekphrastic descriptions of these everyday objects are not essentially different from
the earliest examples of ekphrastic poetry, which were principally
focused on utilitarian objects (urns, shields, cups, garments, and
so on) rather than on paintings or museum pieces. Scott says of
these early manifestations of ekphrasis that "they provide enu-
merations of practical implements, which are meant to communicate to an absent audience the sheer visual appearance of a
thing."[38] There is a striking similarity between Neruda's ekphrastic results and Homer's famous description of Achilles' shield.
We must remember that, as Lessing and many others since have
pointed out, the Greek poet does not present us with a dull inven-
tory of an object's features. Instead, he depicts Vulcan in the
process of making the shield. In the presentation of all three of the
objects described in Neruda's series—the old saddle, the ceramic
piece, and the looms—the emphasis is not on the referential characteristics of form and shape, but on what can only be described
as the "activity" of the object, making it clear that this is no
"mere" object, but a highly charged *form* and a complex symbolic
icon. "Telares," for example, quite positively refers to the whole
topos of the personified artifact, and specifically to the biblical
trope of creation, where instead of God we see the loom forming
and shaping Antartica:

Y allí el telar hilo a hilo, buscando
reconstruyó la flor, subió la pluma
a su imperio escarlata.

(1:536)

[And there the loom, seeking thread by thread,
reconstructed the flower, raised the feather
to its imperial scarlet.]

(221)

Geography and nature ("la primavera oscura del sur" [the South's dark springtime]), along with fauna ("las aves negras" [black birds]), the object ("telar" [loom]), and the human hands all converge in an existential, physical yet transcendental mythical dimension. The narrator does not describe them; he shows us the "manos," the human lives involved in the production of the ekphrastic object. The goal is that the mute object be endowed with a voice, a human status, becoming an iconic symbol, a true poetic emblem independent of the visual referent. These are Neruda's first ekphrastic poems of ordinary and utilitarian objects, and he was to return to and further develop this poetic device in his *Odas elementales*, where even the most humble objects of everyday life become the source of ekphrastic inspiration.

Neruda found in these artifacts the synthesis of primeval man and modern man. Perhaps that is why he was particularly drawn to the Mexican *mercados*, with their abundant variety of popular art objects. The market became for Neruda a symbol of oneness with the silent majority. In Paris around 1950, the same year in which *Canto general* was published, the poet did not feel like he belonged in Europe and was nostalgic for American soil. In "Vámonos al Paraguay" [Let's Go to Paraguay], an article published in *Pro Arte* in Santiago in 1950, the poet explicitly declares:

Yo no soy de estas tierras, de estos bulevares. Yo no pertenezco a estas plantas, a estas aguas. . . . Dónde me llevas? Quiero entrar en esa tela del mercado de México, del mercado sin nombre, del mercado número mil. Quiero tener ese color quemado, quiero ser tejido y destrenzado, quiero que mi poesía cuelgue de los árboles del pueblo, como una bandera, y que cada verso tengo [sic] un peso textil, defienda las caderas de la madre, cubra la crin del agrarista.

[I am not of these lands, these boulevards. I do not belong to these plants, these waters. . . . Where will you carry me? I want to be part of the trapestry of Mexico's markets, a nameless market, the thousandth market. I want to be that burnt color, I want be woven and unraveled, I want my poetry to be strung like banners from the trees in small villages, I want my verse to have the weight of cloth, to protect a mother's flanks, to cover a farmer's mane.][39]

Once again arises the concept of the "poeta cíclico," something like the popular poet found in the *ferias, mercados,* or folkloric celebrations. Orozco often compared the vicarious function of the muralist to the "evangelistas," the name given in Mexico to those who, even today, in the street or a small room, type letters, applications, and documents of all kinds for illiterate peasants and workers. Jean Charlot once declared the following:

For us artisan is the word most closely linked to art. . . . Discarded techniques are resurrected; one tries his hand at fresco, distemper, egg tempera, polychrome carving; some insist on personally preparing their pigments.[40]

Indeed, the fresco technique requires a great deal of physical labor, through which process the role of the artist comes to approximate that of the artisan.

But there were many other ways to reach the masses. The depiction of everyday activities, festivities, and handicrafts was a predominant theme in the work of all the mural painters. Diego Rivera, in particular, shared Neruda's fascination with the *mercados* in Mexico. Many of his best murals set forth in rich colors the variety of objects and people to be found in the market. Although the juxtaposition of past and present is somewhat less conspicuous in Rivera, the market scene inserted in the mural *The Great City of Tenochtitlán* (1945) in the National Palace has many similarities with *El Tianguis* by the same artist in the Ministry of Education of 1924. Nevertheless, the profound dimension given by Neruda to art objects is not present. Infusing an object with such mythical power corresponds to Siqueiros's interpretation of popular art, more closely than to Rivera's. The convergence of man and object (or past and present) in one unified vision resembles Siqueiros's artistic approach. His *Ethnography,* painted in 1939, is a good example of this man-object synthesis. Neruda, like Siqueiros and Charlot, was aware that through handicrafts and popular art the artist can access the essence of the past and its people. He realized, as did Jean Charlot, that "pre-Hispanic and colonial traditions meet and fuse on contemporary terms in the popular arts."[41] In other words, it is the sur-

Diego Rivera, *The Great City of Tenochtitlan*, 1945, The National Palace, Mexico City. Photograph by Marcos Méndez.

Diego Rivera, *El Tianguis* (The Market), 1923–24, The Ministry of Education, Mexico City (INBA).

vival and permanence of popular art that opens up the connection with the past, with the "iniciales perdidas." Like an artisan, Neruda, following the biblical trope of the Adamic figure, wants to give his poetry form and life with his hands and become fused— like the God of Genesis—with the final product so that each poem carries in it a piece of his humanity.

The Poet in the Poem as a Means of Uniting with the Masses

As we have seen, the most obtrusive technique for becoming one with the masses in both Neruda and Rivera's art is the insertion of the artist/poet himself into his own work. In Mexican muralism, Rivera is the painter who most frequently uses, and even abuses, this technique, although Siqueiros and Orozco also resorted to it from time to time. Practically every other frame in the murals of the Ministry of Education and the National Palace, for example, includes either a self-portrait or a likeness of Rivera's wife, Frida Kahlo (see *The Disembarkation in Vercruz* and/or *Dream of a Sunday Afternoon in the Alameda*). The mechanism allows the artist to enter into the events represented as a first-hand observer or chronicler to join with the collectivity as an ordinary member. There is also a theoretical, artistic, and psychological consideration that apparently escapes the artist. The artist/poet constructs himself as the viewing subject and sometimes as the featured object of the painting or poem. In the process, the artist projects a filtered, perhaps idealized image of himself to be imprinted into the work of art. The artist/poet, in other words, assumes the dual position of author/protagonist or subject and object within the same physical space. The poet, like the painter, actively engages in the process of construing his own image as both artist and political *persona*. There is thus a thin line between becoming one with the throng and the purely egocentric impulse of self-aggrandizement.

Throughout *Canto general*, the poet introduces himself or the poetic *persona* into the poem. Sometimes, in order to speak intimately with one of the *libertadores*, the poet engages in a personal dialogue with a hero, a symbolic being or a prosopopeic manifestation. In "Minerales," in the first *Canto*, for example, the poet laments the exploitation of Mother Earth: "Madre de los metales, te quemaron, / te mordieron, te martirizaron" (1:323) [Mother of metals, they burned you, / bit you, martyred you (21)]. In

"Cuauhtémoc," the poetic voice calls the Aztec warrior "joven hermano" [young brother] and tells him in a familiar tone, "en tu mano / recibo el don de tu patria desnuda" (1:376) [in your hand / I receive your naked country's gift].[42] Zapata, O'Higgins, de las Casas, Recabarren, and so on, are all treated in the same familiar apostrophic manner. In other instances, the poetic persona becomes an active participant in the action described, as in the case of *Alturas de Macchu Picchu* or in "Cortés," where the poet, as another member of the indigenous culture, before the devastation of Cholula, warns his fellow *Tlaxcaltecas* against the invader: "Hermano aterrado, no tomes / como amigo al buitre rosado: " (1:348) [Terrified brother, do not / befriend the rosy vulture:] (46). The passive oral participation of the messianic persona, the witness-like chronicler narrating events, is transformed at the end in the poet's active involvement in "El corazón de Pedro de Valdivia." The poet has assumed the dual position of author/protagonist, which allows him to place himself either in or out of the scene of action, at will. The last scene of the poem recreates a human sacrifice similar to those performed by the Aztecs during the *guerra florida*. The poem, which begins in the first person plural, changes to the first person singular in order to present the narrator transformed into a pseudo-Aztec priest taking part in the rite, sharing "[E]l corazón de Pedro de Valdivia":

> Entonces repartimos el corazón sangrante.
> Yo hundí los dientes en aquella corola
> cumpliendo el rito de la tierra:
>
> (1:390)

> [Then we shared the bleeding heart.
> I sank my teeth into that corolla,
> fulfilling the rites of the earth:]
>
> (86)

It must be noted that this is one of the few times in the book that the poet uses the *nosotros* form.

At other times the poet addresses what Jean Franco calls a "público virtual" [virtual public].[43] This particular style, which assumes a "narratee," is used when the poet becomes the redeeming voice in order to communicate his ideological message and encourage the people to strive for a new life. One of the best examples of this style may be found in the first stanza of "Los

muertos de la plaza (28 de enero de 1946, Santiago de Chile)"
[The Corpses in the Plaza (28 January 1946, Santiago de Chile)]:

> Yo no vengo a llorar aquí donde cayeron:
> vengo a vosotros, acudo a los que viven.
> Acudo a ti y a mí y en tu pecho golpeo.
> Cayeron otros antes. Recuerdas? Sí,
> recuerdas.
>
> (1:499)

> [I don't come to weep here where they fell:
> I come to you, I repair to the living.
> I appear to you and me and I beat on your breast.
> Others fell before. Do you remember? Of course you do.]
>
> (186)

If we accept the notion that art is a mirror, a reflection of society with all its customs, beliefs, folklore, superstitions, religions, and so on, *Canto general* would have to assume a similar position insofar as it is concerned with the specular reflection of social reality. In this context, *Canto general* and mural art are an attempt to be mirrors in which not only the spectators see their own reflections, where they find themselves and their identity, but also a space where the artist/poet goes in search of himself and his identity in an effort to define himself in his historical context.

The history, culture, and philosophy of postrevolutionary Mexico offered Neruda a living model of a strong, dynamic society, a society in a continuous process of self-creation and self-definition under the leadership of Lázaro Cárdenas (1934–40). President Cárdenas nationalized the oil industry and enacted the Constitution of 1917, which included agrarian reform. Moreover, Cárdenas's government along with that of the Soviet Union stood alone in support of the Spanish Republic. Neruda paid tribute to Cárdenas and his anti-Fascist stance at the end of *Canto general* in a stanza of "En los muros de México (1943)" (1:707) [On Mexico's Walls (1943)], the poem he recited at his farewell gala in 1943. Mexican muralism expressed the optimism with which the country was facing a new era. For Neruda, this was a strong incentive to continue his political position and to express his new poetic vision in his writing.

He became convinced that the true messianic mission requires the artist to be totally assimilated into the collective, and the fresco technique was for the painters the optimal form of such participation. Poetry, on the other hand, presents a different challenge to achieve the same effect. Neruda uses alternative means such as the transfer of the poetic voice to a member of the masses in an attempt to surrender his individualism and authorship of the work. *La tierra se llama Juan* is the section that best represents this effort. It is a true symphony of voices that at times follows the pattern and oral tradition of the *corrido*. Remarkably, the generating metaphor parallels that of *Los libertadores* (Cuauhtémoc, Lautauro, Zapata, Recabarren, and others). Common people are equated with those historical, quasi-mythical figures who fought for freedom. The poet must play the paradoxical double roles of redeemer and interpreter of the people, and of author and protagonist. Neruda's success, then, is only partial because it is limited to the inclusion of ordinary people. Though he transfers the poetic voice to artisans, workers, or peasants in dramatic monologues, and introduces himself in the scene, the poet remains the sole Author.

Conclusions

Critical Approaches

A CLOSE LOOK AT THE DIFFERENT EXPERIENCES RELEVANT TO THE creation of *Canto general* reveals that most of the poet's critics base their conclusions on rather impressionistic evidence. The most common misconception is that Spain and the Spanish Civil War were key to the inception of *Canto general*. The result has been an overemphasis on the impact of Spain on this book and the marginalization of Neruda's Mexican years, along with the omission of his adherence to Modernist aesthetic values.

The other widespread generalization posits the view of Neruda as an imitator of Andrés Bello (the comparison may have begun with Rodríguez Monegal's *Neruda: el viajero inmóvil*). *Canto general* no doubt belongs to that tradition of Latin American poetry, but Neruda does not pattern his poetry after Bello's.[1] In fact, there are more differences than similarities between the two writers, as Neruda's panoramic view of history, geography and people in *Canto general* contrasts with Bello's stance.[2] The mythical dimension, the inclusion of pre-Colombian cultures, the Conquest, and the colonial period are not part of Bello's project. Speculation regarding Bello's intentions to include these themes is therefore futile. The subtitle of Bello's *Alocución a la poesía* [*Allocution to Poetry*]: "Fragmentos de un poema inédito, titulado 'América'" [Fragments of an unpublished poem titled "America"], at best represents a virtual outline but does not provide proof. In fact, the term "alocución" by definition implies rather a brief speech given by a "superior" to his "súbditos" [subjects] according to the Real Academia's *Diccionario de la lengua española*. Neruda's poetry is affected by Marxist doctrine, Bello's by Catholic pragmatism. Bello used the *silva* because he could not rid himself of form, whereas Neruda breaks with all forms and prefers blank, almost prosaic verse. In fact, what most distances Neruda from Bello is form. Even Araya recognizes a vital difference: the ab-

197

sence in Bello of that cosmogonic component contained in *Canto general*:

> Un elemento de gran importancia en el canto, y que no existió en el proyectado por Bello, es su dimensión cosmogónica, desarrollada sobre todo en la serie XIV, *El gran océano.*

> [An element of great importance in the canto, and one that did not exist in that planned by Bello, is its cosmogonic dimension, as developed especially in series XIV, *The Great Ocean.*][3]

But perhaps the most striking evidence against such generalization, including comparisons of Neruda with Chocano, Gutiérrez, and Lugones, is the poet's embrace of the collectivity, the popular aspect of *poeta del pueblo*, or artisan of words, that Neruda strived to achieve.

Even assuming that Alain Sicard is correct in his conclusion that Neruda discovers History in Spain and that History is the history of class struggle,[4] it is still necessary to explain how Neruda went from *España en el corazón* (1937) to *Canto general* (1950). Other critics, however, have taken a more comprehensive approach to this subject. For example, in his analysis of *Alturas de Macchu Picchu*, Donald Shaw comments:

> Despite the implication of "Explico algunas cosas," in 1937, that a change had already overtaken his work, it was not until after his return to the New World, his stay in Mexico and his senatorial campaign amid the workers of Tarapacá and Antofagasta, that the crucial moment arrives.[5]

Indeed, a careful examination of the textual and biographical evidence vis-à-vis the evolution of Neruda's poetry from *España en el corazón* to the creation of *Canto general* reveals a more crucial role played by the Mexican experience than thought previously.

Textual Evidence

In 1937, Neruda returned from Europe to Chile, where he organized the *Frente Popular* (*Popular Front*) and promoted the cause of the Spanish Republic. In May 1938 his father died, and three months later Neruda also buried his dearest "Mamadre" (his own term of endearment and neologism for his *madrasta*, or stepmother). According to Rodríguez Monegal, "[e]l día mismo de la muerte de su padre comienza a escribir un poema que será el germen primero del *Canto general de Chile* . . ." [the very day of his father's death he began to write a poem that was to be the first germ of *Canto General of Chile* . . .].[6] It has been assumed that this poem is "Almagro" or "Descubridores de Chile" [Chile's Founders] and that because of its theme it was later included in *Los conquistadores* instead of *Canto general de Chile*. I agree that the poem was written about this time because there is nothing else in the text that matches the negative description of the *conquistador* that characterizes this section and sets the tone for all of *Canto general*.[7] In fact, unlike most of the other poems, this one is extremely positive. Its tone and stance vis-à-vis the Spanish condition of the *conquistador* is at odds with the rest of the *canto*. Moreover, as María Magdalena Solá has noted, "[H]ay que señalar la ausencia del americano pre-colombino en este poema y en todo el *Canto general de Chile*."[8] In other words, there is nothing in *Canto general de Chile* that indicates the predominant symbols, images, and motifs characteristic of *Canto general*. The exceptions, of course, are those poems added later in Mexico, two of which are clearly marked as such by the poet. These are "Quiero volver al sur (1941)" [I Want to Return to the South (1941)] and "Melancolía cerca de Orizaba (1942)" [Melancholy Near Orizaba (1942)]. Others, like the fifth poem, a series of stanzas devoted to "Talabatería," "Alfarería," and "Telares," (inserted between "Oceano" and "Inundaciones" [Floods], followed by "Terremoto" [Earthquake]) seem to be out of place, at least thematically. After his stepmother's death in late August 1938, Neruda wrote "La copa de sangre" [The Chalice of Blood].[9] Again, the poem is full of nostalgia for his native land, in the same vein as most of the poems of *Canto general de Chile* (1941).

Canto general de Chile, published in fragments in 1941, at least six months after Neruda's arrival in Mexico in August 1940, evidences the poet's rediscovery of his roots. As has been argued, this identification with his native country denotes the first step toward a more ample commitment. Loyola has stated:

> De este redescubrimiento de Chile, avanza el poeta hacia el redescubrimiento de América Latina, que comienza de veras cuando Neruda se traslada a México en 1940. Porque durante los tres años anteriores, desde mediados de 1937 a mediados de 1940, la voluntad poética de Neruda aparece claramente galvanizada por el afán de redescubrir y revelar la propia patria.

[From this rediscovery of Chile, the poet moves on to a rediscovery of Latin America, which begins in earnest when Neruda takes up residence in Mexico in 1940. Because during the previous three years, from 1937 to mid-1940, Neruda's poetic will clearly seems to be galvanized by this desire to rediscover and reveal his own country.][10]

With the few exceptions just mentioned, *Canto general de Chile* is a section dominated by nostalgia for the past of his homeland. *Canto general de Chile* and the two poems mentioned above ("Descubridores de Chile" and "La copa de sangre") represent the real "núcleo embrionario del futuro *Canto general* de 1950" [embryonic nucleus of the future *Canto general* of 1950].[11]

Clearly, then, the notion that *Canto general* was conceived in Spain begins to lose solid ground and seems totally unfounded. The human and ideological solidarity that Neruda discovered, experienced, and shared in Spain during the Spanish Civil War should not be confused with his renewed commitment to a unified Latin America and the rediscovery of his American identity through the embracing of the indigenous past and the collectivity. Such a commitment entailed the rejection, thematically, of Western—specifically Spanish—culture, which the poet perceived as the source of all maladies. And as we have noted, Rodríguez Monegal points out that Neruda seems to have forgotten his earlier good will toward Spain when he wrote *Canto general,* as he identified with the indigenous people's anger against Spanish paternal imperialism.[12]

But while *Canto general de Chile* can be construed as a rediscovery of Chile, rather than a break with Europe or Spain, Neruda's ekphrastic experience in Mexico was decisive in the shift. Mexican mural art was the cornerstone for Neruda's new vision. The basic images that characterize *Canto general,* such as the mythical dimension of a pristine America and the pre-Colombian cultures, the historical perspective of the continent, and so on, are not present in Neruda's poetry before his stay in Mexico. Even before the publication of the complete volume of *Canto general* in 1950, the poems written and published in Mexico illustrate almost completely the whole array of images, tone, and themes of the book. *América no invoco tu nombre en vano,* for example, was published in Mexico in 1943 and later integrated into *Canto general* as the sixth canto. In my view, it represents Neruda's first attempt to create a unified vision of the continent in all its diversity and richness, but particularly the mythical dimension of the pre-Colombian world: the strong recurring metaphors of the "arcilla"

[clay] and "arena" [sand] of man, the dichotomy of the *libertador* and the *traidor,* and so on, are already present. Another series of poems, "El corazón magallánico" [The Magellan Heart], was published in *Cuadernos Americanos* in 1942. The central theme of these poems relates the violent confrontation between the Spanish invader and the noble American continent. "Dura elegía" [Harsh Elegy], dedicated to the deceased mother of Brazilian leader Luis Carlos Prestes, also appeared in Mexico.[13] Although included in the fifth and final section of *Tercera Residencia* (*Third Residence*) (1942), it foreshadows significant elements of *Canto general.* The basic equation mother = earth, for instance, with its representational codes, is developed here as well as the connection of the metaphor of mother earth with authentic American national heroes such as Cárdenas, O'Higgins, Miranda, and others. Also, the symbolic images of "árbol" [tree] and "raíces" [roots] associated consistently with the *libertador* in *Canto general* appear here for the first time and are used to describe the Brazilian leader:

Señora, hiciste grande, más grande a nuestra América.
Le diste un río puro de colosales aguas:
le diste un árbol alto de infinitas raíces:
un hijo tuyo digno de su patria profunda.

. . . .

Sombras de América, héroes coronados de furia,
de nieve, sangre, océano, tempestad y palomas,
aquí; venid al hueco que esta madre en tus ojos
guardaba para el claro capitán que esperamos:
héroes vivos y muertos de nuestra gran bandera:
O'Higgins, Juárez, Cárdenas, Recabarren, Bolívar,
Martí, Miranda, Artigas, Sucre, Hidalgo, Morelos,
Belgrano, San Martín, Lincoln, Carrera, todos
venid, llenad el hueco de vuestro gran hermano
y que Luis Carlos Prestes sienta en su celda el aire,
las alas torrenciales de los padres de América.

(1:307–8)

[Lady, you made our America great, even greater.
You gave her a pure river of colossal waters:
you gave her a lofty tree of infinite roots:
a son of yours worthy of his depthless country.

. . . .

Spirits of America, heroes crowned with fury,
with snow, blood, ocean, storm, and doves,
here: come to the hollow that this mother in her eyes

kept for the fair captain that we await:
heroes living and dead of our great banner:
O'Higgins, Juárez, Cárdenas, Recabarren, Bolívar,
Martí, Miranda, Artigas, Sucre, Hidalgo, Morelos,
Belgrano, San Martín, Lincoln, Carrera, all,
come, fill the hollow of your great brother
and let Luis Carlos Prestes feel in his cell the air,
the torrential wings of the fathers of America.][14]

The basic polarity or dichotomy between *libertadores* and traitors emerges here as well. During this period, Neruda's new poetic creed is gradually evolving into a more continental view. Mexico's Amerindian heritage, rich history, recent revolution, exotic cultures, and exuberant geography, along with its long tradition of popular art, all filtered and expressed through mural painting, had a remarkable impact on Neruda's personal artistic vision.

Neruda's many references to Mexico reflect not only his great admiration for the country, but also the promise of Mexico as a social paradigm for the rest of Latin America. In a lecture to a group of students at the National University, shortly after his arrival in Mexico, Neruda said:

México, en el Norte, se diferencia de todos, por su vida sacudida y dramática, por su grandioso escenario en que la libertad y la sangre, como grandes estatuas alegóricas, indican los caminos del mundo.

[Mexico, in the North, is different from all the rest, because of its turbulent and dramatic life, because of its grandiose scenario in which freedom and blood, like great allegorical statues, indicate the paths of the world.][15]

Later, in a speech delivered on his return to Chile from Mexico, he reiterates his impression of Mexico's optimism and vitality:

Y no hay en América, ni tal vez en el planeta, país de mayor profundidad humana que México y sus hombres. A través de sus desiertos luminosos, como a través de sus errores gigantescos, se ve la misma cadena de grandiosa generosidad, de vitalidad profunda, de inagotable historia, de germinación inacabable.

[And in America, perhaps even on the planet, there is no country with a more human profoundness than Mexico and her people. Through her luminous deserts, as through her gigantic errors, one can see the same chain of grandiose generosity, profound vitality, unfathomable history, of endless germination.][16]

It may help at this point to consider the historical circumstance of America during the Cold War. By 1940, the only Latin American country that had a "successful" revolution was Mexico. For Neruda, this milestone heralded the prospect of achieving a new communist society on the continent. Although Mexico's government was not socialist in the strictest sense, President Cárdenas' administration had undertaken many reforms that reflected a certain acceptance of some socialist principles. These reforms included nationalization of the oil industry that nearly provoked another war with the United States, a considerable effort to enforce the agrarian reform, and strong support of the Republican government in Spain during the Spanish Civil War. In Neruda's view, the Mexican Revolution and the Cárdenas government represented a victory against the increasing intervention of the United States in Mexico and the rest of the region. In 1943, Neruda praised Mexico's unceasing resistance to its giant neighbor to the north:

> A México correspondió ser el baluarte de nuestra sangre cuando la vida de América le exigió gallardamente imponer las materias fundamentales de la América nuestra, frente al gran país materialista del Norte. Y también a México correspondió levantar las primeras banderas cuando la libertad amenazada en todo nuestro planeta se veía defendida por la alta estirpe de los americanos del Norte.
>
> [It was Mexico's fate to be the bastion of our lifeblood when the survival of America demanded she gallantly reassert the fundamental tenets of our America, opposing the great materialist country to her north. And it was also Mexico which raised the first banners when the liberty of our continent was threatened, and was defended by our valiant northern brothers.][17]

Neruda's newfound optimism and faith in the future may be attributed in part to the vitality and dynamism found in Mexico. This explains his belated conversion to communism in 1945, which indicates that previous to his experience in Mexico the poet had not yet consolidated his political convictions. The years Neruda spent in Mexico were unparalleled in its history as an independent nation. Mexican intellectual, cultural, and artistic movements kept pace with the political and social life of the country, yet Mexican muralism was the artistic medium that best defined and promoted such a national development. The visual power and didactic message of the frescoes were a significant revelation for Neruda, providing him with crucial aesthetic solutions and a format for expressing his new poetic vision. Mural art supplied visual images, figures, themes, and artistic techniques that in fact gave rise to the narrative structure, the content and the tone of *Canto general*. It was the visual impulse, the ekphrastic desire, the archetropic force that moved the poet to transpose into linguistic verbal images the powerful visual text presented in the murals. *Canto general* is the ekphrastic representation of mural painting, sharing the same iconic codes.

In the final analysis, the first half of the book is shown to be an independent complete book, which in general terms follows Diego Rivera's monumental mural at the National Palace. *Canto general* shares with this mural its essential narrative framework, starting before the *Conquista* and ending in the present. Neruda's ekphrastic versions were rather notional than actual, as we have seen, allowing him to borrow liberally from Rivera. The Mexican artist's mark is apparent in certain features of Neruda's poetry: idealization of pre-Columbian civilizations, a panoramic and synchronic view of history, *Canto general's* dialectical and binary structure, the concept of the "poeta del pueblo" or the artist as artisan, and the insertion of the artist in his own art object as a means of communion with the masses, the propagandistic tone that at times seems to cloud the poet's perspective, the avant-garde style, and finally, the encyclopedic nature of the volume.

Neruda's interartistic relation with José Clemente Orozco's work is more conceptual than formal and is of vital importance in the overall configuration of the book. The ambivalent attitude sometimes found in the book, especially in *Alturas de Macchu Picchu*, is the poet's attempt to include the divergent side of reality, and such an approach in Mexican muralism corresponds mainly to Orozco's own artistic vision. As pointed out in chapter three, Orozco focuses not on an idealized vision of the indigenous past, but rather on the cruelty (including human sacrifice) present in the two realities of pre-Colombian cultures and *mutatis mutandis* in contemporary Mexican society. From Orozco, Neruda learned to include the somber and brutal aspects of the American people: the human sacrifice of the ancient cultures is the equivalent of the present oppression of the masses by their own people.

David Alfaro Siqueiros's impact on Neruda is both conceptual and stylistic. To Siquieros is due the mythical, at times expressionist element of *Canto general*. Siquieros's murals are anything but realistic. They resemble volcanic eruptions from the depths of the earth. Their expressionist elements, rich telluric imagery, and violent tone help to produce a mythic dimension in the art object.

History and fiction are combined and (con)fused on the same level to create historical figures of legendary proportions and hopeful outcomes. Neruda captured the tone, the powerful manner of expression, and applied the same techniques to describe history. He realized that the complex and intricate messages imbedded in mural art lacked the articulation that only language—his poetic language—could provide. Neruda understood that the movement's emphasis on official rhetoric and its strong reliance on the visual ran the risk of being labeled manichean or schematic. *Canto general,* then, is the textual ekphrastic equivalent of mural art, a kind of linguistic companion that explicates and elucidates the deeper human complexities inscribed in the murals.

Mexican mural art represents the "artistic vision"—the result of a perceptive and transformational process—that becomes the archetrope, the kinesthetic force, the impulse and motivation which compels and guides Neruda to the artistic image and, ultimately, to the art object or the poem itself.

Appendix: *A Note on Mexican History*

Nᴇxᴛ ᴛᴏ ᴛʜᴇ ɪɴᴅᴇᴘᴇɴᴅᴇɴᴄᴇ ᴍᴏᴠᴇᴍᴇɴᴛ (1810–21), ᴛʜᴇ ᴍᴇxɪᴄᴀɴ Revolution (1910–17) is the most important event in the nation's history. Revolutionary principles, however, had already been out-lined in the Constitution of 1857, promulgated by Benito Juárez during the Reform program. Above all, this constitution estab-lished the separation of church and state through nationalization of ecclesiastical property, elimination of religious orders, and pro-motion of secular education, marriage, and burial. Reformist goals, however, were undermined when the Catholic Church, re-actionaries, and the upper classes joined forces with the French to oppose Mexican liberals. Although defeated momentarily, the conservative forces, with the help of General Porfirio Díaz, man-aged to subvert the army and to overthrow the liberal president Sebastián Lerdo de Tejada, Benito Juárez's successor. Porfirio Díaz, the powerful dictator who ruled Mexico for more than thirty years, renewed friendly international relations, supported indus-try, and protected foreign investment in order to stimulate eco-nomic growth. With primarily United States capital, Mexico constructed a railway system. The country developed into a mod-ern nation.

Díaz's policy of "pan y palo" contributed to one of Mexico's most prosperous periods of industrial advancement. However, in sharp contrast to this wealth, Mexico also continued to experience the same endemic social and economic problems as it had in the past. The basic approach of Díaz's policy meant *pan* for the few and *palo* for the rest. The situation of the poor and the power of the Catholic Church remained unchanged during Díaz's dictator-ship. Moreover, Mexico endured a new hardship: exploitation by foreign investors whose profits did not remain nor were rein-vested in the country.

The Mexican Revolution was mainly triggered not by social or economic conditions but by political aspirations to restore democ-racy and electoral freedom, as set forth in the "Plan de San Luis Potosí," the first manifesto authored by Francisco I. Madero. Under this program, Madero was elected to govern the country on November 3, 1910. At this time the students of San Carlos Academy went on strike and took to the streets to protest out-of-date pedagogical methodology. Hence, Madero's accession to power coincides with the birth of a phenomenom later institution-alized by Ramón Martínez and known as *Aulas al aire libre*, in which students were directed to paint from their own surround-ings. (For more on the onset of the muralist movement in Mexico, see Jean Charlot, *The Mexican Mural Renaissance*.) The following year Emiliano Zapata proclaimed the "Plan de Ayala," reflecting a more populist ideology. Zapata himself was of humble birth and perhaps best represented the aspirations of exploited peas-ants and the revolutionary ideals of the masses. Madero's political and social programs, though generous and well-intentioned, were ineffective. His final contribution to the Revolution was his own death in 1913 at the hands of Victoriano Huerta, a defender of the reactionary groups. During Madero's presidency, Zapata and other revolutionaries such as Pascual Orozco and Pancho Villa, who did not trust Madero's ability to carry out the goals of the Revolution, had kept their armed forces. Huerta was forced to resign in July 1914, and Mexico City was successively occupied by Venustiano Carranza, Zapata, and Villa. The tragic and bloody era of the Mexican Revolution climaxed after Huerta's overthrow, when Carranza, Villa, and Zapata vied to consolidate power.

Unfortunately for Mexico, the more astute, reactionary, and un-scrupulous Venustiano Carranza, who had previously been asso-ciated with the Díaz dictatorship, triumphed. His regime (1915–20) was characterized by corruption and political intrigue. After drafting the Constitution of 1917, defeating Pancho Villa in Celaya, and murdering Zapata in 1919, Carranza's presidency ended the epic conflict and initiated a new civil phase of the Revolution. However, his government was short-lived. Some of his followers coveted power and rebelled against Carranza, who was assassinated in 1920. After the transition period of Adolfo de la Huerta's presidency, Alvaro Obregón was elected president (1920–24). Obregón, like his successor, Plutarco Elías Calles, man-aged to consolidate political power, a process that had begun with Carranza's draft of the new constitution, and the tradition of personal benefit for government service reached new heights.

However, these postrevolutionary regimes made positive con-tributions as well. For example, Obregón's administration calcu-latedly projected the image of a revolutionary regime. His Minister of Education José Vasconcelos, like his predecessor dur-ing the Díaz dictatorship, created an ambitious national cultural agenda. Vasconcelos's program oriented archeology toward the rediscovery of Mexico's pre-Columbian history, religion, literature, music, and popular arts. Calles, well known for his intolerance toward the clergy, helped institute anticlerical legislation, which brought an end to a long period of control by Catholic religious organizations. It must be added, however, that in so doing, he participated in flagrant abuses of personal rights and drove the nation into the Cristero civil wars.

Special emphasis should be placed on Lázaro Cárdenas (1934–40), a populist president who enjoyed the strong support of the masses and who to a certain extent fulfilled Zapata's promises to the Mexican peasantry. Under his leadership, agrarian reform, a program of land redistribution, was implemented in an expeditious manner. Cárdenas advanced the national agenda set by Obregón and Vasconcelos in the early 1920s and earned complete support from all sectors of Mexican society to nationalize the oil industry, which was then in the hands of American companies. Cárdenas, like Zapata before him, was the only leader willing to renounce personal gain and commit his life to the popular cause. Cárdenas was also responsible for creating a national sense of respect for life. His administration was a model of tolerance toward the conflicting forces in the country, by creating an atmosphere in which all political groups could express their views without fear of retaliation by the government in power. During his tenure, Mexico became a mecca for exiles from Spain and the Soviet Union, and for many other foreign refugees. Spanish intellectuals fleeing Franco's nationalist forces found safe haven in Mexico; Soviet dissidents, like Trotsky, were welcomed. Politics became an accepted part of intellectual discussions and no longer implied convulsive personal strife. Such was the political climate before Neruda arrived in Mexico in 1940, at the end of Cárdenas's term.

The Mexican Revolution is one of the most significant socioeconomic events of twentieth-century Latin America. It was an authentic Mexican crusade, without foreign influence of any sort. Its origins, ideology, and results are undeniably Mexican in character. Neither socialist, Marxist, nor communist ideologies have unduly affected the movement's principles or outcome. Even land redistribution, often associated with Russian communism, is, in its ideological nature, purely Mexican, derived from the pseudo-communism of ancient Amerindian cultures. This notion is based on the principle that land belongs to those who cultivate it, rather than on the Soviet view of collective ownership. Other aspects, such as public health care and education and the constitutional amendment declaring that natural resources (minerals, oil, and so on) belonged to the nation, were not drawn from the Soviet model, but were rather a direct outgrowth of the Revolution.

The Mexican Revolution was more than an ideological phenomenon. It was a genuine mass movement in protest of the oppression of the Church, landowners, entrepreneurs, bankers, and foreign companies. Perhaps for this reason, it was possible to create a strong sense of national identity and pride in the ancient history of Mexico.

Notes

Introduction: Neruda in Mexico (1940–1943)

1. Donald L. Shaw, "Interpretations of *Alturas de Macchu Picchu*," *Revista Interamericana de Bibliografía* 38 (1988): 194; Hernán Loyola, "Neruda y América Latina," *Cuadernos Americanos* 218, no. 3 (1978): 176.

2. Frank Riess, *The Word and the Stone: Language and Imagery in Neruda's "Canto general"* (London: Oxford University Press, 1972), xvi.

3. Hernán Uribe, *Fulgor y muerte de Pablo Neruda* (México: El Caballito, 1983), 40.

4. Maurice Halperin, "Pablo Neruda in Mexico," *Books Abroad* 15, no. 2 (1941): 164–68; Wilberto Cantón, "Pablo Neruda en México," in *Posiciones* (Mexico: Imprenta Universitaria, 1950); *Neruda y México,* ed. Manuel Lerin (Mexico: B. Costa-Amic, 1973), (a collection of poems related to Mexico and selected by Lerin); Pablo Neruda, *México florido y espinudo,* with an introduction by Francisco Valero (Mexico: Comisión Nacional Editorial, 1976); Uribe, *Fulgor.*

5. Emir Rodríguez Monegal, *Neruda: el viajero inmóvil,* 2d ed. (Caracas: Monte Avila Editores, 1977), 124–26.

6. Pablo Neruda, *Confieso que he vivido,* 7th ed. (Barcelona: Seix Barral, 1979), 231. Translation from Pablo Neruda, *Memoirs,* trans. Hardie St. Martin (New York: Farrar, Straus & Giroux, 1977), 164.

7. Neruda, *Confieso,* 213; *Memoirs,* 150.

8. Neruda, *Confieso,* 216; *Memoirs,* 152.

9. Neruda, *Confieso,* 216; *Memoirs,* 153.

10. Pablo Neruda, "Algo sobre mi poesía y mi vida," *Aurora* 1 (1954), quoted in Margarita Aguirre, *Genio y figura de Pablo Neruda* (Buenos Aires: Editorial Universitaria, 1969), 146. My translation. Translations from *Canto general* are from Pablo Neruda, *Canto general,* trans. Jack Schmitt, intro. Roberto González Echevarría (Berkeley: University of California Press, 1991). Unless indicated, all other translations are mine.

11. Pablo Neruda, *Para nacer he nacido* (Barcelona: Seix Barral, 1978), 272. Translation from Pablo Neruda, *Passions and Impressions,* ed. Matilde Neruda and Miguel Otero Silva, trans. Margaret Sayers Peden (New York: Farrar, Straus & Giroux, 1983), 250.

12. Wilberto Cantón, *Posiciones* (Mexico: Imprenta Universitaria, 1950), 92.

13. Pablo Neruda, *Confieso,* 216; *Memoirs,* 153.

14. Alfredo Cardona Peña, "Pablo Neruda: Breve historia de sus libros," *Cuadernos Americanos* 9, July–December (1950): 257–89. Later, others would echo the same idea to the point of creating a commonplace.

15. Neruda had also turned down an invitation by Octavio Paz to participate in the 1941 edition of *Laurel, Antología de poesía moderna en lengua española,* which created an even wider gap between them. For Paz's version of this debate or its

causes, see his epilogue to the second edition of this anthology: *Laurel, Antología de la poesía moderna en lengua española* (Mexico: Trillas, 1986).

16. The relationship with José Revueltas had very special meaning for Neruda. Revueltas published a "réplica" (response) to Juan Ramón Jiménez's attacks on Neruda's new indigenist approach. The reader interested in this exchange of attacks can see Juan Ramón Jiménez, "Carta a Pablo Neruda," *Repertorio Americano* 23 (17 January 1942). The same year, Revueltas writes in defense of the Chilean poet, "América sombría" [Dark America], first in *El Popular,* 13 March 1942, and soon after in the same *Repertorio Americano* 23 (9 May 1942). Then Jiménez replies with "¿América sombría?," *Repertorio Americano* 24 (14 August 1943).

17. Octavio Paz, "Respuesta a un Cónsul," *Letras de México,* 15 August 1943, 95.

18. Moreover, in 1963 in Chile, Neruda referred to Ramón López Velarde as the crucial figure who ended *modernismo:* "en la gran triología del modernismo es Ramón López Velarde el maestro final, el que pone el punto sin coma" [in the great trilogy of *modernismo* Ramón López Velarde is the ultimate master, the one who puts the final period]. See Pablo Neruda, Gustavo Ortiz Hernán, Guillermo Atías, *Presencia de Ramón López Velarde en Chile* (Santiago: Fondo del Plan Chileno-Mexicano de Cooperación Fraternal, 1963), 27.

19. Saúl Yurkiévich points to this in his "Mito e historia: dos generadores del *Canto general,*" in *Pablo Neruda,* ed. Emir Rodríguez Monegal and Enrico Mario Santí (Madrid: Taurus, 1980), 198.

20. Ulrich Weisstein, "Literature and the Visual Arts, in *Interrelations of Literature,* ed. Jean-Pierre Barricelli and Joseph Gibaldi (New York: The Modern Language Association of America, 1982), 267. Seznec's comments are from "Art and Literature: A Plea for Humility," *New Literary History* 3 (1972): 569–74.

21. Weisstein, "Literature," 260–61. Wendy Steiner, in her introduction to her special volume of *Poetics Today,* refers to the "imprecision of the notion of *zeitgeist,*" and while acknowledging the problems of periodization, she, like Weisstein, recognizes that our "utter dependence on these notions is equally clear." See "Introduction," *Poetics Today* 10, no. 1 (Spring 1989): 2.

22. Yurkiévich, for example, believes that *Canto general* "carece de articulación rigurosa, de ordenamiento simétrico razonadamente articulado (cronológico, anecdótico o temático) . . . . Responde a una estructura abierta, multiforme, politonal, proclive a las mezclas, a las superposiciones y reiteraciones" [lacks rigorous articulation and a reasonably articulated, chronological, anecdoctic or thematic symmetrical order. . . . It has an open, multiform, politonal structure, inclined toward mixtures, superimpositions and reiterations]. See Yurkiévich, "Mito e historia," 201.

23. Enrico Mario Santí's introduction to his edition of *Canto general* (Madrid: Cátedra, 1990), 57.

24. Enrico M. Santí's introduction to *Canto general,* 84–87.

25. Among the recent appearances are: Amy Golahny ed., *The Eye of the Poet. Studies in the Reciprocity of the Visual and Literary Arts from the Renaissance to the Present* (Lewisburg: Bucknell University Press; London: Associated University Presses, 1996); Murray Krieger, *Ekphrasis. The Illusion of the Natural Sign* (Baltimore: The Johns Hopkins University Press, 1992); Gandelman, Claude, *Reading Pictures, Viewing Texts* (Bloomington and Indianapolis: Indiana University Press, 1991); Norman Bryson, Michael Ann Holy, and Keith Moxey, eds.,

Visual Theory: Painting and Interpretation (Cambridge: Polity, 1991); W. J. T. Mitchell, *Picture Theory* (Chicago: The University of Chicago Press, 1994).

26. *Poetics Today* 10, no. 1 (Spring 1989), special volume ed. by Wendy Steiner.

27. Abigail Rischin, "Beside the Reclining Statue: Ekphrasis, Narrative, and Desire in *Middlemarch*," *PMLA* 111, no. 5 (October 1996): 1121–32.

28. Rosemary Geisdorfer Feal and Carlos Feal, *Painting on the Page. Interartistic Approaches to Modern Hispanic Texts* (Albany: State University Press of New York, 1995).

29. Steiner, "Introduction," *Poetics Today*, 3.

Chapter 1. Image and Text

1. Cited in Edward Allen McCormick, introduction to *Laocoön, An Essay on the Limits of Painting and Poetry*, by Gotthold Ephraim Lessing, trans., intro., and notes by Edward Allen McCormick (1766; reprint, Baltimore and London: The Johns Hopkins University Press, 1984), xii.

2. Henryk Markiewicz, "Ut Pictura Poesis . . . A History of the Topos and the Problem," *New Literary History* 18, no. 3 (Spring 1987): 535. For a comprehensive history of the topos see this article and McCormick. Markiewicz cites the passage from Horace's *Ars Poetica* as it appears in *Classical Literary Criticism: Aristotle, Horace, Longinus*, tran. and ed. T. S. Dorsch (Harmondsworth, 1977): "A poem is like painting: the closer you stand to this one the more it will impress you, whereas you have to stand a good distance from that one; this one demands a rather dark corner, but that one needs to be seen in full light, and will stand up to the keen-eyed scrutiny of the art-critic; this one only pleased you the first time you saw it, but that one will go on giving pleasure however often it is looked at" (535).

3. Lessing, *Laocoön*, 5.

4. McCormick, intro., *Laocoön*, xxv.

5. Lessing, *Laocoön*, 78.

6. Joseph Frank, "Spatial Form: Thirty Years After," in *Spatial Form in Narrative* (Ithaca: Cornell University Press, 1981), 204.

7. Neruda maintained a close and intimate relationship with Eliot in particular, and was well aware of Eliot's interest in painting. In his memoirs, Neruda said of the influential Eliot:

> Todos conocen a Eliot . . . Antes de ser pintor, de dirigir teatros, de escribir luminosas críticas, leía mis versos . . . Yo me sentía halagado . . . Nadie los comprendía mejor . . . Hasta que un día comenzó a leerme los suyos y yo, egoísticamente, corrí protestando: "No me los lea, no me los lea" . . . Me encerré en el baño, pero Eliot,a través de la puerta me los leía . . . Me sentí triste . . . El poeta Frazer, de Escocia, estaba presente . . . Me increpó: "¿Por qué tratas así a Eliot?" . . . Le respondí: "No quiero perder mi lector. Lo he cultivado. Ha conocido hasta las arrugas de me poesía . . . Tiene tanto talento . . . Puede hacer cuadros . . . Puede escribir ensayos . . . Pero quiero guardar este lector, conservarlo, regarlo como planta exótica . . . Tú me comprendes, Frazer" [Everybody knows Eliot . . . Before becoming an illustrator and a playwright, and writing brilliant criticism, he used to read my poems . . . I was flattered . . . No one understood them better . . . Then one day he started to read me his own, and I ran off selfishly, protesting: "Don't read them to me, don't read them to me" . . . I locked myself in the bathroom, but Eliot read them to me through the shut door . . . I was depressed . . . Fraser, the Scottish poet, was there . . . He blasted me: "Why do you treat Eliot like that?" . . . I replied: "I don't want to lose my reader. I have cultivated

him carefully. He has become familiar even with the wrinkles in my poetry . . . Eliot has so much talent . . . He can draw . . . He writes essays . . . But I want to keep this reader, to preserve him, to water him like an exotic plant . . . You understand me, Fraser"] (Neruda, *Confieso*, 359; *Memoirs*, 259–60). For more on Neruda's association with Ezra Pound, see José Miguel Ibáñez Langlois's book, *Rilke, Pound, Neruda: Tres claves de la poesía contemporánea* (Madrid: Rialpe, 1978).

8. Frank, "Spatial Form in Modern Literature," in *The Widening Gyre. Crisis and Mastery in Modern Literature* (New Brunswick: Rutgers University Press, 1963), 10.

9. Walter Sutton, "The Literary Image and the Reader: A Consideration of the Theory of Spatial Form," *Journal of Aesthetics and Art Criticism*, 16 (1957): 112–23. Cited in Frank, "Spatial Form: Thirty Years After," 207.

10. Frank, "Spatial Form: Thirty Years," 207. We cannot avoid thinking here of Lessing's "moment of illusion" in which "we [the reader] should cease to be conscious of the means which the poet uses for this purpose, that is, his work." The poet thus "presents us with images so vivid, that we fancy we have the things themselves before us" (Lessing, *Laocoön*, 85).

11. Frank, "Spatial Form: Thirty Years After," 207.

12. Ibid., 206–7.

13. Ibid., 209.

14. Ibid., 210.

15. Segei Eisenstein, *Film Form and Film Sense,* ed. and trans. Jay Leyda (New York: Meridian Books, 1957), 307. Quoted in Frank, "Spatial Form: Thirty Years After," 210.

16. W. J. T. Mitchell, *Iconology. Image, Text, Ideology* (Chicago and London: The University of Chicago Press, 1986), 98.

17. Ibid.

18. W. J. T. Mitchell, *The Language of Images* (Chicago: The University of Chicago Press, 1980), 291.

19. I use here Ellen Frothingham's translation of Lessing's *Laocoön,* since her translation seems more appropriate. See Lessing, *Laocoön*, tran. Ellen Frothingham (Boston: Little, Brown, 1898), 114. For the reader's benefit, I also cite McCormick's translation: "Homer does not paint the shield as finished and complete, but as a shield that is being made. Thus, here too he has made use of that admirable artistic device: transforming what is coexistent in his subject into what is consecutive, and thereby making the living picture of an action out of the tedious painting of an object. We do not see the shield, but the divine master as he is making it" (Lessing, *Laocoön*, tran. McCormick, 95).

20. Lessing, *Laocoön*, 78.

21. Mitchell, *Iconology*, 99.

22. Wendy Steiner, *The Colors of Rhetoric* (Chicago and London: The Chicago University Press, 1982), 46.

23. Lessing, *Laocoön*, 85.

24. Ibid.

25. Ibid., 78.

26. Ibid.

27. Mitchell, *Iconology*, 101.

28. Ibid., 101–2.

29. Ibid., 102.

30. Ibid.

31. Ibid., 112.

32. Ibid., 105.

33. Grant F. Scott, "The Rhetoric of Dilation: Ekphrasis and Ideology," *Word and Image* 7, no. 4 (October–December 1991): 301–10.

34. Jay asserts that "our postmodern society is essentially oculocentrist"—that is, "it is the sense of sight and the visual that are overduly privileged." See Gandelman, *Reading Pictures*, 151.

35. Mitchell, *Picture Theory*, 95–96. A number of studies have been published on the psychology of visual response to texts/reading. See Mitchell, *Picture Theory*, 96 n.23 and María Carmen Africa Vidal Claramonte, *Arte y literatura* (Madrid: Palas Atanea, 1992), 22 n.11.

36. Mitchell, *Picture Theory*, 5.

37. Steiner, *Colors*, 2.

38. Golahny, *The Eye of the Poet*, 12.

39. George Saintsbury, *A History of Criticism and Literary Taste in Europe*, vol. 1 (London, 1992), 491. Quoted in Scott, "The Rhetoric," 301.

40. Krieger, *Ekphrasis*, 6.

41. Jean H. Hagstrum, *The Sister Arts. The Tradition of Literary Pictorialism and English Poetry from Dryden to Gray* (Chicago: The University of Chicago Press, 1958), 18 n.34.

42. Hagstrum, *Sister Arts*, 18–19.

43. Steiner, *Rhetoric*, 41.

44. Paraphrased by Kreiger, *Ekphrasis*, 6.

45. Mitchell, alluding to this tendency by semioticians, notes, "Signs are everywhere; there is nothing that is not potentially or actually a sign." See *Iconology*, 62.

46. Nelson Goodman, *Languages of Art. An Approach to a Theory of Symbols* (Indianapolis, New York, Kansas City: Bobbs-Merrill, 1968).

47. See Mitchell, *Iconology*, 55.

48. Krieger, *Ekphrasis*, 4.

49. "In other words, instead of asking all the arts—even the verbal—to seek to become natural signs, we are told to move beyond the naiveté of such a semiotic, to accept the arbitrary and conventional character of *all* aesthetic signs—even the visual—and make the most of it, recognizing that pictures, no less than verbal structures, are human inventions and, as such, are products of an artificial making process." Krieger, *Ekphrasis*, 4.

50. Ibid., 11.

51. Ibid., 16.

52. Ibid., 9.

53. Ibid., 23.

54. Ibid., 14.

55. Ibid., 15.

56. Ibid.

57. Ibid., 16.

58. Cited by Golahny, *The Eye*, 13.

59. John Hollander, who also discusses this subject, speaks of a *"notional* ekphrasis, in which the descriptive passage applies to an image whose existence depends upon the text, and of *actual* ekphrasis, in which the image is known, and exists independently of the text." See Hollander, "The Poetics of Ekphrasis," *Word and Image* 4 (1988): 109–19. Quoted in Golhany, *The Eye*, 13.

60. Krieger, *Ekphrasis*, 18–19.

61. Ibid., 19.

62. Ibid., 21.

63. Ibid., 19.

64. Here I am adopting the concept of "suture" as it is used in film theory, and as W. J. T. Mitchell applies it to his study of Blake's illuminated books. That is, "suture" is "that which 'fills in' the gaps between images and shots by constructing a subjective sense of continuity and absent positionality." See Mitchell, *Picture*, 91–92, n.15.

65. Concrete poetry or poems-as-figures are the literal expression of this artistic desire.

66. Krieger, *Ekphrasis*, 263. Clearly, this notion of the circular is very similar to Joseph Frank's vision of the synchronic that calls for the ability of a poem to undermine the temporality of language.

67. Ibid., 265.

68. Ibid., 266.

69. Ibid., 265–66.

70. Sigurd Burkhardt, "The Poet as Fool and Priest," *ELH* 23 (December 1956): 280. Quoted in Krieger, *Ekphrasis*, 266.

71. Mitchell, *Picture*, 154.

72. Ibid., 112.

73. Ibid., 152.

74. Ibid., 154.

75. Ibid., 156.

76. Ibid., 157.

77. Ibid.

78. Ibid., 161.

79. Ibid., 159.

80. Ibid., 162.

81. Ibid., 163.

82. Franklin Rogers, *Painting and Poetry: Form, Metaphor, and the Language of Literature* (Lewisburg, PA: Bucknell University Press; London: Associated University Presses, 1985), 71.

83. Ibid., 74.

84. Ibid., 122.

85. Ibid., 107.

86. Ibid., 121.

87. Max Black, *Models and Metaphors: Studies in Language and Philosophy* (Ithaca: Cornell University Press, 1962), 41. Quoted in Rogers, 117.

88. Rogers, 116.

89. Ibid., 111.

90. Mitchell, *Picture*, 164.

91. Ibid.

92. Rudolf Arnheim, "The Images of Pictures and Words, *Word and Image* 2, no. 4 (1986): 310.

93. Steiner, *Colors*, 61.

94. Ibid.

95. Ibid., 64. Steiner quotes from Luce Marinetti Barbi, "Marinetti and Futurism," *Structuralist* 12 (1972–73): 52.

96. René Wellek, "The Parallelism between Literature and the Arts," in René Wellek and Austin Warren, *Theory of Literature* (New York: Harcourt, 1962), 119. Quoted in Ulrich Weisstein, "Literature and the Visual Arts," in *Interrelations of*

Literature, ed. Jean-Pierre Barricelli and Joseph Gibaldi (New York: The Modern Language Association of America, 1982), 259.

97. Weisstein, "Literature," 259.

98. Ibid., 260.

99. Wellek, "The Parallelism," 122.

100. Wendy Steiner, "Introduction," *Poetics Today,* 2.

Chapter 2: Neruda and the Mural Phenomenon

1. Saúl Yurkiévich, "Mito e historia," 198.

2. Several studies have been written on Alberti's poetry and its correspondence to his own plastic work, as well as to that of other painters. For a comprehensive study of the dual trajectory of Rafael Alberti as a poet and as a painter, see Luis Lorenzo-Rivero, "Rafael Alberti: pintura, poesía y política," *Letras de Deusto* 15, no. 31–33 (1983): 5–25.

3. We have mentioned previously the ample knowledge and friendship that Neruda established with such Modernist writers as T. S. Eliot and Ezra Pound. See chapter 1, note 7.

4. Rene de Costa, *Vicente Huidobro* (Oxford: Oxford University Press, 1984).

5. Octavio Paz, "Poesía, pintura, música, etcétera. Conversación con Manuel Ulacia." *Vuelta* 155 (October 1989): 17.

6. According to Jean Franco, it was José Carlos Mariátegui who "realized more clearly than any other the connection between Indianism and the European fashion for exotic art". Jean Franco, *The Modern Culture of Latin America: Society and the Artist* (London: Pall Mall Press, 1967), 106.

7. Some of his most representative paintings of this period are: *Carmélina,* 1903, Museum of Fine Arts, Boston; *L'Algérienne,* 1909, Musée National d'Art Moderne, Paris; and all those paintings dealing with the African and Asian themes such as *Les Marocains,* 1916, Museum of Modern Art, New York. The reader interested in this period of Matisse work may consult *Homage to Henri Matisse,* ed. by Lazzaro [?] (New York: Tudor Publishing Co., 1970).

8. Hoog, Michael. *Paul Gauguin. Life and Work* (New York: Rizzoli International Publications, 1987), 256. Gauguin's paintings mentioned above also belong to this edition.

9. Octavio Paz has already pointed out Rivera's connection to the French and Italian schools, and has also described this artist as "el pintor que prologó la visión de Gauguin—árboles, hojas, agua, flores, cuerpos, frutos—y la hizo reflorecer" [the painter who prefaced Gauguin's vision—trees, leaves, water, flowers, bodies, fruits—and made it flourish]. See Octavio Paz, *Los privilegios de la vista. Arte de México,* México en la obra de Octavio Paz, vol. 3 (Mexico City: Fondo de Cultura Económica, 1987), 26–27.

10. Quoted in Hoog, *Paul Gauguin,* 257.

11. Paz, *Privilegios,* 45.

12. Ibid., 46.

13. Quoted in Jean Charlot, *The Mexican Mural Renaissance. 1920–1925* (New Haven and London: Yale University Press, 1963), 73.

14. Quoted in Charlot, *The Mexican Mural Renaissance,* 10–11.

15. Roland Barthes, *Elements of Semiology,* trans. Annette Lavers and Colin Smith (New York: Hill & Wang, 1968; reprint 1977), 10–11. Quoted in Mitchell, *Iconology,* 56.

16. Sigmund Freud, *The Interpretation of Dreams* (New York: Avon Books, 1965), 347. Quoted in Mitchell, *Iconology*, 45. Interestingly, Mitchell uses as one of his examples, these comments from Freud: "The plastic arts of painting and sculpture labour, indeed, under a similar limitation as compared with poetry, which can make use of speech. . . . Before painting became acquainted with the laws of expression by which it is governed, it made attempts to get over this handicap. In ancient paintings small labels were hung from the mouths of the persons represented, containing in written characters the speeches which the artist despaired of representing pictorially" (Freud, *Interpretation*, 347).

17. Sergio Montecino, "Pintura y poesía (Neruda y los pintores)," *Atenea* 450 (1984): 122.

18. Mitchell, *Picture*, 164. See the complete discussion on ekphrasis in chapter 2.

19. Angel Valbuena Briones, *Literatura Hispanoamericana*, 4th ed. (Barcelona: Gustavo Gili, 1969), 5:475.

20. Ibid., 475.

21. Peña, "Pablo Neruda," 286.

22. Luis Cardoza y Aragón, *El Río: Novelas de caballería* (México: FCE, 1986), 691.

23. Giuseppe Bellini, intro. and comp., *Pablo Neruda*, by Pablo Neruda (Milan: Nuova Accademia Editrice, 1960), 34.

24. Roberto Fernández Retamar, intro. and comp., *Poesías*, by Pablo Neruda (La Habana: Casa de las Américas, 1972), xiii.

25. Juan Villegas, *Estructuras míticas y arquetipos en el "Canto general" de Neruda* (Barcelona: Planeta, 1976), 49.

26. Villegas, *Estructuras*, 49.

27. Referring to these years and to Mistral's Mexican experience, Jaime Concha points out:

A través del muralismo mexicano; en su mirada atenta a las formas plásticas de la cerámica y del arte popular; . . . la Mistral descubrirá caminos de expresividad que le señalan un rumbo: poner su poesía en sintonía con la intensidad de la lírica azteca, con la potencia enigmática de las estelas mayas, con el puro brotar sentimental de las canciones quechuas.

[Through Mexican muralism—in its attentive focus on the plastic forms of ceramics and popular art—Mistral was to discover paths of expression that gave her a direction: to place her poetry in harmony with the intensity of the Aztec lyricism, with the enigmatic power of the Mayan steles, with the pure sentimental outpouring of the Quechua songs.]

See *Gabriela Mistral* (Barcelona: Júcar, 1987), 37.

28. Manuel Pedro González, *Trayectoria de la Novela en México* (México: Botas, 1951), 99. As we said earlier, mural art was the favored form of artistic expression which condensed the images, figures, and topoi of the Mexican Revolution, becoming literally the driving force for all other artistic media. See the comments in the following pages by Pedro González and Desmond Rochfort on the artistic impact of the movement.

29. Enrique Pupo-Walker has examined the works of Rulfo and Ferretis in this light, and has also compared Mariano Azuela's novel, *Los de abajo* with the murals of Orozco. The references are as follow: "*Los de abajo* y la pintura de Orozco: un caso de correspondencias estéticas," *Cuadernos Americanos* 44, no. 5

(1967): 237–54; "Personajes y ambiente en *Pedro Páramo*," *Cuadernos Americanos* 47 (1969): 194–204; "La transposición de valores pictóricos en la narrativa de Ferretis y Rulfo," *Nueva Narrativa Hispanoamericana* 1, no. 1 (1971): 95–103.

30. González, *Trayectoria*, 100.

31. Ibid., 100–101.

32. Desmond Rochfort, *The Murals of Diego Rivera* (London: Journeyman, 1987), 95.

33. In the case of *Los de abajo* (1915) by Mariano Azuela, and other early novels, obviously the line of influence could be reversed. See Enrique Pupo Walker, "*Los de abajo* y la pintura de Orozco: un caso de correspondencias estéticas," *Cuadernos Americanos* 44, no. 5 (1967): 237–54. Thus, there is a thematic continuity associated with history, in which muralism adopts the historical vision and the narrative elements of the novel, including its human and physical environment. This is why we talk about the narrative structure of muralism, of whose discourse or code *Canto general* becomes a part.

34. Quoted in Cardoza y Aragón, *El Río*, 689.

35. In a conversation with Manuel Ulacia published in *Vuelta* in 1989, Octavio Paz said:

"En México, cuando yo era muchacho, se hablaba muchísimo de la pintura mural mexicana. Se decía que México era un país de pintores, no de poetas ni escritores. Ahora vemos que eso nunca fue cierto y hoy menos que nunca. En mi juventud tuve que enfrentarme a la realidad y al mito de la pintura mural mexicana. Realidad poderosa y mito no menos poderoso. . . . Preferí la mirada crítica a la mirada beata: el movimiento había degenerado en academia estética y en dogma político. Me atreví a decirlo y me excomulgaron."

[In Mexico, when I was a child, Mexican mural painting was discussed very often. It was said that Mexico was a country of painters, not poets or writers. Now we see that this was never true, and less so now than ever. In my youth I had to confront the reality and the myth of Mexican mural painting. A powerful reality and a no less powerful myth. . . . I preferred a critical eye to a sympathetic one: the movement had degenerated into academic aesthetics and political dogma. I dared to say so, and was excommunicated for it.]

See Octavio Paz, "Poesía," 15.

36. González, *Trayectoria*, 93–94.

37. Luis Cardoza y Aragón, *Pintura contempóranea de México*, 2d ed. (Mexico: Era, 1988), 98–99.

38. For an overview of the artistic production of this period, see Dawn Ades. *Art in Latin America. The Modern Era, 1820–1980* (New Haven: Yale University Press, 1989), 27–36, 101.

39. Ibid., 32.

40. Cardoza y Aragón, *Pintura*, 99.

41. Rochfort, *The Murals of Diego Rivera*, 15.

42. Quoted by Charlot, *The Mexican Mural Renaissance*, 61.

43. Ibid., 71.

44. Leonard Folgarait, *So Far From Heaven: David Alfaro Siqueiros' "The March of Humanity" and Mexican Revolutionary Politics* (Cambridge: Cambridge University Press, 1987), 1.

45. Charlot, *The Mexican Mural Renaissance*, 47.

46. Lessing, *Laocoön*, 95.

47. Folgarait, *So Far From Heaven*, 1. As previously stated, at least Rivera and Siqueiros were not quite departing from the avant-garde, but furthering a very avant-garde aesthetic trend. Therefore, what seems to Folgarait to be a return to a "pre-modernist aesthetic" is in fact part of the avant-garde in Europe that coincides with modernism in the United States.

48. Neruda, *Confieso*, 216–17; *Memoirs*, 153.

49. Neruda, *Confieso*, 219; *Memoirs*, 155.

50. Folgarait, *So Far From Heaven*, 1. We have already expressed disagreement with the concept of a "realistic narrative style."

51. Cited by Pupo-Walker, "Los de abajo," 241.

52. David Elliott, ed., *¡Orozco! 1883–1949. An Exhibition Organized by the Ministry of Foreign Affairs and the Institute of Fine Arts, Mexico* (Oxford: Museum of Modern Art Oxford, 1980), 116.

53. Ibid.

54. Ibid.

55. Ibid.

56. See the discussion in the introduction regarding Santí's idea that the book can be divided in two parts, each one with a common center (section VIII). Later on, he will acknowledge that such lineal design of the first unit is only apparent. See Santí, ed., *Canto* 57–58, 81.

57. Nathaniel Tarn, "Neruda and the Indigenous Culture," *Sulfur* 15 (1986): 170.

58. It has already been pointed out that the perspective of the speaker is contemporary. Thus, the linearity of the first text, as in the case of mural painting, is only apparent.

59. Fernando Alegría, ed., *Canto general* 2d ed. (Caracas: Biblioteca Ayacucho, 1981), xvii.

60. Santí, *Canto*, 57.

61. Such discontinuity has been also underlined by Villegas. The critic affirms: "Pese a que se dan algunos de los motivos característicos de la dualidad central que hemos descrito en todo el *Canto*, éstos no conforman lo esencial de esta sección. Lo que puede deberse a que lo compuso aisladamente, mucho antes de haber escrito la totalidad del *Canto*" [In spite of the fact that one can find some of the characteristic motifs of the central duality that we have described in the entire *Canto*, these are not the essential basis of this section. This could be explained by the fact that he composed it on isolated occasions, much earlier than the writing of the whole *Canto*]. Villegas, *Estructuras*, 62.

62. "The common characteristic of these later murals," says Rochfort, "is his concentration on pre-Colombian life and civilisations." Rochfort, *The Murals of Diego Rivera*, 81.

Chapter 3: The Indigenous Theme and the Search for Roots

1. James E. Miller, *The American Quest for a Supreme Fiction* (Chicago: University of Chicago Press, 1979).

2. Frank, "Spatial Form: Thirty Years After," 207.

3. Ibid., 210.

4. I have previously mentioned Neruda's relationship with these writers. Modernism, as the term is used in this context, differs from the Latin American

modernismo. Modernism in the United States corresponds more to the *vanguard-ista* movements in Spain and Latin America and, in general, to the European avant-garde. It is for this reason that I emphasized earlier that Neruda, Rivera, and Siqueiros are very much part of a continuation of these movements.

5. Villegas, *Estructuras,* 51.

6. Rochfort, *The Murals of Diego Rivera,* 21.

7. Charlot relates the Mexican philosopher's disappointment: "The Byzantine hue of the mural in the making had left Vasconcelos unconvinced. Rivera himself was beginning to look his own country in the face and to find her beautiful, and his Italian memories gradually faded." Charlot, *The Mexican Mural Renaissance,* 143.

8. Diego Rivera, *Arte y política,* ed. Raquel Tibol (Mexico: Grijalbo, 1979), 49.

9. Ibid., 49–50.

10. Pablo Neruda, *Obras completas,* 4th ed., vol. 1 (Buenos Aires: Losada, 1973), 315. Further references to Neruda's poetry are taken from this edition and are indicated in parentheses by volume and page number. The English version is from Jack Schmitt's translation of *Canto general,* 13. Further references to this translation are indicated by page number in parentheses.

11. Nelly E. Santos, "Génesis de una concepción del compromiso poético en el *Canto general,*" *Cuadernos Americanos* 4–6 (1983): 234.

12. Frank, "Spatial Form: Thirty Years After," 210.

13. Ibid.

14. Max Black, *Models and Metaphors,* 41. Quoted in Rogers, *Painting and Poetry,* 117.

15. Rogers, *Painting and Poetry,* 107.

16. In his eagerness to capture, record, and document every single specimen of American flora and fauna, Neruda undertakes a naturalist project similar to Carolus Linnaeus's classification of plants and animals in the eighteenth century. Like Linnaeus, the Chilean attempts to register not only every plant, bird, or animal in his exploration of the continent, but also rivers, mountains, minerals, and even civilizations. Luis Enrique Délano, who was Neruda's personal secretary before and during his stay in Mexico, underlines the impact of the Mexican years: "todo el mundo sabe que, aparte de poeta, Pablo Neruda fue un excelente naturalista y estamos ciertos de que comenzó a tocar ese *violon d'Ingres,* a desempeñar esa "segunda profesión," en México. . . . En los años que siguen, en realidad, escribe sobre árboles, ríos, animales . . . su afición por las conchas marinas, de las que llegó a tener con el tiempo una extraordinaria colección . . . nació en México. [Everyone knew that, besides being a poet, Pablo Neruda was an excellent naturalist and we are certain that he began to play that *violon d'Ingres,* to practice that "second profession," in Mexico. . . . In the subsequent years, as a matter of fact, he wrote about trees, rivers, animals . . . his passion for seashells, of which he came to have an extraordinary collection . . . was born in Mexico.] See Luis Enrique Délano, "La raíz volcánica de la poesía de Pablo Neruda," *Cuadernos Americanos* 4–6 (1981): 92.

17. Rochfort, *The Murals of Diego Rivera,* 44.

18. The term "literary competence" is used here as defined by Michael Riffaterre in his book, *Semiotics of Poetry* (Bloomington: Indiana University Press, 1984), 5. According to this theoretician, literary competence "is the reader's familiarity with the descriptive systems, with themes, with his society mythologies, and above all with other texts. Wherever there are gaps or compressions in the text—such as incomplete descriptions, or allusions, or quotations—it is

this literary competence alone that will enable the reader to respond properly and to complete or fill in according to the hypogrammatic model" (5).

19. Shaw, "Interpretations," 8.

20. Establishing a bond with the ancient history of Amerindian cultures is a mythic gesture based on ideological impulse and is quite similar to the response in the Independence period to the cultural dilemma of that time: how should the descendants of the Spanish in America reject Spain and, by extension, Western civilization?

21. Claude Levy-Strauss, *Structural Anthropology* (New York: Basic Books, 1963) 1:224.

22. Rochfort, *The Murals of Diego Rivera,* 81.

23. Rogers, *Painting and Poetry,* 122.

24. Mitchell, *Picture,* 154.

25. Arnheim, "Images," 310.

26. Krieger, *Ekphrasis,* 266.

27. Sigurd Burckhardt, who is convinced that "words already have what the artist first wants to give them—body," has also proposed "that the nature and primary function of the most important poetic devices—especially rhyme, meter and metaphor—is to release words in some measure from their bondage to meaning, their purely referential role, and to give or restore to them the corporeality which a true medium needs." See "The Poet as Fool and Priest" *ELH* 23 (December 1956): 280. Quoted in Krieger, *Ekphrasis,* 266.

28. Villegas, *Estructuras,* 52.

29. Ibid., 53.

30. Angus Wilson, *The Wild Garden* (Berkeley and Los Angeles: University of California Press, 1963), 149. Quoted in Rogers, *Painting and Poetry,* 48.

31. Cardona Peña, "Pablo Neruda," 280.

32. Ibid., 280.

33. Villegas, *Estructuras,* 55.

34. *Canto general*'s second edition of Biblioteca Ayacucho (1981) changes the date to 1519, the actual year Cortés's expedition landed in Veracruz. Santí's edition of Cátedra (1990), however, maintains the original date (1493), adding only in a footnote Cortés's date of disembarkation in Mexico. Perhaps a typographical mistake, Santí's date of 1547 is incorrect. The precise date should be 1519, the date adopted by the Ayacucho's edition, and by Jack Schmitt, the translator.

35. Rochfort, *The Murals of Diego Rivera,* 59.

36. In this context, José Vasconcelos, one of the architects of postrevolutionary Mexico, was described by Paz as "Ministro de una Revolución triunfante" [Minister of a triumphant Revolution] who "soñaba con el renacer de nuestro pueblo y de nuestra cultura" [dreamed of the rebirth of our people and of our culture]. Then Paz adds, "Probablemente es más exacto hablar de una *fundación* que de un *renacimiento*" [It is probably more exact to speak of a *foundation* than of a *renaissance*]. See Paz, *Privilegios* 20; emphasis added.

37. Paz, *Privilegios,* 45–46.

38. Gabriela Mistral was similarly moved by the visual force of the murals; Jaime Concha notes: "Indirectamente, esta compenetración con el indio generará en ella una visión negativa de la conquista, decididamente anti-hispánica" [Indirectly, this co-penetration with the Indian was to generate in her a negative, decidedly anti-Hispanic vision of the Conquest]. See Concha, *Gabriela Mistral,* 37.

39. Quoted in Rodríguez Monegal, *Neruda: el viajero inmóvil*, 125.

40. Rodríguez Monegal, *Neruda: el viajero inmóvil*, 126.

41. Pablo Neruda, "El corazón magallánico," *Cuadernos Americanos* 2 (March-April 1942).

42. Quoted in Cardona Peña, "Pablo Neruda," 280.

43. I use the term "iconic" in the context described by Jean Hagstrum in *The Sister Arts*, 18–19.

44. Francoise Metzer, *Salome and the Dance of Writing* (Chicago: The University of Chicago Press, 1987), 102.

45. Krieger, *Ekphrasis*, 11.

46. Ibid., 16.

47. Ibid., 9.

48. Ibid., 15.

49. Cardona Peña, "Pablo Neruda," 280.

50. Giuseppe Bellini, "Pablo Neruda fundador de utopias," *Actas del VIII Congreso de la Asociación Internacional de Hispanistas* (Providence: Comisión Editorial del VIII Congreso de la A.I.H.; Madrid: Ediciones Istmo, 1986), 7.

51. Bellini, "Pablo Neruda fundador," 7–8.

52. Villegas explains: "La estructura mítica que estructura el conjunto explica no sólo la composición y la funcionalidad de los rasgos con que se caracteriza al mundo y a los personajes, sino que también justifica el optimismo que aureola el libro aún en los momentos más depresivos para la historia de América" [The mythic structure of the whole explains not only the composition and functionality of the characteristics given to the world and the people, but also justifies the optimism that glows in the book even in the most depressing moments of the history of America] (Villegas, *Estructuras*, 46).

53. Villegas, *Estructuras*, 46.

54. Hugo Rodríguez-Alcalá, *Narrativa hispanoamericana* (Madrid: Gredos, 1973), 167.

55. Rochfort, *The Murals of Diego Rivera*, 101, n. 4.

56. Neruda, *Confieso*, 216–17; *Memoirs*, 153.

57. Charlot, *The Mexican Mural Renaissance*, 2.

58. Quoted by Miguel Bueno, "El arte de Diego Rivera atacado por el genial artista C. Orozco," *El Imparcial* (22 November 1926).

59. Quoted by Miguel Bueno, "El arte de Diego Rivera."

60. Charlot, *The Mexican Mural Renaissance*, 12.

61. Rochfort, *The Murals of Diego Rivera*, 59.

62. Indeed, Enrico Mario Santí proposes "that the meaning of Latin American literature lies on the form of its debate with the Western tradition, and that the critic's principal task is to study that form." See Santí, *Pablo Neruda. The Poetics of Prophecy* (Ithaca, London: Cornell University Press, 1982), 9.

63. Octavio Paz, "A Literature of Foundations," *The Siren and the Seashell, and Other Essays on Poetry and Poetics*, tran. Lysander Kemp and Margaret Sayers Peden (Austin: University of Texas Press, 1976), 179.

64. Pablo Neruda, "Algunas reflexiones improvisadas sobre mis trabajos," *Mapocho* 2, no. 3 (1964): 181.

65. Nelly E. Santos, "Génesis de una concepción," 242–43.

66. As González Echevarría has said: "He is not a voice one can hope to imitate, emulate or compete with. Neruda's voice has biblical resonances, . . . only as part of the throng's roar or cry can we hope to reach the resonance, the

volume and the tone of the voice in *Canto general*." Roberto González Echevarría, intro. to *Canto general*, tran. Jack Schmitt, 7.

67. According to Charlot, "[E]arly in this century, when the Parisian vanguard, having hacked its way through uncharted stylistic jungles, proudly returned with strange trophies, the displayed grotesquerie looked familiar and somewhat tame from such an Amerindian vantage point." Charlot, *The Mexican Mural Renaissance*, 10.

68. For further discussion of this, see Octavio Paz's *Los privilegios de la vista*, particularly the chapter on "La piedra y el movimiento."

69. For more on the impact of these figures in Latin America, see Jean Franco, *Modern Culture*, 104–7.

70. Seymour Menton, "La novela indigenista: el indio y las corrientes literarias," *América Indígena* 38, no. 1 (1978): 233.

71. Rodríguez Monegal, *Neruda: el viajero inmóvil*, 15.

72. Menton, "La novela indigenista," 233.

73. Phyllis W. Rodríquez-Peralta, *José Santos Chocano* (New York: Twayne, 1970), 145.

74. Rodríquez-Peralta, *José Santos Chocano*, 145.

75. González Echevarría, introduction to *Canto general*, 7.

76. Hernán Loyola, *Ser y morir en Pablo Neruda (1918–1945)* (Santiago: Santiago, 1967), 182.

77. According to Rodríguez Monegal, who bases his assertion on biographical data, *Canto general de Chile* was written in 1938 (see Rodríguez Monegal, *Neruda: el viajero inmóvil*, 311). Referring to this *Canto*, María Solá concludes that both this poem and the entire *Canto general de Chile* lack the presence of the indigenous theme. "Hay que señalar la ausencia del americano pre-colombino en este poema y en todo el *Canto general de Chile*" [We must point out the absence of the pre-Colombian American in this poem and in all of *Canto General of Chile*]. See María M. Solá, *Poesía y política en Pablo Neruda* (San Juan: Editorial Universitaria, 1980), 46.

78. Neruda, *Confieso*, 235; *Memoirs*, 165.

79. I must clarify that an effort has been made to present Neruda's views on the Araucanian and other pre-Columbian cultures, using his poetry and published commentaries.

80. Quoted by Leticia Alonso de Lozano, "México en la obra de Gabriela Mistral," (diss., University of Colorado, 1987), 31. Commenting on Mistral's fascination with the Mexican indigenous past, Jaime Concha notes, "Será México, donde fascinada y en conmoción, la mujer experimentará la revelación poderosa de lo indígena y de su enorme legado humano y cultural" [It was in Mexico, where she was fascinated and in turmoil, that she was to experiment the powerful revelation of the indigenous people and their enormous human and cultural legacy] (Concha, *Gabriela Mistral*, 34).

81. Pablo Neruda, "Discurso," *Tierra Nueva* 2, no. 9–10 (1941): 121.

82. During and after the presidency of Lázaro Cárdenas (1934–40), Mexico underwent an intense era of construction. Délano states that "el impacto que provocó en Neruda fue casi instantáneo y ciertamente muy profundo. . . . Todo lo sorprendía y lo impresionaba: los indios; las ruinas prehispánicas y coloniales, la arquitectura en general, las pirámides, las montañas, los volcanes, . . . las flores, los insectos." [the impact that it had on Neruda was almost instantaneous and certainly very profound. . . . Everything surprised and impressed him: the Indians; the pre-Hispanic and colonial ruins, the architecture in general, the

pyramids, the mountains, the volcanoes, . . . the flowers, the insects.] (Délano 91).

83. The concept of "Gran Lengua" is used in this sense by Giuseppe Bellini. For him: "en esa extraordinaria 'overture' al *Canto general* que es 'Amor América,' el poeta afirma, diría con orgullo, su condición de 'Gran Lengua,' a la manera indígena, o sea de intérprete sagrado de su mundo, con una expresión sencilla que lo distingue de entre la multitud y lo aísla por encima de los signos del tiempo" [in that extraordinary overture to *Canto General* that is 'Amor America,' the poet affirms, I would say with pride, his role as a 'Gran Lengua,' in the indigenous manner, that is as a sacred interpreter of his world, with a simple expressiveness that distinguishes him from the multitude and isolates him above the signs of time]. Bellini, "Pablo Neruda," 7.

84. Pedro Henríquez Ureña, "La utopía de América," *Plenitud de América: ensayos escogidos* (Buenos Aires: Peña del Giudice, 1952), 11. Quoted in Franco, *The Modern Culture*, 71.

85. Tarn, "Neruda," 171.

86. Neruda, *Confieso*, 235; *Memoirs* 165–66.

87. Menton, "La novela indigenista," 233.

88. Julio Rodríguez-Luis, *Hermenéutica y praxis del indigenismo* (Mexico: Fondo de Cultura Económica, 1980), 10.

89. Tarn, "Neruda," 170.

90. Ibid.

Chapter 4: The Panoramic View

1. Rochfort, *The Murals of Diego Rivera*, 58.

2. Lecture in the University of Chile in 1954, cited by Margarita Aguirre, *Genio y figura de Pablo Neruda*, 134.

3. Cardona Peña, "Pablo Neruda," 278.

4. Ibid.

5. Aguirre, *Genio y figura de Pablo Neruda*, 146.

6. Scott, "The Rhetoric," 302.

7. Ibid., 302–3. It is also interesting that Mitchell's history of the discipline considers that the "earliest examples of ekphrastic poetry are not, it seems, principally associated with painting, but are on utilitarian objects . . . various sorts of weapons and armor and architectural ornaments like friezes, reliefs, frescoes, and statues *in situ*." Like Scott and Krieger, Mitchell notes that, at first, ekphrastic poetry originates as "an ornamental and subordinate part of larger textual units like the epic or pastoral." See Mitchell, *Picture*, 165.

8. Angelo Marchese and Joaquín Forradellas, *Diccionario de retórica, crítica y terminología literaria* (Barcelona: Ariel, 1989), 120–30.

9. For more on the subject of ex–votos and popular manifestations of this sort, see Dawn Ades, *Art in Latin America*, esp. pp. 91–94. For Posada's impact on Mexican mural painting, see chapter 5 of the same study. Regarding the influence on muralism of the colonial pictorial tradition dominated by religious themes, see also Jean Charlot's personal account, *The Mexican Mural Renaissance*, esp. p. 27.

10. Ades, *Art in Latin America*, 125.

11. Ibid., 130.

12. We must once again clarify that we are not referring to the "modernista" movement of Darío and Martí in Latin America, but to the movement in American and English literature that corresponded roughly to the European avant-garde.

13. Frank, "Spatial Form in Modern Literature," 59–60.

14. Ibid., 60.

15. See the discussion of this idea in chapter 2. Whether or not the supplanting of history by the sense of mythic time is accomplished in *Canto general* or mural art is certainly debatable. What we are arguing here is the artistic interest in the mythical imagination, in the aesthetic simulacrum. It is of interest to add that Frank extends this aesthetic principle outside the English language by quoting a passage from *Rayuela* (*Hopscotch*) by Julio Cortázar in order to demonstrate how widespread was the practice. See note 7 of Frank, "Spatial Form: Thirty Years After," 209.

16. Villegas, *Estructuras*, 117.

17. The ambiguous treatment, in many cases, of the pre-Colombian cultures was discussed in the previous chapter. Sections 9, 10, 12, 13, and 15 also deal with different aspects of history: from past to present and from personal to continental. However, we concentrate here on sections 4 and 5 because of their close relationship to the panoramic view of history contained in Rivera's murals.

18. I use Wordsworth's metaphor in the same way that Krieger does in his critique of the English poet's manipulation of time and space in poetry. According to Krieger, in many of Wordsworth's poems, "the moment celebrated is a conjunction of two occasions, one far past with one present. The recurrence of experience, of identical stimulus, modified by the severe changes time has wrought in the experiencing subject, permits the simultaneous perception of motion and stasis." See *Ekphrasis*, 279.

19. For additional information on this technique, both in painting and in literature, see Helmut A. Hatzfeld, *Literature Through Art. A New Approach to French Literature* (New York: Oxford University Press, 1952), 55–56.

20. María Rosa Olivera-Williams, "Las series III, IV y V del *Canto general*," *Texto Crítico* 7, no. 22–23 (1981): 143.

21. Villegas, *Estructuras*, 57.

22. Riess, *The Word and the Stone*, 9.

23. Guillermo Barzuna Pérez, "Concepción del libertador americano en un poem de Pablo Neruda," *Káñina* 8, no. 1–2 (1984): 43.

24. Laurence E. Schmeckebier, *Modern Mexican Art* (Minneapolis: University of Minnesota Press, 1939), 129.

25. Rochfort, *The Murals of Diego Rivera*, 48.

26. Villegas, *Estructuras*, 58.

27. Riess, *The Word and the Stone*, 9.

28. The image of the storm as representative of the proximity of the revolution can be found, for example, in Agustín Yáñez's *Al filo del agua* [*The Edge of the Storm*]. The author has said of the title that "*Al filo del agua* es una expresión campesina que significa el momento de iniciarse la lluvia, y—en sentido figurado, muy común—la inminencia o el principio de un suceso" [*Al filo del agua* is a *campesino* expression that indicates the moment when it begins to rain, and—in a very common figurative sense—the imminence or beginning of an event]. See Agustín Yáñez, *Al filo del agua*, ed. Antonio Castro Leal, 19th ed. (Mexico: Porrúa, 1986), 2.

29. I share González Echevarría's opinion that "the foundational story of the *Canto general* is one of betrayal. Betrayal is important because it sets up the mood of the *Canto,* which is one of outrage, and its promise, which is one of restoration" (9).

30. There is an error in Schmitt's translation of this passage. He understands the second and third lines to read "Moctezuma is not extinct / like a fallen chalice." A closer reading reveals that Cuauhtemoc, not Moctezuma, is the subject of "No es," setting up the contrast of a dead figure (Moctezuma) with a very much alive warrior (Cuauhtemoc)—a reading that is commensurate with the images that Mexicans and other Latin Americans have of the two men.

31. Jorge García Antezana, "Intertextualidad mítica en *Alturas de Macchu Picchu," Revista de Crítica Literaria Latinoamericana* 11, no. 21–22 (1985): 75.

32. Donald L. Shaw has stated in relation to this aspect of *Canto general* in *Alturas de Macchu Picchu* that "If Neruda adopts in any sense at all a Christ-like stance here, it is the stance of Christ as "hijo de hombre" as in Roa Bastos' famous left-wing novel." See Shaw, "Interpretations," 194.

33. Edwin M. Moseley, *Pseudonyms of Christ in the Modern Novel* (New York: University of Pittsburgh Press, 1962), 216.

34. Elliott, ¡*Orozco!,* 116.

35. Schmeckebier, *Modern Mexican Art,* 129.

36. Charlot, *The Mexican Mural Renaissance,* 25.

37. Quoted by Charlot, Ibid.

38. Charlot, *The Mexican Mural Renaissance,* 27.

39. Neruda, *Confieso,* 219; *Memoirs,* 155. The construction of the school was sponsored by Lázaro Cárdenas's administration.

40. Velodia Teitelboim, "El arte público del pintor David Alfaro Siqueiros," *Vida y obra de David Alfaro Siqueiros,* ed. Angélica Arenal de Siqueiros (Mexico: Fondo de Cultura Económica, 1975), 51.

41. Arnheim, "Images," 310.

42. See Cardona Peña, "Pablo Neruda," 280.

43. Frank, "Spatial Form: Thirty years After," 209. Wendy Steiner seems to share the critical assumption we see in Modernist aesthetics—a reflection of the realist, omniscient perspective in art that had prevailed from the Renaissance to the end of the nineteenth century: "With Modernism, the trend [that of the Renaissance] seems to have reversed itself. Literature became obsessed with first person narrative and the limitations of knowledge implicit in it, whereas painting became much more intent on omniscient perspective." See *Colors,* 64. It is at this point that she quotes Marinetti's daughter as claiming that futurism fought for the "interpenetration of the figure and its surroundings, insertion of the spectator into the middle of the picture (Marinetti Barbi, "Marinetti," 52; cited by Steiner, *Colors,* 64). This strengthens the argument that Neruda and the muralists in fact employed avant-garde strategies.

44. Mitchell, *Picture,* 92.

45. Diego Rivera, *My Life, My Art,* ed. Gladys March (New York: Citadel Press, 1960), 134. Quoted by Rochfort, *The Murals of Diego Rivera,* 24.

46. González Echevarría, introduction to *Canto general,* 7.

47. Cardona Peña, "Pablo Neruda," 281.

48. Villegas, *Estructuras,* 41.

49. González Echevarría, introduction to *Canto general,* 9.

50. Olivera-Williams, "Las series," 136.

51. Cardona Peña, "Pablo Neruda," 280. Whether or not the previous assumptions are based on purely impressionistic evidence, nonetheless they are common beliefs among Latin Americans even today.

52. For more on Neruda's ambivalent role as historian or as chronicler, see Santí's introduction to *Canto general*, 86.

53. Alain Sicard, *El pensamiento poético de Pablo Neruda* (Madrid: Gredos, 1981), 258.

54. Villegas, *Estructuras*, 73.

55. Eugenia Neves, "La ideología de la independencia en *Canto general* de Pablo Neruda," *Homenaje a Noël Solomon*, ed. Alberto Gil Novales (Barcelona: Universidad Autónoma de Barcelona, 1979), 286.

56. Yurkiévich, "Mito e historia," 201.

57. Villegas, *Estructuras*, 41.

58. Olivera-Williams, "Las series," 156.

59. Villegas, *Estructuras*.

60. Yurkiévich, "Mito e historia," 211.

61. Rafael Bosch, "El *Canto general* y el poeta como historiador," *Revista de Crítica Literaria Latinoamericana* 1 (1975): 70–71.

62. Bosch, "El *Canto general*," 71.

63. Elliott, *¡Orozco!*, 116.

64. Ibid.

65. Jean Franco, *The Modern Culture*, 72.

66. Jean Pierre Feber, "La Guerre D'Araucanie dans le *Canto general* de Pablo Neruda, *Hommage de Hispanistes Français a Noël Salomon* (Barcelona: LAIA, 1979), 308.

67. Feber, "La Guerre D'Araucanie," 307.

68. Sarandy Cabrera, "Primera teoría del *Canto general*," *Número* 13–14 (1951): 193.

69. I believe that this also explains what Santí calls "errores de documentación histórica en que incurre el cronista" [errors of historical documentation in which the chronicler incurs]. See Santí's introduction to *Canto general*, 88.

Chapter 5: The Poet and the People

1. Ades, *Art in Latin America*, 130.

2. Ibid.

3. Jean Franco, *César Vallejo: La dialéctica de la poesía y el silencio* (Buenos Aires: Editorial Sudamericana, 1984), 214.

4. Mitchell, *Iconology*, 5.

5. Ibid., 164.

6. Ibid., 2.

7. Ibid., 38.

8. Ibid., 4.

9. Ibid., 119.

10. Ibid., 165.

11. It is well known that Neruda always felt a strong commitment to the Republican cause in Spain. We are not trying to deny that or to detract from it. For Neruda, as for many Spanish intellectuals, there were two Spains. One was dominated by the violence of Franco's Nationalist forces, evoking the imperial past and the glorious Spain of the sixteenth century; the other Spain was repre-

sented by the Republicans and Socialist intellectuals who were persecuted and forced into exile. Neruda rejected the former and defended the latter. That is why Miguel Otero Silva, Rafael Alberti, and Miguel Hernández are included in section XII, *Los ríos del canto*, of *Canto general*. But, on the whole, *Canto general* is an American product.

12. Jean Franco, "Orfeo en Utopía: El poeta y la colectividad en el *Canto general*," *Simposio Pablo Neruda*, Isaac Jack Lévy and Juan Loveluck, eds. (Columbia: Dept. of Foreign Languages and Literatures, University of South Carolina, 1975), 286.

13. González, *Trayectoria*, 100.

14. Quoted in Rochfort, *The Murals of Diego Rivera*, 24.

15. For commentary on this notion, see Paz, *Privilegios*, 66–61.

16. Cantón, *Posiciones*, 103–4.

17. See Paz, *Privilegios*, 95, and the introduction of this study.

18. Quoted in Rodríguez Monegal, *Neruda: el viajero inmóvil*, 137.

19. In her excellent analysis of this subject, Franco explains the oral nature of the book: "La lectura en voz alta que influía tanto en *Canto general* representa el polo opuesto al orfeísmo que destacaba al poeta como ser extraordinario" [The act of reading aloud that so influenced *Canto General* represents the opposite pole to Orpheism, which exalted the poet as an extraordinary being]. See Franco, "Orfeo," 287.

20. Franco, "Orfeo," 287.

21. Schmeckebier, *Modern Mexican Art*, 128.

22. Quoted in Cardona Peña, "Pablo Neruda," 281.

23. Quoted by Santí, introduction to *Canto general*, 73–74. Also evident are the underpinnings for the testimonial novel of writers like Elena Poniatowska and the poetic concept of anti-poetry preferred by Nicanor Parra. I would argue that the indirect source of both is Mexican mural art because many of its themes, figures, and characters are literally drawn from common, ordinary people. Moreover mural painters, were routinely assisted by masons, house painters, and artisans who served as models for future murals.

24. Quoted in Santí, introduction to *Canto general*, 64–65.

25. Santí, introduction to *Canto general*, 65.

26. Lessing, *Laocoön*, 67.

27. Ibid., 155.

28. See ibid., 240.

29. Villegas, *Estructuras*, 141.

30. Schmeckebier, *Modern Mexican Art*, 129.

31. Cabrera, "Primera teoría," 195.

32. Santí, introduction to *Canto general*, 64–66.

33. González, *Trayectoria*, 100.

34. Franco, "Orfeo," 283.

35. Ibid.

36. Santí, introduction to *Canto general*, 74.

37. Riess, *The Word and the Stone*, 29.

38. Scott, "The Rhetoric," 303.

39. Neruda, *Para nacer*, 164–65. *Passions and Impressions*, 153. A good idea of the important role played by the visual in Neruda's art can be extrapolated from his memoirs in which he talks about the *mercados* in Mexico:

Lo recorrí por años enteros de mercado a mercado. . . . México es una tierra de pañolones color carmín y turquesa fosforescente. México es una tierra de vasijas y cántaros

y de frutas partidas bajo un enjambre de insecto. México es un campo infinito de
magüeyes (sic) de tinte azul acero y corona de espinas amarillas.
Todo esto dan los mercados más hermosos del mundo. La fruta y la lana, el barro y
los telares, muestran el poderío asombroso de los dedos mexicanos fecundos y eternos.
See *Confieso*, 213.
[I traveled through it for years, from market to market. . . . Mexico is a land of
crimson and phospherescent shawls. Mexico is a land of earthen bowls and pitchers,
and fruit lying open to a swarm of insects. Mexico is an infinite countryside of steel-
blue century plants with yellow thorns.
The most beautiful markets in the world have all this to offer. Fruit and wool, clay
and weaving looms, give evidence of the incredible skill of the fertile and timeless
fingers of the Mexicans.]
See *Memoirs*, 150.
40. Charlot, *The Mexican Mural Renaissance*, 75.
41. Ibid., 28.
42. Schmitt's translation of this line is "I read your / naked country's gift on
your hand" (21). I prefer "receive" to "read" for "recibo."
43. Franco, "Orfeo," 283–84.

Conclusion

1. González Echevarría is of this opinion: "There are really no antecedents
in Spanish for this kind of poem, or even book, except perhaps in those colonial
histories mentioned, or in Bello. But Bello's neoclassical rhetoric gets in the way
too often." See the introduction to *Canto general*, 7.
2. See the differences and affinities between Neruda and Bello listed by
Araya on pages 75–76 of his article. Guillermo Araya, "Destierro y poesía, Bello
y Neruda," *Hommage des Hispanistes Français à Noël Salomon* (Barcelona: LAIA,
1979), 74.
3. Ibid., 76.
4. See Sicard, *El pensamiento poético*, 258, and our discussion of this critic's
conclusion in chapter 4 of this study.
5. Shaw, "Interpretations," 194.
6. Rodríguez Monegal, *Neruda: el viajero inmóvil*, 122.
7. The poem is chronologically the earliest included in *Canto general*. It was
published in 1940 in Chile, under the title "Almagro," in *La hora* (21 July 1940)
and was later included in *Canto general de Chile, Fragmentos* (Mexico 1943). See
Santí's comments in his edition of *Canto general*, 169.
8. Solá, *Poesía y política*, 46.
9. Loyola, *Ser y morir*, 182.
10. Hernán Loyola, "Neruda y América Latina," *Cuadernos Americanos* 218,
no. 3 (1978): 176.
11. Loyola, *Ser y morir*, 185.
12. Rodríguez Monegal, *Neruda: el viajero inmóvil*, 126.
13. Luis Carlos Prestes was imprisoned at the time of his mother's death in
Mexico. The Brazilian government had refused to grant permission for the leader
to travel and attend his mother's funeral.
14. Translation from Pablo Neruda, *Residence on Earth (Residencia en la tierra)*,
trans. Donald D. Walsh (New York: New Directions, 1973), 349–51.
15. Neruda, "Discurso," 121.

16. Quoted in Loyola, "Neruda," 179.

17. Neruda, *Para nacer,* 169; *Passions and Impressions,* 157. From the context it seems that Neruda could have been referring to the Mexican-American war in the 1840s, and to Cárdenas's initiative to condemn the growing ethnic, racist, and ideological intolerance in the world.

Works Cited

Ades, Dawn. *Art in Latin America. The Modern Era, 1820–1980.* New Haven and London: Yale University Press, 1989.

Agosin, Marjorie. *Pablo Neruda.* Translated by Lorraine Roses. TWAS. Boston: Twayne, 1986.

Aguayo, Rafael. *Neruda. Un hombre de la Araucanía.* Concepción, Chile: LAR, 1987.

Aguirre, Margarita. *Genio y figura de Pablo Neruda.* 3d. ed. Buenos Aires: Editorial Universitaria de Buenos Aires, 1969.

Alegría, Fernando. Prologue to *Canto general,* by Pablo Neruda. 2d. ed. Caracas: Biblioteca Ayacucho, 1981.

Alonso de Lozano, Leticia. "México en la obra de Gabriela Mistral." Diss., University of Colorado, 1987.

Araya, Guillermo. "El *Canto general* de Neruda: poema épico-lírico." *Revista de Crítica Literaria Latinoamericana* 4, no. 7–8 (1978): 119–52.

———. "Destierro y poesía. Bello y Neruda." *Hommage des Hispanistes Français a Noël Salomon.* Barcelona: LAIA, 1979: 73–90.

Arnheim, Rudolf. "The images of pictures and words." *Word & Image* 2, no. 4 (1986): 306–10.

Barthes, *Elements of Semiology.* Translated by Annette Lavers and Colin Smith. New York: Hill & Wang, 1968; 1977.

Barzuna Pérez, Guillermo. "Concepción del libertador americano en un poema de P. Neruda." *Káñina* 8, no. 1–2 (1984): 39–44.

Becco, Horacio Jorge. *Pablo Neruda. Bibliografía.* Buenos Aires: Casa Pardo, 1975.

Bellini, Guiseppe, comp. and ed. *Pablo Neruda. Il Mosaico dei Poeti.* Milan: Nuova Accademia Editrice, 1960.

———. "Pablo Neruda fundador de utopias." *Actas del VIII Congreso de la Asociación Internacional de Hispanistas: 22—27 agosto, 1983, Brown University.* Providence: Comisión Editorial del VIII Congreso de la A.I.H.; Madrid: Ediciones Istmo, 1986: 3–19.

Black, Max. *Models and Metaphors: Studies in Language and Philosophy.* Ithaca: Cornell University Press, 1962.

Bosch, Rafael. "El *Canto general* y el poeta como historiador." *Revista de Crítica Literaria Latinoamericana* 1 (1975): 61–72.

Bryson, Norman, Michael Ann Holy, and Keith Moxey, eds. *Visual Theory: Painting and Interpretation.* Cambridge: Polity, 1991.

Bueno, Miguel. "El arte de Diego Rivera atacado por el genial artista C. Orozco." *El Imparcial* (22 November 1926).

Burkhardt, Sigurd. "The Poet as Fool and Priest." *ELH* 23 (December 1956).

Cabrera, Sarandy. "Primera teoría del *Canto general.*" *Número* 13–14 (1951): 189–95.

Cano Ballesta, Juan. "Miguel Hernández y su amistad con Pablo Neruda (Crisis estética e ideológica a la luz de unos documentos)." *Rodríguez Monegal and Santí,* 143–74.

Cantón, Wilberto. *Posiciones.* Mexico: Imprenta Universitaria, 1950.

Cardona Peña, Alfredo. "Pablo Neruda. Breve historia de sus libros." *Cuadernos Americanos* 9 July-December (1950): 257–89.

———. *Pablo Neruda y otros ensayos.* Colección Studium 7. Mexico: Ediciones de Andrea, 1955.

Cardoza y Aragón, Luis. *El río. Novelas de caballería.* Mexico: Fondo de Cultura Económica, 1986.

———. *Pintura contemporánea de Mexico.* Mexico: Ediciones Era, 1974.

Castro Leal, Antonio. "Nota sobre el *Canto general.*" *Revista de Bellas Artes* 11–12 (1973): 72–73.

Charlot, Jean. *The Mexican Mural Renaissance. 1920–1925.* New Haven and London: Yale University Press, 1963.

Concha, Jaime. *Gabriela Mistral.* Madrid: Ediciones Júcar, 1987.

De Costa, Rene. *Vicente Huidobro.* Oxford: Oxford University Press, 1984.

Delano, Luis Enrique. "La raíz volcánica de la poesía de Pablo Neruda." *Cuadernos Americanos* 4–6 (1981): 83–96.

Di San Lazzaro, Gualtieri, ed. *Homage to Henri Matisse.* New York: Tudor Publishing, 1970.

Díaz Casanueva, Humberto. "En el aniversario de la muerte de Pablo Neruda (Comentario a su 'Canto a Bolívar')." *Arieto* 9, no. 35 (1983): 26–28.

Dorsch, T. S., tran. and ed. *Classical Literary Criticism: Aristotle, Horace, Longinus.* Harmondsworth: Penguin, 1974.

Durán, Manuel. "Pablo Neruda y la tradición romántica y simbolista." *Cuadernos Americanos* 39 (1980): 187–99.

Eisenstein, Segei. *Film Form and Film Sense.* Translated and edited by Jay Leyda. New York: Meridian Books, 1957.

Elliot, David, ed. *¡Orozco! 1883–1949. An Exhibition Organized by the Ministry of Foreign Affairs and the Institute of Fine Arts, Mexico.* Oxford: Museum of Modern Art, Oxford, 1980.

Febrer, Jean Pierre. "La guerre d'Araucanie dans le *Canto General* de Pablo Neruda (L'altération de l'histoire au service de l'Histoire)." *Hommage des Hispanistes Français a Noël Salomon.* Barcelona: LAIA, 1979: 307–19.

Fernández-Retamar, Roberto. Introduction to *Poesías* by Pablo Neruda. La Habana: Casa de las Américas, 1972.

Folgarait, Leonard. *So Far From Heaven. David Alfaro Siqueros' "The March of Humanity" and Mexican Revolutionary Politics.* Cambridge: Cambridge University Press, 1987.

Franco, Jean. *César Vallejo. La dialéctica de la poesía y el silencio.* Buenos Aires: Editorial Sudamericana, 1984.

———. *The Modern Culture of Latin America. Society and the Artist.* London: Pall Mall Press, 1967.

————. "Orfeo en Utopía: El poeta y la colectividad en el *Canto general.*" In *Simposio Pablo Neruda. Actas,* edited by Isaac Jack Lévy and Juan Loveluck, 269–289. Hispanic Studies. New York, Madrid: University of South Carolina, Las Americas, 1975.

Frank, Joseph. "Spatial Form in Modern Literature." In *The Widening Gyre: Crisis and Mastery in Modern Literature.* New Brunswick: Rutgers University Press, 1963.

————. "Spatial Form: Thirty Years After." In Smitten, 1981: 202–43.

Freud, Sigmund. *The Interpretation of Dreams.* New York: Avon Books, 1965.

Gandelman, Claude. *Reading Pictures, Viewing Texts.* Bloomington and Indianapolis: Indiana University Press, 1991.

García Antezana, Jorge. "Intertextualidad mítica en *Alturas de Macchu Picchu.*" *Revista de Crítica Literaria Latinoamericana* 2, no. 21–22 (1985): 75–83.

Geisdorfer Feal, Rosemary, and Carlos Feal. *Painting on the Page. Interartistic Approaches to Modern Hispanic Texts.* Albany: State University Press of New York, 1995.

Golahny, Amy, ed. *The Eye of the Poet. Studies in the Reciprocity of the Visual and Literary Arts from the Renaissance to the Present.* Lewisburg: Bucknell University Press; London: Associated University Presses, 1996.

Goldfarb, Marcos. "Neruda: El poeta comunista." *Revista de Crítica Literaria Latinoamericana* 2, no. 21–22 (1985): 101–7.

González, Manuel Pedro. *Trayectoria de la novela en México.* Mexico: Botas, 1951.

González Echevarría, Roberto. Introduction to *Canto general,* by Pablo Neruda. Translated by Jack Schmitt. Berkeley: University of California Press, 1991.

Goodman, Nelson. *Languages of Art. An Approach to a Theory of Symbols.* Indianapolis, New York, and Kansas City: Bobbs-Merrill Company, 1968.

Hagstrum, Jean H. *The Sister Arts. The Tradition of Literary Pictorialism and English Poetry from Dryden to Gray.* Chicago: The University of Chicago Press, 1958.

Halperin, Maurice. "Pablo Neruda in Mexico." *Books Abroad* 15, no. 2 (1941): 164–68.

Hatzfeld, Helmut A. *Literature Through Art. A New Approach to French Literature.* New York: Oxford University Press, 1952.

Hollander, John. "The Poetics of Ekphrasis." *Word and Image* 4 (1988): 209–19.

Hoog, Michael. *Paul Gaugin. Life and Work.* Translated by Constance Devanthéry-Lewis. New York: Rizzoli, 1987.

Ibáñez Langlois, José Miguel. *Rilke, Pound, Neruda: Tres claves de la poesía contemporánea.* Madrid: Rialpe, 1978.

Jiménez, José Olivio, comp. and ed. *Antología crítica de la poesía modernista hispanoamericana.* Madrid: Hiperión, 1985.

Jiménez, Juan Ramón. "Carta a Pablo Neruda." *Repertorio Americano* 23 (17 January 1942).

————. "¿América sombría?," *Repertorio Americano* 24 (14 August 1943).

Karsen, Sonja. "Neruda's *Canto general* in Historical Context." *Symposium* 32, no. 3 (1978): 221–35.

Krieger, Murray. *Ekphrasis. The Illusion of the Natural Sign.* Baltimore: The Johns Hopkins University Press, 1992.

Larrea, Juan. *Del surrealismo a Machupicchu.* Serie del volador. Mexico: Joaquín Mortiz, 1967.

Lazo, Raimundo. *La novela andina. Pasado y futuro.* 2d ed. Mexico: Porrúa, 1973.

Leal, Luis. *Historia del cuento hispanoamericano.* Historia Literaria de Hispanoamérica 2. Mexico: Ediciones de Andrea, 1966.

Lerín, Manuel, comp. and ed. *Neruda y México.* Mexico: B. Costa-Amic, 1973.

Lessing, Gotthold Ephraim. *Laocoön. An Essay on the Limits of Painting and Poetry.* Translation, introduction, and notes by Edward Allen McCormick. 1766. Baltimore and London: The Johns Hopkins University Press, 1984.

———. *Laocoön. An Essay on the Limits of Painting and Poetry.* Translated by Ellen Frothingham. Boston: Little, Brown & Company, 1898.

Lévy-Strauss, Claude. *Structural Anthropology.* Vol. 1. New York: Basic Books, 1963.

Lorenzo-Rivero, Luis. "Rafael Alberti: Pintura, poesía y política." *Letras de Deusto* 15, no. 31–32 (1985): 5–25.

Loveluck, Juan. "*Alturas de Macchu Picchu:* Cantos I–V." *Revista Iberoamericana* 39 (1973): 175–88.

Loyola, Hernán. "Neruda y América Latina." *Cuadernos Americanos* 218, no. 3 (1978): 175–97.

———. *Ser y morir en Pablo Neruda 1918–1945.* Santiago: Editora Santiago, 1967.

Lozada, Alfredo. "Visión degradada/error visionario. Desconstruyendo la modalidad profética en la poesía de Pablo Neruda." *Revista Iberoamericana* 52 (1986): 963–70.

Mangini González, Shirley. "Mitología y cosmología en Gabriela Mistral y Pablo Neruda." *Discurso Literario* 2, no. 2 (1985): 439–55.

Marchese, Angelo and Joaquín Forradellas. *Diccionario de retórica, crítica y terminología literaria.* Barcelona: Ariel, 1989.

Marcos, Juan Manuel. "Vallejo y Neruda: La Guerra Civil española como profecía hispanoamericana." *Cuadernos Americanos* 44 (1985): 217–24.

Markiewicz, Henryk. "Ut Pictura Poesis . . . A History of the Topos and the Problem." *New Literary History* 18, no. 3 (Spring 1987): 535–58.

Matos Moquete, Manuel A. "Mito y unidad americana en el *Canto general* de Pablo Neruda." *Cuadernos de Poética* 1, no. 1 (1983): 12–16.

McCormick, Edward Allen. Introduction to *Laocoön. An Essay on the Limits of Painting and Poetry.* Lessing 1984.

Menton, Seymour. "La novela indigenista: el indio y las corrientes literarias," *América Indígena* 38, no. 1 (1978): 231–240.

Metzer, Francoise. *Salome and the Dance of Writing.* Chicago: The University of Chicago Press, 1987.

Micheli, Mario de. *Siqueiros.* Translated by Ron Strom. New York: Harry N. Abrams, 1968.

Miller, James E. *The American Quest for a Supreme Fiction.* Chicago: University of Chicago Press, 1979.

Mitchell, W. J. T. *Iconology. Image, Text, Ideology.* Chicago and London: The University of Chicago Press, 1986.

———. *The Language of Images.* Chicago: The University of Chicago Press, 1980.

———. *Picture Theory.* Chicago: The University of Chicago Press, 1994.

Montecino, Sergio. "Pintura y poesía (Neruda y los pintores)." *Atenea* 450 (1984): 115–24.

Moseley, Edwin M. *Pseudonyms of Christ in the Modern Novel.* New York: University of Pittsburgh Press, 1962.

Munro, Thomas. *The Arts and Their Interrelations.* New York: The Liberal Arts Press, 1949.

Neruda, Pablo. "Algunas reflexiones improvisadas sobre mis trabajos," *Mapocho* 2, no. 3 (1964).

———. *Canto general.* Translated by Jack Schmitt, introduction by Roberto González Echevarría. Berkeley and Los Angeles: University of California Press, 1991.

———. *Canto general.* Edited and introduction by Enrico Mario Santí. Madrid: Cátedra, 1990.

———. *Carta a México.* Mexico: Fondo de Cultura Popular, 1947.

———. *Confieso que he vivido. Memorias.* Barcelona, Mexico: Seix Barral, 1987.

———. "Discurso." *Tierra Nueva* 2 (1944): 120–22.

———. "El corazón magallánico." *Cuadernos Americanos* 2 (March-April 1942).

———. *Memoirs.* Translated (of *Confieso que he vivido*) by Hardie St. Martin. New York: Farrar, Straus & Giroux, 1977.

———. *México florido y espinudo.* Introduction by Francisco Valero. Mexico: Edimex, 1976.

———. *Obras completas.* 4th ed. Buenos Aires: Losada, 1973.

———. *Para nacer he nacido.* Edited by Matilde Neruda and Miguel Otero Silva. Biblioteca Breve. Barcelona: Seix Barral, 1977.

———. *Passions and Impressions.* Edited by Matilde Neruda and Miguel Otero Silva and translated (of *Para nacer he nacido*) by Margaret Sayers Peden. New York: Farrar, Straus & Giroux, 1983.

———. *Residence on Earth.* Translated (of *Residencia en la tierra*) by Donald D. Walsh. New York: New Directions, 1973.

Neruda, Pablo, Gustavo Ortiz Hernán, and Guillermo Atías. *Presencia de Ramón López Velarde en Chile.* Santiago: Fondo del Plan Chileno-Mexicano de Cooperación Fraternal, 1963.

Neves, Eugenia. "La ideología de la Independencia en *Canto general* de Pablo Neruda y la segunda declaración de la Habana." *Homenaje a Noël Salomon: Ilustración española e Independencia de América.* Edited by Alberto Gil Novales. Barcelona: Universidad Autónoma de Barcelona, 1979: 283–88.

Olivera-Williams, María Rosa. "Las series III, IV y V del *Canto general.*" *Texto Crítico* 7, no. 22–23 (1981): 134–62.

Orozco, José Clemente. *Autobiografía.* 2d ed. Serie Crónicas. Mexico: Ediciones Era, 1985.

Paz, Octavio. *Laurel, Antología de poesía moderna en lengua española.* Mexico: Trillas, 1986.

———. "A Literature of Foundations," *The Siren and the Seashell, and Other Essays on Poetry and Poetics.* Translated by Lysander Kemp and Margaret Sayers Peden. Austin: University of Texas Press, 1976: 173–79.

———. "Pablo Neruda en el corazón." *Ruta* 4 (1938): 25–33.

————. "Poesía, pintura, música, etcétera. Conversación con Manuel Ulacia." *Vuelta* 155 (October 1989): 14–23.

————. *Los privilegios de la vista. Arte de México.* México en la obra de Octavio Paz, III. Mexico: Fondo de Cultura Económica, 1987.

————. "Respuesta a un consul." *Letras de México* 15 August (1943): 95.

Pring-Mill, Robert D. F. "Neruda y el original de 'Los libertadores'." *Actas del Sexto Congreso Internacional de Hispanistas celebrado en Toronto del 22 al 26 agosto 1977.* Toronto: Dept. of Spanish and Portuguese, University of Toronto, 1977: 587–88.

Pupo-Walker, C. Enrique. "La transposición de valores pictóricos en la narrativa de Ferretis y Rulfo." *Nueva Narrativa Hispanoamericana* 1, no. 1 (1971): 95–103.

————. *"Los de abajo* y la pintura de Orozco: Un caso de correspondencias estéticas." *Cuadernos Americanos* 5, no. 154 (1967): 237–54.

————. "Personajes y ambiente en *Pedro Páramo.*" *Cuadernos Americanos* 47 (1969): 194–204.

Revueltas, José. "América sombría." *El Popular* (13 March 1942).

————. "América sombría." *Repertorio Americano* 23 (9 May 1942).

Riess, Frank. *The Word and the Stone. Language and Imagery in Neruda's "Canto General."* London: Oxford University Press, 1972.

Riffaterre, Michael. *Semiotics of Poetry.* Reprint, 1978. Bloomington: Indiana University Press, 1984.

Rischin, Abigail S. "Beside the Reclining Statue: Ekphrasis, Narrative, and Desire in *Middlemarch.*" *PMLA* 111, no. 5 (October 1996): 1121–32.

Rivera, Diego. *Arte y política.* Edited and introduction by Raquel Tibol. 2d ed. Mexico: Grijalbo, 1978.

Rochfort, Desmond. *The Murals of Diego Rivera.* Chronology by Julia Engelhardt. London: Journeyman, 1987.

Rodríguez-Alcalá, Hugo. *Narrativa hispanoamericana.* Madrid: Gredos, 1973.

Rodríguez-Peralta, Phyllis W. *José Santos Chocano.* TWAS. New York: Twayne, 1970.

Rodríguez-Luis, Julio. *Hermenéutica y praxis del indigenismo. La novela indigenista de Clorinda Matto a José María Arguedas.* Mexico: Fondo de Cultura Económica, 1980.

Rodríguez Monegal, Emir. *Neruda: El viajero inmóvil.* Rev. ed. Caracas: Monte Avila, 1977.

Rodríguez Monegal, Emir and Enrico Mario Santí. *Pablo Neruda. El escritor y la crítica.* Madrid: Taurus, 1985.

Rogers, Franklin R. *Painting and Poetry. Form, Metaphor, and the Language of Literature.* Assisted by Mary Ann Rogers. Lewisburg: Bucknell University Press; London, Toronto: Associated University Presses, 1985.

Saintsbury, George. *A History of Criticism and Literary Taste in Europe.* Vol. 1. London, 1992.

Santí, Enrico Mario. Introduction to *Canto general* by Pablo Neruda. Edited by Enrico Mario Santí. Madrid: Cátedra, 1990.

————. *Pablo Neruda. The Poetics of Prophecy.* Ithaca, London: Cornell University Press, 1982.

Santos, Nelly E. "Génesis de una concepción del compromiso poético en el *Canto general.*" *Cuadernos Americanos* 4–6 (1983): 228–45.

Schmeckebier, Laurence E. *Modern Mexican Art.* Minneapolis: University of Minnesota Press, 1939.

Scott, Grant F. "The Rhetoric of Dilation: Ekphrasis and Ideology." *Word and Image.* 7, no. 4 (October–December 1991): 301–310.

Seznec Jean. "Art and Literature: A Plea for Humility." *New Literary History* 3 (1972): 569–74.

Shaw, Donald L. "Interpretations of *Alturas de Macchu Picchu.*" *Revista Interamericana de Bibliografía* 38 (1988): 186–95.

Sicard, Alain. *El pensamiento poético de Pablo Neruda.* Translated by Pilar Ruiz Va. Madrid: Gredos, 1981.

Smitten, Jeffrey R. and Ann Daghistany, eds. Foreword by Joseph Frank. *Spatial Form in Narrative.* Ithaca and London: Cornell University Press, 1981.

Solá, María Magdalena. *Poesía y política en Pablo Neruda (Análisis del "Canto general").* Río Piedras: Editorial Universitaria, Universidad de Puerto Rico, 1980.

Solís, Ruth, comp. and ed. *Vida y obra de David Alfaro Siqueiros.* Prologue by Angélica Arenal de Siqueiros. Mexico: Fondo de Cultura Económica, 1975.

Steiner, Wendy. *The Colors of Rhetoric.* Chicago and London: The University of Chicago Press, 1982.

———. "Introduction." Special issue edited by Wendy Steiner. *Poetics Today* 10, no. 1 (Spring 1989): 1–3.

Sutton, Walter. "The Literary Image and the Reader: A Consideration of the Theory of Spatial Form." *Journal of Aesthetics and Art Criticism* 16 (1957): 112–23.

Tarn, Nathaniel. "Neruda and Indigenous Culture." *Sulfur* 15 (1986): 169–73.

Teitelboim, Velodia. "El arte público del pintor David Alfaro Siqueiros." *Vida y obra de David Alfaro Siqueiros.* Edited by Angélica Arenal de Siqueiros. Mexico: Fondo de Cultura Económica, 1975.

Uribe, Hernán. *Fulgor y muerte de Pablo Neruda.* Mexico: Editorial El Caballito, 1983.

Valbuena Briones, Angel. *Literatura Hispanoamericana.* 4th ed. Vol. 5. Barcelona: Gustavo Gil, 1969.

Veas Mercado, Fernando. "*Canto general.* La ideología y su proyección imaginaria. La epopeya actual." *Revista de Crítica Literaria Latinoamericana* 2, no. 21–22 (1985): 59–74.

Vidal Claramonte, María Carmen Africa. *Arte y literature.* Madrid: Palas Atanea, 1992.

Villegas, Juan. *Estructuras míticas y arquetípicos en el "Canto general" de Neruda.* Barcelona: Planeta, 1976.

Wellek, René. "The Parallelism between Literature and the Arts." In René Wellek and Austin Warren. *Theory of Literature.* 3d. ed. New York: Harcourt, 1962.

Weisstein, Ulrich. "Literature and the Visual Arts." In *Interrelations of Literature,* edited by Jean-Pierre Barricelli and Joseph Gibaldi, 251–77. New York: The Modern Language Association of America, 1982:

Wilson, Angus. *The Wild Garden.* Berkeley and Los Angeles: University of California Press, 1963.

Woodbridge, Hensley C., and David S. Zubatsky. *Pablo Neruda. An Annotated Bibliography of Biographical and Critical Studies.* New York, London: Garland Publishing, 1988.

Yáñez, Agustín. *Al filo del agua.* Edited by Antonio Castro Leal. 19th ed. Mexico: Porrúa, 1986.

Yurkiévich, Saúl. "Mito e historia: dos generadores del *Canto general.*" In *Pablo Neruda. See* Rodríguez Monegal and Santí 1985, 198–218.

Index

Alberti, Rafael, 46, 50, 164, 216 n. 2
Alturas de Macchu Picchu: poems, section II, 84; section XI, 98
Alvarado, Pedro de, 98
American art, 48, 59
Apollinaire, Guillaume, 47, 50
Araucanía, 16; Araucanians, 149
Archetrope: archetropic experience, 40, 41, 57, 60, 63, 99, 152, 156; archetropic impulse, 90; and metaphor, 40; and the metaphoric process, 40
arena traicionada, La,: and its structure, 158
arena traicionada, La,: poems, "Los muertos de la plaza (28 de enero de 1946, Santiago de Chile)," 195; "Las oligarquías," 161–63; "Poetas celestes," 170, 175, "Promulgación de la ley del embudo," 163–64
The artist/poet inside the art object, 149–50

Baudelaire, Charles, 47
Bello, Andrés, 113–14, 118, 182, 197–98, 229 n. 1; and *Alocución a la poesía*, 197
Beltrán, Carlos, 52
Best Maugard, Adolfo, 59
Bilbao, Francisco de, 147
Blake, William, 30, 37, 50
Bolshevik Revolution, 112, 113
Borges, Jorge Luis, 41, 50
Botero, Fernando, 91, 110; *The Presidential Family,* 110
Breton, André, 47

Calles, Plutarco Elías, 207–8; and the Church, 208
Canto general: and Christ-like figures, 138–39 (*see also* Christ-like figures); and Christian ideology, 171–72 (*see also* Christian ideology); as chroni-

cle, 21; and the Cold War, 203 (*see also* Cold War); and the epic tradition, 123–26, 177, 183–84 (*see also* Epic tradition); and European Avant-garde, 172–73, 226 n. 43 (*see also* European avant-garde); and fascism, 167; first edition, 17, 51–52; and its formal structure, 19, 21, 63, 65–66, 96, 104, 110, 123, 124, 164, 211 n. 22; history and myth in, 125–28, 200, 225 n. 15 (*see also* History and myth); as an iconoclastic work, 172, 174–75; and medieval (artistic) tradition, 127, 150–51, 183–84; and Modernist aesthetics, 169, 172–73, 197, 219 n. 47 (*see also* Modernism); and the mythical dimension of pre-Hispanic cultures, 68–91, 200 (*see also* pre-Hispanic cultures); and social realism, 126–27, 173 (*see also* Social realism); and the theme of betrayal, 138, 158, 168, 226 n. 29
Canto general: cantos, *Alturas de Macchu Picchu*, 14, 80, 104, 106, 170, 186, 194, 198 (see also *Alturas de Macchu Picchu*); *América, no invoco tu nombre en vano*, 65, 66, 69, 200; *La arena traicionada*, 65, 128, 158–68 (see also *La arena traicionada*); *Canto general de Chile*, 14, 65, 69, 114, 118, 199–200 (see also *Canto general de Chile*); *Los conquistadores*, 91–103 (see also *Los conquistadores*); *El fugitivo*, 184 (see also *El fugitivo*); *El gran océano*, 69; *La lámpara en la tierra*, 68–91 (see also *La lámpara en la tierra*); *Los libertadores*, 120, 128–58, 196 (see also *Los libertadores*); *Que despierte el leñador*, 110; *La tierra se llama Juan*, 66, 112, 125, 169, 176, 196 (see also *La tierra*

239

se llama Juan); *Yo soy,* 117, 179 (see also *Yo soy*)

Canto general de Chile: poems, "Alfarería,"65, 186–87, 188; "Himno y regreso," 114–15; "Inundaciones," 199; "Melancolía cerca de Orizaba (1942)," 199; "Océano," 199; "Quiero volver al sur (1941)," 199; "Talabartería," 65, 186, 188, 199; "Telares," 65, 187–89, 199

Cardenas, Lázaro, 152, 167, 195; and the Spanish Republic, 203, 208

Carranza, Venustiano, and the Constitution of 1919, 207

Caupolicán, 133, 147

Charlot, Jean, 60, 61, 106, 190, 207; *Massacre in the Templo Mayor*, 91

Chillán (Chile), 124; Siqueiros's murals in, 17, 66, 91, 144

Chocano, Santos, 113–14, 198

Christ-like figures, 147; Cuauhtémoc, 138

Christian iconography, 47, 48; in Communist doctrine, 133, 141–43; in mural art, 64, 65, 66, 72, 133; inversion and transgression of, 170; in Western literature and culture, 141

Christian iconology, 171

Christian ideology: in Mexican culture and art, 142–43, 172

Chronicler, the poet as, 73, 110

Cold War, 21; in Neruda, 21, 165

Colonia, La, as a historical parenthesis, 147, 159–61

Colonial art and muralism, 142–43

Colonial art in Mexico: religious paintings, 126, 142–43; medieval tradition of painting in, 126

Conceptual space, 41, 148, 164; and the concept of palimpsest, 41; and reader's response, 41

Concrete poetry, 47; imagist poetry, 44

Conquistadores, Los,: poems, "A pesar de la ira," 91, 93–94, 103–4; "Las agonías," 97; "Ahora es Cuba," 79; "El corazón magallánico (1519)," 94–95, 115, 201; "Cortés," 120, 194; "Descubridores de Chile" (originally titled "Almagro"), 94, 199, 229n. 7; "Homenaje a Balboa," 98; "Llegan al mar de México (1493),"

92–93; "Se unen la tierra y el hombre," 115; "Un obispo," 97; "Vienen por las islas (1493)," 96–97

Conventionalism, 33, 50

Cortés, Hernán, 98, 92

Cristero civil war, 208

Cuauhtémoc, 124, 133, 147, 152

cummings, e. e., 28

Da Vinci, Leonardo, 31

Dante Allighieri, 125

Darío, Rubén, 113; and *modernismo*, 225n. 12

Díaz del Castillo, Bernal, 98

Díaz, Porfirio, 206

Doctor Atl (Gerardo Murillo), 60

Ekphrastic: desire, 46, 70; fear, 38, 39; hope, 38, 39, 41, 52, 67; independence, 35; indifference, 38, 39; poetry, 28, 32, 39, 41, 73, 88, 124, 151, 188, 224n. 7; principle, 33, 35, 36, 102; process, 31, 88

Ekphrasis, 28, 31, 32–41, 52, 102, 124; actual, 99, 130, 148, 151, 214n. 59; direct, 66; and the epic tradition, 125; and the epigram, 43, 44, 51, 102; fictive, 35, 99–102; literary, 35, 99–102, 130; as literary topos, 124–25; and mixed media, 39; notional, 99, 214n. 59; and the poem-as-emblem, 35, 36, 37, 43, 102; and semiotics, 33, 36, 39

Eliot, T. S., 25, 37, 68, 125, 127, 151, 212–13n. 7

Enciso, Jorge, 58

encomienda, La, 160

Epic narrative, 114

Epic panorama of history, 123, 133

Epic poetry, 43, 50; and medieval tradition, 14

epic tradition: in *Canto general*, 123–25; and history as myth, 125; and the mythical of dimension of history, 125–26; in poetry, 125

Ethnic theme, 15–16, 96, 121, 216n. 6; as foundation in *Canto general*, 124

Ethnography, 121

Ethnic cultures, 81

European artistic models, rejection of, 105, 109, 112, 170; adoption of, 56–58